Image Testimonies

Recent political conflicts signal an increased proliferation of image testimonies shared widely via social media. Although witnessing with and through images is not a phenomenon of the internet era, contemporary digital image practices and politics have significantly intensified the affective economies of image testimonies. This volume traces the contours of these conditions and develops a conception of image testimony along four areas of focus.

The first and second section of this volume reflects the discussion of image testimonies as an interplay of evidential qualities and their potential to express affective relationalities and emotional involvement. The third section focuses on the question of how social media technologies shape and subsequently are shaped by image testimonies. To further complicate the ethical position of the witness, the final section looks at image testimony at the intersection of creation and destruction, taking into account the perspectives of different actors and their opposed moral positions.

With an emphasis on the affectivity of these images, *Image Testimonies* provides new and so far overlooked insights in the field. It will appeal to students and researchers interested in fields such as Sociology and Social Policy, Media and Communications, Visual Arts and Culture and Middle East Studies.

Kerstin Schankweiler is an art historian and postdoctoral researcher at the Collaborative Research Center Affective Societies at Freie Universität Berlin, Germany.

Verena Straub is an art historian and research associate at the Collaborative Research Center Affective Societies at the Freie Universität Berlin, Germany.

Tobias Wendl is Professor for the Arts and Visual Cultures of Africa at the Institute of Art History, Freie Universität Berlin, Germany.

Routledge Studies in Affective Societies

Series Editors:

Birgitt Röttger-Rössler
Professor of Social and Cultural Anthropology at Freie Universität Berlin, Germany

Doris Kolesch
Professor of Theater and Performance Studies at Freie Universität Berlin, Germany

Routledge Studies in Affective Societies presents high-level academic work on the social dimensions of human affectivity. It aims to shape, consolidate and promote a new understanding of societies as Affective Societies, accounting for the fundamental importance of affect and emotion for human coexistence in the mobile and networked worlds of the 21st century. Contributions come from a wide range of academic fields, including anthropology, sociology, cultural, media and film studies, political science, performance studies, art history, philosophy, and social, developmental and cultural psychology. Contributing authors share the vision of a transdisciplinary understanding of the affective dynamics of human sociality. Thus, *Routledge Studies in Affective Societies* devotes considerable space to the development of methodology, research methods and techniques that are capable of uniting perspectives and practices from different fields.

1   **Affect in Relation**
     Families, Places, Technologies
     Edited by Birgitt Röttger-Rössler and Jan Slaby

2   **Image Testimonies**
     Witnessing in Times of Social Media
     Edited by Kerstin Schankweiler, Verena Straub and Tobias Wendl

3   **Affective Societies**
     Key Concepts
     Edited by Jan Slaby and Christian von Scheve

4   **Analyzing Affective Societies**
     Methods and Methodologies
     Edited by Antje Kahl

For more information about this series, please visit: www.routledge.com/ Routledge-Studies-in-Affective-Societies/book-series/RSAS

Image Testimonies

Witnessing in Times of Social Media

Edited by Kerstin Schankweiler,
Verena Straub and
Tobias Wendl

Routledge
Taylor & Francis Group

LONDON AND NEW YORK

First published 2019
by Routledge
2 Park Square, Milton Park, Abingdon, Oxon OX14 4RN

and by Routledge
52 Vanderbilt Avenue, New York, NY 10017

Routledge is an imprint of the Taylor & Francis Group, an informa business

British Library Cataloguing-in-Publication Data
A catalogue record for this book is available from the British Library

Library of Congress Cataloging-in-Publication Data
A catalog record has been requested for this book

ISBN: 978-1-138-34306-1 (hbk)
ISBN: 978-0-429-43485-3 (ebk)

Typeset in Times New Roman
by Wearset Ltd, Boldon, Tyne and Wear

Contents

Contributors

Jonas Bens is an anthropologist/lawyer and postdoctoral research fellow at the Collaborative Research Center Affective Societies, Freie Universität Berlin, Germany. He specializes in legal and political anthropology with a research focus on indigeneity, transitional justice, democracy, and the politics of affect and emotion. His publications include "Sentimentalising persons and things: Creating normative arrangement of bodies through courtroom talk" (*Journal of Legal Anthropology*, 2018) and the upcoming monograph *The Indigenous Paradox: Rights, Sovereignty, and Culture in the Americas* (University of Pennsylvania Press).

Tom Bioly has studied Arab Studies and Comparative Religions in Jena and Leipzig and is currently a PhD student at the Institute for Near Eastern Studies of the University of Jena, Germany (Professor Dr Tilman Seidensticker). Having dealt with the destruction of cultural properties by the Islamic State in his master's thesis, his dissertation is now treating the Jihadist claim to Islamic authenticity. Apart from Jihadism, Salafism and Wahhabism, his main research interests consist of religious, political and social developments in the Arabian Peninsula, the Quran as well as pre- and early Islamic history. Tom Bioly is receiving a scholarship from the Konrad-Adenauer-Stiftung.

Simon Faulkner is a Senior Lecturer in Art History and Visual Culture at Manchester School of Art (Manchester Metropolitan University), UK. His recent individual research has been focused on relationships between visual practices and the Israeli–Palestinian conflict. This research has addressed a range of artistic and photographic work, and has been particularly concerned with the ways that visual images have been used for political purposes within the divided geography of Israel/Palestine. This work has resulted in a number of publications, including the book *Between States* (Black Dog Publishing, 2015), written with Israeli artist David Reeb. Since 2014, he has also been a member of the Visual Social Media Lab, the work of which is focused on researching social media images.

Paul Frosh teaches in the Department of Communication and Journalism at the Hebrew University of Jerusalem, Israel. His research spans visual culture, media aesthetics, media witnessing and moral concern. His books include *The Image Factory: Consumer Culture, Photography and the Visual Content Industry* (2003) and *Media Witnessing: Testimony in the Age of Mass Communication* (2009, edited with Amit Pinchevski). His most recent book is *The Poetics of Digital Media* (Polity, 2018).

Christoph Günther is the Principal Investigator of the Junior Research Group "Jihadism on the Internet: Images and Videos, their Appropriation and Dissemination", at the Department of Anthropology and African Studies, Johannes Gutenberg University Mainz, Germany. His research interests include religio-political movements in the modern Middle East, visual cultures and iconography, and the sociology of religion. He has extensively published on the evolution, ideology, and political iconography of the Islamic State and its predecessors, including his latest monograph *Ein zweiter Staat im Zweistromland? Genese und Ideologie des "Islamischen Staates Irak"* (Ergon, 2014).

Marianna Liosi is an independent curator and researcher based in Berlin, Germany. She graduated in Visual Arts at IUAV, Venice and she is currently a PhD candidate in Humanities, University of Ferrara (Italy). In her research she explores the aesthetics of social, economic and political dynamics, with specific attention to media, technology and the question of spectatorship and its generative role. She has curated exhibitions, film programmes and workshops, among the most recent: "Tentative Matters", D21 Kunstraum, Leipzig, 2017; "Between Broadcast", in collaboration with Between Bridges, Berlin, 2016; "Regarding Spectatorship: Revolt and the Distant Observer", in collaboration with Boaz Levin, Kunstraum Kreuzberg/Bethanien, Berlin, 2015; "Leisure Complex", Savvy Contemporary, Berlin, 2014.

Amer Matar is a Syrian documentary filmmaker, journalist, writer and cultural activist. He started as a freelance journalist in 2005, writing political satire and cultural reviews for national newspapers. With the uprising in Syria, he started documentary filmmaking. He co-directed and produced short documentaries that were broadcast by regional Pan-Arab TV stations. Several of his films have been screened internationally, notably *Azadi*, which won the Silver Hawk prize at Rotterdam IFF in 2011 (co-directed with Talal Derki). Amer is a board member of the Syrian Journalist League, head of the Syrian Aljazeera Media Group, co-founder and chairman of Al sharee for Development & Media 2011, and co-founder of the Syria Mobile Film Festival, launched in 2014. In 2012 he was awarded a scholarship from Heinrich-Böll-Stiftung. He was also a beneficiary of the prestigious PEN scholarship program, "Writers in Exile" (2012–2015).

Guevara Namer is a photographer and documentary filmmaker from Syria. She moved to Germany in 2013 and became a co-founder of DOX BOX e.V. She is moderating the online platform "The Community", a based-on-membership platform for documentary film professionals from the Arab world. Her

previous experiences include documentary film productions, capacity building in Syria and across the MENA region, as well as photography training
programs for citizen journalists and video activists in Syria.

Penelope Papailias is an associate professor of social anthropology at the
Department of History, Archaeology and Social Anthropology at the University of Thessaly, Greece, where she also directs the Laboratory of Social
Anthropology. Her monograph *Genres of Recollection: Archival Poetics and
Modern Greece* (2005) explores the politics of cultural memory and popular
practices of historical documentation and archiving. She is the author of
numerous articles on the cultural politics and media technologies of witnessing. She has co-authored an online, open-access textbook in Greek, entitled
Digital Ethnography (2015), is co-founder of the Pelion Summer Lab for Cultural Theory and Experimental Humanities, and is on the editorial board of
the online, open-access Greek feminist journal *φεμινιστιqά/feministiqá*.

Michael Richardson is Senior Lecturer in Media in the School of the Arts and
Media, UNSW, Australia. His transdisciplinary research investigates the intersection of affect and power in media, literature, politics and culture. He is currently working on a project about drones and witnessing in war and culture. He
is the author of *Gestures of Testimony: Torture, Trauma and Affect in Literature* (Bloomsbury, 2016) and co-editor of *Traumatic Affect* (2013).

Kerstin Schankweiler is an art historian and currently postdoctoral researcher
in the project "Affective Dynamics of Images in the Era of Social Media" at
the Collaborative Research Center Affective Societies at Freie Universität
Berlin, Germany. Her research areas include image practices in social media,
contemporary art from Africa, and art history in a global context. She is the
author of *Die Mobilisierung der Dinge* (Transcript, 2012) and co-curated the
exhibition "Affect Me. Social Media Images in Art" (KAI 10 Düsseldorf, 11
November–10 March 2018).

Sascha Simons teaches media studies at the University of Bonn, Germany, and
recently finished his PhD thesis on Critical Media Events and the politics of
web video witnessing. He is interested in the aesthetics, theory and history of
digital media and the interplay of media and social morphology. Sascha takes
part in the editorial collective of *spheres – Journal for Digital Cultures* and
the editorial board of the book series *Digital Cultures* (meson press). His
latest publications are "The ornament of mass customization. On the collective consciousness of dispersed examiners" in *Social Media—New Masses*;
and "Mobilizing memes. The contagious socio-aesthetics of participation" in
ReClaiming Participation.

Verena Straub is an art historian, working in the Collaborative Research Center
Affective Societies at the Freie Universität Berlin, Germany, on a project
entitled "Affective Dynamics of Images in the Era of Social Media". Her

research areas include visual culture, art and science, and the role of images in political conflicts. She is currently completing her PhD thesis on the video testimonies of suicide bombers and their adaptation in contemporary art. Her latest publications include "The making and gendering of a martyr: Images of female suicide bombers in the Middle East" in J. Eder and C. Klonk (eds), *Image Operations. Visual Media and Political Conflict* (Manchester University Press 2016).

Tobias Wendl is Professor at the Institute of Art History (KHI), Freie Universität Berlin, Germany, where he holds the Alfried Krupp von Bohlen und Halbach Chair for African Arts and Visual Cultures. He received his PhD in anthropology from the University of Munich in 1990 and is a founding member of the Collaborative Research Center Affective Societies. His books include *9/11 and its Remediations in Popular Culture and Arts in Africa* (Lit, 2015); *Snap Me One! Studiofotografen in Afrika* (1998, both with Heike Behrend); *Black Paris: Kunst und Geschichte einer schwarzen Diaspora* (Hammer, 2006, with Bettina von Lintig and Kerstin Pinther); *Africa Screams: Das Böse in Kino, Kunst und Kult* (Hammer, 2004).

Acknowledgements

The idea for this collective volume comes out of our research within the project "Affective Dynamics of Images in Times of Social Media" that is part of the Collaborative Research Centre Affective Societies at the Freie Universität Berlin. In this context we organized the international symposium "Image Testimonies—Witnessing in Times of Social Media" in Berlin in July 2017. The current book is based on the papers that were presented at this symposium and is the result of many lively discussions.

A large number of people and institutions have contributed to the successful completion of this publication and we would like to thank them for their encouragement, support and continuous interest in the project. We are very grateful to the Collaborative Research Centre Affective Societies and the German Research Council (DFG), for providing the framework and funding that made our research, the symposium and this volume possible. We would also like to thank the editors of the Routledge book series Affective Societies, Birgitt Röttger-Rössler and Doris Kolesch, for their support. Our sincere thanks go to Emily Briggs and Elena Chiu from Routledge who have been more than helpful during the process of publication. Tamar Blickstein, Landon Little, Pete Waterhouse, Katharina Jörder and Eva Wiegert provided excellent copy editing and put the finishing touches on the manuscript. We owe enormous gratitude to Linda Huke, the student assistant in our team, who has helped us throughout the project with an immense commitment and patience. Last but not least, we are deeply grateful to all contributors to this volume who have maintained the wonderful and inspiring spirit of the conference throughout the publication process. We thank them for their excellent and dedicated work as well as for their involvement in shaping the ideas we wanted to bring forth with this book. The collaboration was a delightful experience for us.

Berlin, July 2018
Kerstin Schankweiler, Verena Straub and Tobias Wendl

Chapter 1

Image testimonies

Witnessing in times of social media

*Kerstin Schankweiler, Verena Straub, and
Tobias Wendl*

The currency of image testimonies

Recent political conflicts have signaled an increased proliferation of image testimonies that are shared widely via social media. Although witnessing with and through images is not a phenomenon of the internet era (Zelizer 2007), image practices and politics in social media have significantly intensified the affective economies of image testimonies that are circulated in "real time" on Facebook, YouTube, Twitter and other social media platforms. New technologies have enabled individuals to record, upload, and share images directly via mobile devices, which make nearly everyone a potential witness at any given time. Since the so-called Arab Spring, it has become evident that audiovisual accounts of witnessing are circulated under new conditions that fundamentally reshape not only the practices of witnessing and testifying with images but also the testimonies as such. The Egyptian Uprising 2011 has been called the "Facebook Revolution"—not without contestation (Lim 2012)—and the Syrian conflict, for example, was described as the "the first YouTube war" (cited in Al-Ghazzi 2014, p. 441). This already indicates the assumed privileged role of social media in political conflict today. At the same time, social media and digital communication networks are integral parts of our current visual culture, characterized by the ubiquity of digital photography and imaging (Hand 2012). This new dominance of the visual and visuality has significantly transformed practices of witnessing and therefore calls for a new theoretical approach to testimony as image testimony. The current volume traces the contours of these conditions and attempts to develop a concept of image testimony that contributes to the ongoing debate on witnessing and testifying as contemporary image practices in the context of social media.

Towards a concept of image testimony

Our notion of image testimonies draws from a variety of theoretical strands and positions that crystallize around the two terms under question: image and testimony. Combining the two into a compound term first of all underscores the fact that testimony includes language-based as well as image-based exemplars and that their modulations oscillate between the registers of the verbal and the visual. Language-based testimonies on the one hand refer to scripted speech acts that were originally associated with either religious or legal contexts (such as giving a fervent expression of faith or making a solemn declaration in court). Image-based testimonies on the other hand show a less concise genealogy, though they have precursors in discursive practices that evolved in journalism (Zelizer 2007), as well as early visual anthropology using photographic images as an analytical tool and as evidence.[1] Testimonies, of course, have been recorded and transmitted in different and diverse media, embracing the media landscape as it developed. They have been communicated as spoken or written accounts, as literary texts,[2] illustrations, photographs or moving images. Regardless of modality, the social practice of testifying, in a basic understanding, includes the following parameters; a subject who acts as testifier, an event (or certain facts of this event) that form the content of the testimony, the testimony itself, as well as an audience to which the testimony is addressed, and, last but not least, a media infrastructure in which the testimony is articulated and circulated. As the chapters in our volume demonstrate, however, these parameters are not fixed entities but are constantly transformed and contested.

Through the proliferation of digital image technologies, growing transnational media connectivity and the increasing amount of images fluxing and refluxing around the globe, human experience has become much more visual (and visualized) than ever before. As a response, scholars in the 1990s made visual culture a new field of inquiry. Shifting their focus from the verbal to the visual, from text to image, they engaged in exploring how people seek information, meaning and pleasure in the interface with visual technologies and environments (Mirzoeff 1999, p. 3). Although images have thereby often been addressed as if they were texts, made up of discrete entities (signs, symbols), unfolding in a narrative plane, there are good reasons for trying to overcome such a textual bias. W.J.T. Mitchell (1986, p. 9) has stressed the agency of images that can make them grow into "actors on the historical stage," but he has also pointed to the difficulties of drawing neat demarcation lines between images and texts as they more often than not intermingle and interact. According to Mitchell (1994, p. 5),

> the "differences" between images and language are not merely formal matters; they are, in practice, linked to things like the difference between the (speaking) self and the (seen) other; between telling and showing, between "hearsay" and "eye-witness" testimony; between words (heard, quoted, inscribed) and objects, actions (seen, depicted, described); between sensory channels, traditions of representation, and modes of experience.

Current testimonial practices can mostly be described as a combination and interplay of image and text. This interplay shows considerable variations, from photographs that include written statements, audio-visual witnessing accounts and video footage to complexly layered multimedia contexts in the internet. Therefore, to speak of an image testimony does not proclaim the absence of language and text.

Witnessing and testimony have been theorized within a broad framework of epistemological, philosophical, ethical, and media-theoretical perspectives as well as in journalism and communication studies. Political scientist Michal Givoni (2011, p. 150) has observed: "Since the last third of the twentieth century, testimony has enjoyed unprecedented popularity as a philosophical theme, as an artistic gesture, and a political strategy." An important and influential body of literature on testimony has been developed in relation to the issue of trauma and the Holocaust (e.g. Felman & Laub 1992; Agamben 1999; Wieviorka 2006). While this strand of research focuses on the figure of the survivor-witness, other scholars aimed at expanding and differentiating a variety of witnessing figures, including the martyr, the juridical, historical or moral witness, and eyewitnessing versus fleshwitnessing (Fassin 2008; Assmann 2008; Harari 2009). The conceptual field of witnessing is characterized by a complex multiplicity of terms that are often not clearly distinguished and used synonymously, such as the witness, witnessing, bearing witness, to testify and testimony (Givoni 2011; Peters 2001; Tait 2011). John Durham Peters points to the double meaning of the verb *to witness*, "the passive one of seeing and the active one of saying" (Peters 2001, p. 709). Notions such as eyewitnessing or bearing witness seem to account for this ambiguity by differentiating between more passive and more active dimensions of witnessing. Understood as a social relational practice, witnessing always depends on its mediation through testimony (Frosh & Pinchevski 2009, p. 1). In our digital visual culture today, images have definitely become the dominant means of mediating witnessing. Our volume's focus on image testimonies acknowledges and highlights this central role of mediation, enabling witnessing accounts to move through space and time somewhat independently from the human witness.

In this context, it is worth noting that from early on, visuality and vision, image, and imaging technologies have shaped theories of testimony. In discourses of witnessing, seeing has been attributed a privileged role, compared with other senses of perception (Zelizer 2007, p. 410). Both in journalism and communication studies as well as in historical sciences, eyewitnessing gained importance as a key concept in relation to the account of events (Zelizer 2007; Burke 2001). In the most basic sense, eyewitnessing as "a social archetype" (Givoni 2011, p. 149) requires being physically present at an event, which unfolds before one's own eyes. According to John Durham Peters (2001, p. 720), "to be there, present at the event in space and time is the paradigm case [of witnessing]." This "being there" provides the legitimacy and reliability of the eyewitness. While the act of eyewitnessing is not detachable from the human body and its co-presence at the event, testimonies are mediations of this act, a result or product of eyewitnessing. Image testimonies, such as drawings, paintings or photographs were then valued analogously to archeological objects and artifacts as historical sources, as "objets témoin" (Gabus 1975) or "mute witnesses" (Burke 2001, p. 14), whose evidential qualities were at the same time doubted, just as the eyewitnesses' claim to authority. This doubt accompanied most of the historical discourse around eyewitnessing and was dependent on developments of imaging techniques used as "eye-witnessing tools" (Zelizer 2007, p. 418). As Renaud Dulong observes in his book, *Le témoin oculaire*, it was the camera that played an especially significant role in shaping our modern understanding of the eyewitness. With the emergence of photography, the eyewitness as a central figure in testimony theory was confronted with the ideal and model of the camera to register reality in a seemingly objective way (Dulong 1998). In contrast, Dulong as well as other researchers elaborated a different understanding of the eyewitness as an ethical figure with the ability to judge. This gave way to conceptualizations of the witness beyond the paradigm of the eyewitness (Givoni 2011). In view of current image practices, the dilemma of the eyewitness presents itself in a new light. With the mobile phone camera always at hand, witnessing practices today often combine both the ethical position of the human and the recording techniques of the camera. The resulting images document the events as much as they mark subjective positions and ethical engagements.

The topic of visual media again became center stage in theories that analyze mass mediated forms of witnessing. Building on John Ellis' idea of second-hand witnessing, which assumes that distant viewers "are drawn into the position of being witnesses" themselves (Ellis 2000, p. 10), Paul Frosh and Amit Pinchevski have coined the term "media witnessing" (Frosh & Pinchevski 2009). They elaborated on the ubiquity of "media witnessing performed *in*, *by* and *through* the media" (Frosh & Pinchevski 2009, p. 1). Shifting the focus away from the eyewitness to "witnessing as receptivity," Paul Frosh reminds us that "'bearing witness,' … is an act performed not by a witness but by a witnessing text" (Frosh 2006, p. 274). This shift makes it necessary to bring this witnessing text itself into focus. In light of the current primacy of the visual, it becomes obvious that the "witnessing text" today is predominantly image-based.

Although visuality and image practices represent a recurring theme in research on witnessing and testimony, the analysis of the images themselves has not been at the center of attention. Only a few publications, especially within art history and visual culture studies, have foregrounded the potential of images in bearing witness and addressed images as the subject of investigation (e.g., Guerin & Hallas 2007; Behrmann & Priedl 2014; Richardson 2016). Frances Guerin and Roger Hallas (2007, p. 4) insist on "the agency of the material image," which "is grounded in the performative (rather than constative) function of the act of bearing witness. Within the context of bearing witness, material images do not merely depict the historical world, they participate in its transformation." This body of literature does not yet account for witnessing in times of social media. Our volume therefore aims at expanding this discussion and at re-conceptualizing image testimony in the digital age.

Image testimony in the social media era

Research on witnessing and testimony has often revolved around turning points in history that have impacted practices of witnessing. Times of eminent crises have always given rise to a proliferation of testimonies. The Holocaust and 9/11 are two of the most prominent examples often referred to in testimony theory. A similar paradigm shift in witnessing practices can be attributed to a wave of new social movements that started only a decade after the terror attacks in New York and Washington with the uprisings in North Africa and the Arab World. These movements gained their paradigmatic status and momentum by the unprecedented use of mobile devices as tools of witnessing and social media networks, producing a hitherto unknown global visibility. This new visual culture of witnessing also spilled over to other parts of the globe—just think of the Occupy movement, the Gezi Park protests, Euromaidan, or ongoing activism such as #BlackLivesMatter. Many assumptions about witnessing and testimony need to be reconsidered in light of these recent developments, both in the political as well as in the media sphere of our networked world.

Works focusing on the digital turn and the creation of connectivity and connectedness via social media networks are particularly fruitful in this context. Several scholars (van Dyke 2008; Gunthert 2015; Gerling, Holschbach & Löffler 2018) emphasized the fact that digital photography has experienced a major change from its former memorial and commemorative functions to a more communication-oriented use. André Gunthert (2014) has introduced the concept of "conversational images," thus highlighting the new practices of photo sharing as a means to trigger conversations. Taking the events during the Egyptian revolution as their example, Florian Ebner and Constanze Wicke (2013) have suggested that the increasing connectedness of photographers, activists and citizen journalists with social media platforms has bestowed photography with a new testimonial layer and quality. This goes particularly for the unfolding of civic protest movements, when the digital devices connected to social media platforms, provide the witnesses, participating in the events on the ground, with a means for testifying. Kari Andén-Papadopoulos (2013), for example, has coined the term "citizen camera witnessing" in relation to embodied practices of witnessing in recent uprisings. Mette Mortensen (2015) has referred to this new condition as "connected witnessing," in which the former temporal and spatial division of witnessing and testifying increasingly dissolves. Mortensen (2015, p. 1403) explains:

> By placing emphasis on the participatory aspect, connective witnessing not only captures ongoing changes to acts of witnessing and political participation but also accentuates the increasing overlap between the two. Depending on focus, one may speak of witnessing as a personalized form of political participation or personalized political participation in the form of witnessing.

Considering the timeliness of the topic—with new technologies, practices and genres of image testimonies emerging as we write—our volume aims at laying the foundation for a relevant new field of research.

Pluralities of witnessing and evolving genres

The causes and motivations for producing image testimonies today are manifold and wide-ranging. Political activists and dissidents might use their mobile phone cameras as a means of resistance against oppressive regimes. Equally, regime loyalists, militant actors and terror groups employ digital media for their purposes (Al-Ghazzi 2014). Opposing actors often circulate their image testimonies with very different intentions on the same social media platforms. While some image testimonies are used as weapons with distinct aims, others seem to be recorded accidentally and without any clear intention by people who happen to be at the site of the witnessed event. Theorizing image testimonies in a globalized world needs to start by acknowledging the plurality of witnessing practices. While testimony theory has mostly emphasized the moral and ethical integrity of the witness, only recently have scholars challenged this conception in which "to witness means to be on the right side" (Peters 2001, p. 714) and instead highlighted the heterogeneity of witnessing agents. The field of perpetrator testimony has contributed to complicate the ethical position of the witness (Schmidt 2017). Likewise, Omar Al-Ghazzi (2014, p. 441) has criticized the often Eurocentric discourse around notions of citizen journalism for their "universalist assumptions about participation, democratization, and inclusion." Ideas of non-human witnessing (such as drone images) even more radically challenge the human and moral nature of the witness as such. With the broad spectrum of case studies and examples presented in this volume, we want to suggest that image practices of witnessing are not per se morally right or wrong, but can be employed for different political agendas and take on multiple forms of meaning depending on their specific context of production and reception. This becomes even more important in times of social media when it is almost impossible to trace and identify the intentions connected with image testimonies. Along with the heterogeneity of agents, social web image testimonies encompass a whole range of genres, such as images of protest, war, and human rights violations (see chapters by Simons, Bens, Schankweiler, Faulkner and the conversation between Liosi, Namer and Matar), selfies (chapter by Papailias), suicide bombers' video testimonies (chapter by Straub), or videos of the destruction of cultural goods (chapters by Günther & Bioly, and Wendl), and drone images (chapter by Richardson) and screenshots (chapter by Frosh).

Affective dimensions of image testimony

Besides their claim to "show the truth" or their aim to address political problems, the special efficacy of image testimonies seems to lie in their ability to affect, to move, or to mobilize. Especially in the context of social media, it becomes clear that image testimonies are embedded in a complex network of relationality that is characterized by processes of affecting and being affected. Our understanding of affect is grounded in the theoretical work carried out at the Collaborative Research Center Affective Societies at the Freie Universität Berlin, out of which this volume took shape. One of the main theoretical claims is

> that affect and emotion are relational phenomena unfolding in interaction and are not reducible to individual mental states or corporeal comportment. Even if viewed as a "bodily capacity" in a broad sense, affect can only be understood as a relational dynamic between actors and the complex socio-material environments in which they are embedded.
>
> (Röttger-Rössler & Kolesch 2018, p. xiii)

In a similar way, witnessing and testifying are necessarily relational acts that create ties between events, people and testimonies. Given the theoretical assumption that affectivity is the basis for the emergence of all social relations, it becomes obvious that affect needs to be conceptualized as a key concept for the understanding of the relationality of witnessing (Richardson & Schankweiler 2019). Our volume encompasses practices of image production, circulation and sharing as well as reception and appropriation, thereby underlining images as a focal point in the relational network of affective witnessing. The various case studies demonstrate that image testimonies not only serve as vectors of affectivity, but also play a major role in communicating affect and are therefore central for analyzing "affective societies" in our increasingly mobile and connected world today.

Temporalities of witnessing

The temporality of witnessing and testimony gains new relevance, given the infrastructure of social media networks. The digital cultural space is characterized by (the possibility of) processing in real time that coincides with an effect of actuality. This also provides a new framework for the specific temporalities that play out in image testimonies and that many chapters address. As the chapters by Schankweiler and Papailias show, for example, mobile phone witnessing in social media stand out due to a simultaneity of giving and seeing testimony. Other chapters question the conventional chronology of witnessing and testimony and provide examples where temporalities are reversed. Whereas in Frosh's case study, witnesses of the present become witnesses of the past (Yolocaust project), the suicide bombers that Straub discusses, are portrayed as witnesses of their own future martyrdom. The coexistence of images from all times and spaces on the internet and the possibility of seeing image testimonies again and again, increasingly complicates temporalities. When Paul Frosh and Amit

Pinchevski state that "space-time parameters have been utterly transformed" (Frosh & Pinchevski 2009, p. 8) in media witnessing, then the extension of space and time that accompanies image testimony is taken to the extreme in times of social media.

Analyzing image testimonies—structure of the volume

Part I—epistemologies of testimonies

The first part of the book sets the stage for some of the fundamental issues in relation to witnessing and image testimonies. In his contribution "Credibility in crisis: contradictions of web video witnessing," Sascha Simons provides a profound overview of the theoretical debates on the trustworthiness of testimonies, situating this within a "current crisis of media credibility." He shows how web videos intensify the epistemological and political contradictions inherent in media witnessing and tackles issues of reliability, politics, and aesthetics that prove highly relevant for the discussion of image testimonies as a whole. Revisiting John Fiske's aesthetic category of the "videolow" from 1996, Simons introduces the new term "datalow," thereby taking into account the "datafication" of video testimonies in the social media era.

The courtroom is the site par excellence when discussing the evidential potential of image testimonies. Jonas Bens' chapter "Affective images and the political trial" is based on courtroom ethnography at the International Criminal Court in The Hague and the trial against former LRA commander Dominic Ongwen, who was accused of committing war crimes in Northern Uganda. Bens examines the uses of images as evidence in court and argues that one needs to focus on their affective dimensions in order to understand the performative power these images hold. His analysis challenges established assumptions about the court's supposed objectivity and rationality and explores the role of non-humans giving testimony. By providing a bridge to Part II "Affective Witnessing," Bens' chapter exemplifies how image testimonies combine evidential qualities and the potential to create affective relationalities and emotional involvement.

In conversation

The interview "Fearless filming: video footage from Syria since 2011" captures the perspective of activists and practitioners and expands on the topics addressed in Part I. This chapter is based on a discussion between curator Marianna Liosi held with Syrian filmmakers Guevara Namer and Amer Matar, both living and working in exile in Berlin. Drawing on their experiences in Syria, Namer and Matar address the social and political conditions that filmmakers and citizen witnesses have been facing since the uprising in 2011. Their film projects and statements open up a number of questions concerning the expectations and frustrations of mobile phone witnessing in Syria: What is the efficacy of video testimonies in promoting actual political change? How have previously high expectations of video testimonies changed over the course of the Syrian conflict? From a personal point of view, Namer and Matar discuss to what extent video production works as an emancipatory gesture for Syrians—despite all fallen hopes and disappointments. Their perspectives also call into question a clear distinction between practices of citizen witnessing and artistic practices of filmmaking.

Part II—affective witnessing

Whereas affect surfaces throughout the volume, the chapters combined in Part II put special focus on an elaborated discussion of affect theory in relation to witnessing. Drawing from a case example from Morocco, Kerstin Schankweiler reads media witnessing of police violence as a practice and a politics of affecting. In her chapter "'Moroccan Lives Matter': practices and politics of affecting" she focuses on the aesthetic quality of videos testifying to police brutality, arguing that what is witnessed is mainly the videographer and other eyewitnesses being affected. Schankweiler describes this as a specific mode of "affective media witnessing" that is powerful in mobilizing a community of solidarity, political protest and dissent. By focusing on mobile phone image practices in which seeing and testifying happens at the same time and place, the dilemma of the "veracity gap" (Peters 2001, p. 711) presents itself in a new light.

Like Schankweiler, Michael Richardson elucidates the central relevance of affectivity to processes of witnessing and testifying. In his chapter "Drone's-eye view: affective witnessing and technicities of perception," he discusses drone images as a form of non-human testimony, that is closely tied to digital mediations of social media and its currency: affect. Extending the human perception, the apparatus of the drone with its iconic view from above brings into being an entirely new form of affective witnessing. This is not only used for military purposes but also by activists and artists alike, portraying drone witnessing as ambivalent, oscillating between weapons of death and means of resistance.

Part III—social media practices

The question of how social media technologies shape and, in turn, are shaped by image testimonies is the focus of Part III. Simon Faulkner's text "Photographic witnessing, the occupation and Palestinian politics" revolves around a specific genre of social media images: Facebook Cover Photos. He analyzes how Palestinian photographers and photojournalists portray themselves as activists putting their lives at risk to document the Israeli occupation. The (photo)journalist has been a key figure in testimony theory and has often been discussed as a supposedly impartial eyewitness. His position was recently challenged by new practices of citizen journalism and video activism. Faulkner's close-readings of photographs from Palestine expose this blurred distinction between professional journalism and politically and emotionally involved activism. He makes an argument for an approach to photography that focuses on the cultural meaning and value of these witnessing practices.

In her contribution "Witnessing to survive: selfie videos, live mobile witnessing and black necropolitics," Penelope Papailias focuses on yet another social media tool gaining relevance in practices of witnessing. She analyzes the Facebook Live video of Philando Castile's shooting by police. Besides an exploration of the specific temporalities and potentials of live mobile witnessing, her chapter refers to practices of visualization associated with the Black Lives Matter movement and problematizes colorblind theorizing of mobile citizen witnessing.

As an important expansion of witnessing in times of social media, Paul Frosh shifts the perspective from witnessing *in* social media to witnessing *of* social media. His chapter "Eye, flesh, world: three modes of digital witnessing" looks at social media not as a means for circulating testimonies but as image testimonies in and of themselves. Based on three case studies—the "Yolocaust" website by Israeli artist Shahak Shapira, Noa Jansma's Instagram account called #dearcatcallers, and a screenshot from WhatsApp used in a newspaper to report on the death of an Israeli soldier—Frosh maps out three modes of witnessing. He shows how the established modes of eye-witnessing and flesh-witnessing are reshaped in the context of social media. In addition, he introduces the new mode of world-witnessing, arguing that "digital networks themselves constitute witnessable worlds."

Part IV—witnessing destruction

To provide a more differentiated take on witnessing in its plurality, Part IV looks at image testimony at the intersection of creation and destruction, taking into account the perspectives of different actors and their contrary moral positions. As a special genre of perpetrator testimony, Verena Straub discusses the videotaped messages of suicide bombers in which various modes of witnessing are at play. Her chapter "'Living martyrs': testifying what is to come" foregrounds the unique temporality of these testimonies, which—instead of providing evidence for a past incident—anticipate the future suicide attack and set the stage for it to happen. Since the temporalities of testimony play out in reverse, Straub suggests considering these types of videos as forms of "anticipatory image testimony."

The intricate relationship between idolatry and iconoclasm is central to the final two chapters of the volume. In their contribution "Testimonies for a new social order: the Islamic State's iconic iconoclasm," Christoph Günther and Tom Bioly demonstrate how the so-called Islamic State uses videos and photographs testifying to the destruction of cultural goods as a means to promote social change. The authors highlight the violent quality of these image testimonies by

framing them as instances of "enforced witnessing" that make it almost impossible for viewers to take a neutral position. By turning the iconoclastic acts into
iconic images themselves, the Islamic State attempts to stabilize its claim to
power as sanctioned by divine ordinances.

In his chapter "From Cape Town to Timbuktu: iconoclastic testimonies in the
age of social media," Tobias Wendl presents three case studies of recent political
and religious iconoclasm in South Africa and Mali (the #RhodesMustFall campaign, the vandalizing of Brett Murray's painting "The Spear" and the destruction of Sufi mausoleums in Timbuktu). He argues that the destruction of images
simultaneously unmasks and enhances the power of images and that the very act
of destruction in itself provides a testimony to antecedent conflict. Particular
emphasis is given to the analysis of subsequent secondary image testimonies and
re-enactments in which after-images of the iconoclastic defacement and annihilation have emerged and were widely shared, heavily fueled by the immediacy
promise of the social media and their potential to communicate a multiplicity of
voices and viewpoints.

Although dealing with a variety of case studies and perspectives, the geographical scope throughout this volume is somewhat biased on the MENA
region and sub-Saharan Africa. Yet we do not see this as a limitation. In light of
political conflicts and the relevance of citizen media witnessing in these regions
we argue that a special focus on the economy of image testimonies originating in
countries such as Syria, Iraq, Israel and Palestine, or Morocco, Mali, Uganda
and South Africa, is highly appropriate and topical. A geographical focus also
fosters the coherence and dialogue between the individual chapters. However, as
many chapters show, a discussion of image testimony in social media does by no
means confine itself to any regional context. Rather, the scope of case studies
demonstrate that image testimony is a global phenomenon characterized by
transnational entanglements and a variety of local appropriations that need to be
contextualized respectively.

The lines of thought that we outlined as key elements of image testimony, cut
across the different sections and chapters of this volume and work as common
threads. The guiding themes of plurality, affectivity and temporality shape a new
approach on testimony theory. Together, the contributions create a kind of
mosaic that provides a more nuanced picture of what we conceptualize as image
testimony in times of social media.

Notes

1 Connections can be established to social documentary photography as it evolved in the
  depression-era of the 1930s in the US, patronized by the Farm Security Administration
  (FSA) and associated with the names of Walker Evans, Dorothea Lange and Gordon
  Parks. Another precursor is the photography-based research monograph *Balinese Character: A Photographic Analysis* by Gregory Bateson and Margret Mead 1942).
2 A special case of literary testimony is the genre of *testimonio* in Latin America, see
  Beverley (2004).

References

Agamben, G. (1999). *Remnants of Auschwitz: The Witness and the Archive*. New York: Zone Books.

Al-Ghazzi, O. (2014). "Citizen journalism" in the Syrian Uprising: Problematizing Western narratives in a local context. *Communication Theory*, 24(4), pp. 435–454.

Andén-Papadopoulos, K. (2014). Citizen camera-witnessing: Embodied political dissent in the age of "mediated mass self-communication". *New Media & Society*, 16(5), pp. 753–769.

Assmann, A. (2008). Vier Grundtypen von Zeugenschaft. In U. Petzold & C. Trouvé (eds), *Zeugen und Zeugnisse: Bildungsprojekte zur NS-Zwangsarbeit mit Jugendlichen*, pp. 12–26. Berlin: Stiftung Erinnerung, Verantwortung und Zukunft.

Bateson, G. & Mead, M. (1942). *Balinese Character: A Photographic Analysis*. New York: New York Academy of Science.

Behrmann, C. & Priedl, E. (eds) (2014). *Autopsia: Blut- und Augenzeugen. Extreme Bilder des christlichen Martyriums*. München: Wilhelm Fink Verlag.

Beverley, J. (2004). *Testimonio: On the Politics of Truth*. Minneapolis: University of Minnesota Press.

Burke, P. (2001). *Eyewitnessing: The Uses of Images as Historical Evidence*. London: Reaction Books.

Dulong, R. (1998). *Le témoin oculaire: Les conditions sociales de l'attestation personnelle*. Paris: L'École des Hautes Etudes des Sciences Sociales.

Ebner, F. & Wicke, C. (eds) (2013). *Cairo: Open City. New Testimonies from an Ongoing Revolution*. Leipzig: Spector Books.

Ellis, J. (2000). *Seeing Things: Television in the Age of Uncertainty*. London: I.B. Tauris.

Fassin, D. (2008). The humanitarian politics of testimony: Subjectification through trauma in the Israeli–Palestinian conflict. *Cultural Anthropology*, 23(3), pp. 531–558.

Felman, S. & Laub, D. (1992). *Testimony: Crises of Witnessing in Literature, Psychoanalysis, and History*. New York: Routledge.

Frosh, P. (2006). Telling presences: Witnessing, mass media, and the imagined lives of strangers. *Critical Studies in Media Communication*, 23(4), pp. 265–284.

Frosh, P. & Pinchevski, A. (2009). Introduction: Why media witnessing? Why now? In P. Frosh & A. Pinchevski (eds), *Media Witnessing: Testimony in the Age of Mass Communication*, pp. 1–19. Basingstoke: Palgrave Macmillan.

Gabus, J. (1975). *L'objet témoin: Les références d'une civilisation par l'objet*. Neuchâtel: Ides et calendes.

Gerling, W., Holschbach, S. & Löffler, P. (2018). Bilder verteilen: Fotografische Praktiken in der digitalen Kultur, Bielefeld: Transcript.

Givoni, M. (2011). Witnessing/testimony. *Mafte'akh: Lexical Review of Political Thought*, 2, pp. 147–169.

Guerin, F. & Hallas, R. (2007). *The Image and the Witness: Trauma, Memory and Visual Culture*. London: Wallflower.

Gunthert, A. (2014). The conversational image: New uses for digital photography. *Études photographiques*, 31 (Spring), pp. 54–71.

Gunthert, A. (2015). *L'image partagée: La photographie numérique*. Paris: Textuel.

Hand, M. (2012). *Ubiquitous Photography*. Cambridge, UK: Polity.

Harari, Y.N. (2009). Scholars, eyewitnesses, and flesh-witnesses of war: A tense relationship. *Partial Answers: Journal of Literature and the History of Ideas*, 7(2), pp. 213–228.

Lim, M. (2012). Clicks, cabs, and coffee houses: Social media and oppositional movements in Egypt, 2004–2011. *Journal of Communication*, 62(2), pp. 231–248.

Mirzoeff, N. (1999). *Introduction to Visual Culture*. London and New York: Routledge.

Mitchell, W.J.T. (1986). *Iconology: Image, Text, Ideology*. Chicago: University of Chicago Press.

Mitchell, W.J.T. (1994). *Picture Theory: Essays on Verbal and Visual Representation*. Chicago: University of Chicago Press.

Mortensen, M. (2015). Connective witnessing: Reconfiguring the relationship between the individual and the collective. *Information, Communication & Society*, 18(11), pp. 1393–1406.

Peters, J.D. (2001). Witnessing. *Media, Culture & Society*, 23(6), pp. 707–723.

Richardson, M. (2016). *Gestures of Testimony: Torture, Trauma, and Affect in Literature*. New York: Bloomsbury.

Richardson, M. & Schankweiler, K. (2019). Affective witnessing. In J. Slaby & C. von Scheve (eds), *Affective Societies: Key Concepts*. London: Routledge.

Röttger-Rössler, B. & Kolesch, D. (2018). Affective societies: Introduction to the book series. In B. Röttger-Rössler & J. Slaby (eds), *Affect in Relation: Families, Places, Technologies*, pp. xii–xv. London: Routledge.

Schmidt, S. (2017). Perpetrators' knowledge: What and how can we learn from perpetrator testimony? *Journal of Perpetrator Research*, 1(1), pp. 85–104.

Tait, S. (2011). Bearing witness, journalism and moral responsibility. *Media, Culture & Society*, 33(8), pp. 1220–1235.

van Dyke, J. (2008). Digital photography: Communication, identity, memory. *Visual Communication*, 7(1), pp. 57–76.

Wieviorka, A. (2006). *The Era of the Witness*. Ithaca, NY: Cornell University Press.

Zelizer, B. (2007). On "having been there": "Eyewitnessing" as a journalistic key word. *Critical Studies in Media Communication*, 24(5), pp. 408–428.

Part I

Epistemologies of testimonies

Chapter 2

Credibility in crisis

Contradictions of web video witnessing

Sascha Simons

The current public debates about media witnessing lie at the heart of a controversy. What is at stake is the function of public media as a fourth estate. While a generalized distrust against those in power has been an impetus of this function, it now seems this distrust has reversed against the representatives, conventions, and forms of established media institutions themselves, forging a veritable crisis of credibility. In the context of this crisis, media witnesses not only report on events, but also testify to an ongoing social and media upheaval. Digital and social media not only raise the question of how a particular event has taken place, but also of who may speak or make herself heard in a rapidly changing socio-technical environment.

Videos often play a privileged role in this process. They qualify as witnesses not because of their ontological properties, but because of cultural ascriptions that are inherently linked to their discursive history. Although an awareness of digital image manipulation has become commonplace, and despite the fact that analogue video technology already lacks the ontological qualities of the photographic index, the promise of a mechanical, true-to-life representation still permeates cultural conceptions of video recordings (Nichols 1994, p. 29). Not least, it fosters the imagination of governments and their civic counter cultures using videos as a means of surveillance or of subversive sousveillance (Mann, Nolan & Wellmann 2003). This latter subversive appropriation gained momentum during the so-called Green Revolution in the streets of Teheran in 2009, and has shaped our perception of the manifold protest movements ever since. Ubiquitous and numerous camera lenses seem to promise a multi-perspective, unfiltered, first-hand experience of whatever may be happening, and an authentic expression of an otherwise ignored political discontent.

This process is not new. It transposes the high hopes and emancipatory claims of the 1970s Video Guerrilla and 1980s Camcorder Revolution to the sphere of media distribution. Nowadays, not only audio-visual production and reproduction are affordable for an increasing number of customers. Further, social media networks currently mediate the means of circulation. In contrast to their predecessors, today's video witnesses can share their audio-visual footage via a variety of ready-made streams and archives.

This proliferation of audio-visual testimonies and sources has changed the way media events unfold (Andén-Papadopoulos 2014, p. 759). But it has also destabilized the very conventions and institutions designed to guarantee the validity of media testimonies, such as the juridical distinction of witnesses, victims and offenders (Krämer 2015, p. 147). With the rise of web videos, we are no longer just "witnesses without a tribunal", but are becoming witnesses through the eyes of victims who might as well be perpetrators (Peters 2009 [2001], p. 39). Facing a situation where neutrality and objectivity give way to subjective involvement and affective contagion, what we need are witnesses for the witness. Web videos have therefore intensified a general unreliability of witnessing that arises from the notorious difficulty of translating lived experience into discursive form. This "veracity gap" calls for a new social epistemology of witnessing that bears an ethical claim (Peters 2009, p. 48; Schmidt 2011, p. 50; Krämer 2015, p. 160). The following sections therefore reconstruct how the current crisis of credibility is inherently linked to this socio-technical redistribution, and consider what an ethics of web video witnessing might look like.

Unreliability of the witness

The lone witness has always been unreliable—not at least due to her mediality, as most notably John Durham Peters has argued in a widely cited essay. He defines the witness as "the paradigm case of a medium: the means by which experience is supplied to others who lack the original" (Peters 2009 [2001], p. 26). In order to function as "surrogate sense organs of the absent", witnesses need to translate a subjective experience into a discursive form that can be filed and stored, processed and distributed, publicly shared or challenged (Peters 2009 [2001], p. 25). However, this translation is a tricky task that raises a banal but inevitable epistemological problem: "Words can be exchanged, experiences not" (Peters 2009 [2001], p. 26).

This epistemological problem hints at the truism in media theory that any translation or mediation alters or even constitutes what is to be translated or mediated: in this case a subjective perception. Therefore, even if we set aside deliberate false testimonies, already sincere witnesses are likely to fail in giving truthful accounts of a given event, because their initial perception has been washed away by oblivion or trauma, overlaid with memories, biased by over-ambitious criminal prosecutors, contradicted by other witnesses—or just has not been that accurate in the first place.[1]

Inaccurate first-hand accounts are anything but an exception, since observers become witnesses unexpectedly and retroactively. At the time of witnessing, they are not aware of being expected to testify about what they have seen or heard, or of the details to which they will be expected to have paid more attention.

> [T]hey are elected after the fact. [...] In testifying we must take responsibility for what we once took little responsibility for. We must report on

events, the details of which have assumed as massive an importance as they were once trivial. [...] Testifying has the structure of repentance: retroactively caring about what we were once careless of.[2]

(Peters 2009 [2001], p. 40)

Sybille Krämer takes Peters' notion of the mediality of the witness one step further. In her media philosophy of the messenger, she systematically unfolds his more or less rambling observations. For her, the media function confronts the witness with a double bind. In order to give an accurate account of an occurrence, witnesses would have to function like mere recording devices—an impossible task for obvious reasons. On the contrary, they can only comply with this demand if they trade in their personal credibility for the validity of their testimonies. Therefore, following Krämer, the witness embodies two contradictory demands.

The fundamental dilemma of witnessing consists of the Janus-faced role of the witness, which implies and requires being a medium and likewise being a person. Personality and depersonalisation are *both* necessary to make the mediality of the witness possible.

(Krämer 2015, p. 153)

However, even what Peters terms "a mere tablet of recording" cannot evade this epistemological paradox (Peters 2009 [2001], p. 33), as Rudolf Arnheim argues transferring the witnessing paradox to photographic authenticity (Arnheim 1997, p. 53). In this perspective, what has been said about the mediality of the (human) witness holds true for media testimonies as well, to which Peters and Krämer pay less attention. In either case, witnessing translates subjective veracity into objective truth. The aforementioned epistemological gap is thus also an ethical one, which the witness only can bridge thanks to what Krämer calls the social epistemology of witnessing (Krämer 2015, p. 160).

Put simply, witnesses need someone to trust them. And since—to misquote Lenin—confidence is good but control is better, both witnesses and their addressees can make use of a whole apparatus of more or less institutionalized procedures to vouch for witness credibility (Peters 2009 [2001], p. 29). If witnessing according to Peters "is a discourse with a hole in it that awaits filling" (Peters 2009 [2001], p. 26), Krämer suggests such filling can only be accomplished through a social endeavour, since the witness is confronted with a task she cannot solve on her own. Thus, in speaking about the mediality of the witness, one speaks about social conditions as much as epistemological ones.[3]

The politics of witnessing

Mediality thus implies that bearing witness is subject to the social distribution of power. This draws our attention to two political dimensions of witnessing, comprising its political effects on one hand, and its social conditions on the other. One needs to combine both angles to do justice to the crucially changing socio-technical environment of audio-visual witnessing. Thus, the following paragraphs tackle the interplay of these perspectives, looking at shifts in the distribution of witnessing capacities, and at how these changes shape the roles, modes and rhetoric of video witnessing and activism.

First, witnessing can have political consequences. In light of the political agency of the witness, the epistemological *catch 22* reveals a political equivalent. Sybille Schmidt and Ramon Voges note that the political significance of the witness is bound to her apolitical being (Schmidt & Voges 2011, p. 13). Again, the authority of witnesses is contingent on their impartiality, which is why, for example, victims in court make weak witnesses (Krämer 2015, p. 149). It is thanks to this impartiality that witnessing can unfold its persuasive and ultimately mobilizing power. As will be shown below with regards to video activism, this obviously poses a problem for political practices of witnessing that deliberately take sides. Insofar as witnessing is used as a rhetorical means serving a political agenda, this impartiality diminishes, as does the source of the witness' authority. Therefore, following Hannah Arendt, Schmidt and Voges locate the witness on the margins of the social and economic centres (Schmidt & Voges 2011, p. 10). In this view, witnesses are deprived from actual power, but are able to cross the borders between political, epistemological, and ethical discourses.

Second, Tamar Ashuri and Amit Pinchevski approach this boundary space from the opposite side. They are not so much concerned about the political outcome of witnessing, as by its social conditions. They take seriously the aforementioned exposure of the witness to social power relations, and map this relational space as a social field in the sense of Pierre Bourdieu (1993, p. 72). For them, the field of witnessing is composed of eyewitnesses, mediators and audience. Eyewitnesses connect event and discourse, while mediators—like mass media institutions—connect discourse to meaning, and the audience, in turn, transforms meaning into judgements (Ashuri & Pinchevski 2009, p. 142). Each translation depends on trust, which can be considered as the ultimate symbolic capital of the field.

> It follows that being a witness is subject to struggle, not privilege; it is something to be accomplished, not simply given. [...] We propose that the game being played in the witnessing field is a game of trust in which agents compete to gain the trust of their designated audiences.
>
> (Ashuri & Pinchevski 2009, p. 136)

This competition, as Ashuri and Pinchevski (2009, p. 146) continue, "makes witnessing a political arena" that takes place both "across zones and between zones". This means that eyewitnesses may compete with each other, but also with mediators or the audience. Furthermore, the competitive field of witnessing is organized hierarchically "with the mediator at the top" (Ashuri & Pinchevski

2009, p. 146), since the aesthetic capacity to transform a sensual experience into a public testimony assures a privileged, albeit contested, position in the field.

> Thus, while the mediators are arguably the dominant agent in the field, their privilege is forever tainted by their reliance on eyewitnesses insofar as providing the one thing the mediator will always lack—presence at the event. The distinctive quality of "being there" is therefore the eyewitness's exclusive resource, which secures for them an integral, if limited, point of ascendancy within the field.
>
> (Ashuri & Pinchevski 2009, p. 146)

In sum, witnessing has always been a precarious practice, because witnesses are epistemologically and politically ambivalent figures. This picture is already complex when we treat witnesses as media, as we have done thus far. However, this complexity is greatly amplified as soon as we consider audio-visual testimonies as media witnesses, as we do below.

The resurrected "videolow"

The aforementioned contradictions have come to a head, since ubiquitous handheld cameras and social media services have made the means of audio-visual reproduction and distribution available on a large scale. Consequently, it has never been so easy to fill the contested role of a witness. Potential witnesses are ready to shoot and share whatever may transpire anywhere their camera-packed and networked handheld devices may go. For better or worse, this media re-distribution has irreversibly altered the socio-aesthetic distribution of witnessing. And it has left Ashuri's and Pinchevski's fragile equilibrium between eyewitnesses, mediators and audiences out of balance (Andén-Papadopoulos 2014, p. 758).

This equilibrium relied on an uneven distribution of technology. In Ashuri's and Pinchevski's schematic triad, eyewitnesses are deprived of technological means. And as a result, the transformation of witnesses into testimonies is exclusively performed by mediators.

> Granting an eyewitness the status of testimony is the mediator's prerogative. In terms of the field, one is an eyewitness only insofar as one is found qualified by the mediator. Hence, an eyewitness who fails to gain the status of testimony does not figure in the field and is consequently condemned to silence.
>
> (Ashuri & Pinchevski 2009, p. 144)

But eyewitnesses with access to the requisite media technology are much less likely to be "condemned to silence". When the mediators lose their technological monopoly, the clear boundaries drawn by Ashuri and Pinchevski become blurry.

This kind of audio-visual enunciation, which is primarily shot with handheld cameras, clearly differs from classical media coverage. Its shaky and blurry images evoke a more tactical and subjective participant's feel than the distant, strategic gaze of the TV news.[4] It commits itself to the performative aesthetics of authenticity that John Fiske tagged as the "videolow" of witness videos over 20 years ago.

> [T]heir lower-quality images, poor but closely involved vantage points, moments of loss of technical control (blurred focus, too-rapid pans, tilted or dropped cameras), and their reduced editing all serve to reveal the discursive control that official news exerts over the events it reports. Videolow shows that events can always be put into discourse differently from videohigh, and this enhances its sense of authenticity.
>
> (Fiske 1996, p. 159)

This aesthetic continuity is anything but self-evident, and points to at least two significant technological innovations. The first concerns the videos' aesthetics and the conceptual status of witnessing. By replacing the optical viewfinder, the display liberates the cameras from the human eye, further merging them with the filming bodies. In the words of Rabih Mroué they become "eyes implanted in their hands" (Mroué 2012, p. 30). The recordings of these optical prostheses always show traces of the filming body and its environment, and never conceal the *hors-champ* in front of or beyond the camera (Thiele 2010, p. 290; Krautkrämer 2014, p. 119).[5] With the filming body and its environment so evidently inscribed into the audio-visual forms, the difference between witnesses and audio-visual testimonies is suspended. The more entangled camera and body become, the smaller the threshold between witness and testimony.[6]

The second technological innovation concerns the structure of distribution, and bears mainly political consequences. The video witnesses of the 1970s and 1980s that Fiske is concerned with are constantly struggling with how to share their footage (Fiske 1996, p. 160; Sorensen 1991, p. 33; Holmes n.d.) Nowadays, in contrast, video witnesses have access to various means of distribution as well. One could say that the videolow has been resurrected under the conditions of social media and its imperative of spreadability,[7] thus fortifying the role of the witnesses at the expense of their mediators (Andén-Papadopoulos 2014, pp. 755, 759). Nonetheless, it would be far too hasty to speculate about a technologically driven empowerment of an autonomous eyewitness who dispensed with her mediators. As the next section shows, such a notion of radical autonomy ignores the aforementioned epistemological and political paradoxes of witnessing, potentially exacerbating the crisis of credibility even more.

Crisis readiness and the dilemma of strategic witnessing

This revival of the videolow corresponds with a cultural transformation of witnessing caused by the ubiquity of both cameras and video footage. As Kari

Andén-Papadopoulos points out, "the very handiness of the mobile is in itself trans-formative", since there seems to be nothing unworthy of being filmed and shared (Andén-Papadopoulos 2014, p. 760). Whenever something more or less extra-ordinary happens, people spontaneously draw their camera-phones to document the events and authenticate their participation in it. Witnessing becomes a routine reflex for coping with the interruptions of the everyday routine. In a broader perspective, it conforms to a cultural instability that Paul Frosh and Pinchevski describe as crisis readiness. As they note, crisis is no longer an interruption of the routine, but has become the routine itself (Frosh & Pinchevski 2009a, p. 295).

> In highly complex and over-determined social structures, virtually every moment thus becomes potentially crucial—critical, to return to our original etymology—to the future well-being of political, social, and economic systems. Modern audio-visual technologies that render reality in new units of time (the freeze frame and the slow motion, for instance) which can be given sudden, decisive significance, and whose indexical recording of inci-dentals escapes the particular intentionality of those deploying them, are particularly suited to this sense of the pregnancy of any moment as the har-binger of crisis.
>
> (Frosh & Pinchevski 2009a, p. 298)[8]

This "perpetual condition of transformative possibility" (Frosh & Pinchevski 2009a, p. 303) reverses Peters' notion that "witnessing is always a state of exception, an emergency" (Peters 2009, p. 47). Instead, it becomes a ritual in which witnesses are no longer exclusively "elected after the fact" (Peters 2009 [2001], p. 40), but "wilfully assume" their role and ultimately anticipate the events they are supposed to reconstruct.

> Activists and protestors are performing not only in front of, but for the camera which, in turn, is suggestive of the increasing extent to which "ordinary" people are now socialized into crisis recording and reporting.
>
> (Andén-Papadopoulos 2014, p. 764)

They thereby blur the line between witnessing and political action, and render witnessing a strongly self-referential practice.[9]

Video activism can serve as a prime illustration of this development. Since its heydays in the 1970s and 1980s, the promise of video activism has relied on its capacity to publicly expose social and political grievances, of which the mass media publics would otherwise be unaware. For this purpose, it connects discur-sive topoi of counter-surveillance with counter-publics. This means that video activism was intended to invert media surveillance techniques in the name of the civil rights, for the purpose of changing the shape of public debate (Garrin 1992, p. 33; Fiske 1996, p. 158). Its videos oblige its viewers to engage in a moment of discursive and media reflexivity, as they challenge hegemonic perspectives and aesthetics. Characterized by the Fiske quote above as aesthetics of authenticity, these unorthodox media forms can ignite an affective, contagious force that is hard to predict and even harder to control.[10] However, videolow's alleged authenticity and its political agency are fed by the prefix "counter" (Fiske 1996, p. 157). As such, videolow echoes the witness's position at the margins, far from the power centre of the field. Hence, video activism is driven by the same "imperative of speaking out against unjust power" that is often thought to strengthen the witness' stance (Andén-Papadopoulos 2014, p. 757). If Peters (2009 [2001], p. 30) is right that "to witness means to be on the right side", video activists should make confident witnesses since they take sides by definition, as do their videos. Nevertheless, they remain witnesses with interests and, as such, need to be aware of the ambivalences imposed by the political practice of witnessing. This means that inasmuch as video activists claim the role of an eyewitness, they have to deal with its epistemological and political contradictions. This problem comes to the fore when the former exceptional and granted occasion of being a witness becomes a ritualized, conscious and potentially instrumental act—and even more when witnesses' interests become subjects of strategic concerns following more or less formalized aesthetic protocols.

In this sense, Sandra Ristovka tackles the ongoing professionalization of video activism with the term "strategic witnessing". In her understanding, such witnessing follows a more utilitarian approach and "illustrates a shift away from witnessing of to witnessing for" (Ristovka 2016, p. 1041). Her observations build on an analysis of the non-governmental organization Witness, founded by former Genesis singer Peter Gabriel in the aftermath of the Rodney King incident. She reconstructs how the organization's approach has changed over time. After trusting that cameras in the right hands would do the job more or less on their own until the early 2000s, Witness has since extended its technology-driven approach to include hands-on support, such as on-the-ground-training or legal counselling. This support focuses on the videos' "context, message, and call for action" rather "than merely documenting violence and suffering" (Ristovka 2016, p. 1042). Media witnessing is not constituted or limited by the connection to a witnessed event, but rather "signals a strategic position in regards to an audience" and calls for rhetorical and aesthetic strategies appealing this envisioned audience (Ristovka 2016, p. 1044). In consequence, the audience ultimately replaces the witnessed event as the end of the organization's means.

> In this context, professionalization downplays the traditional paradigm of video activism as a public assemblage of critical voices and the historical function of witnessing where the imperative to bear witness is of uppermost ethical importance. Instead, the key focus is how to render activist witnessing legible to relevant stakeholders. Witnessing, therefore, gets confined to institutional parameters. What could potentially get lost, then, is a broader public cognizance of a traumatic occurrence.
>
> (Ristovka 2016, p. 1036)

But this is not the only thing that could get lost, if one insists on the aforementioned paradoxical structure of witnessing, which entails serving as an epistemological subject and object at the same time. By reconstructing significant modifications in the field of witnessing thus far, we have mainly dealt with the second dimension of political witnessing. To complement that perspective, it is now necessary to discuss political witnessing through the lens of the epistemologically derived dilemma outlined by Schmidt and Voges. If the political efficacy of witnessing stems from its apolitical position, then neglecting the latter strategic witnessing runs the risk of upsetting the balance between poles of apolitical impartiality (or objectivity) and political influence (or subjectivity). Although this utilitarian approach may produce its intended impact, it runs the long-term risk of undermining the authority of witnessing. If the power of activist video comes at this price, it ultimately cuts off one of its main and initial sources.[11]

New mediators and the datalow

Interestingly, Ristovka's analysis suggests that it is now the audience, rather than the witnesses, who stand to profit most from this media crisis. Hinting at the limits of the witnesses' emancipation, she implicitly conforms well to Ashuri's and Pinchevski's field theory. By loosening established bonds of trust among witnesses, mediators and the audience, strategic witnessing contributes to a profound revaluation of the field's capital. Following Bourdieu, one of the best ways to change the rules of the game played in a particular field is to devaluate the dominant capital (Bourdieu & Wacquant 1992, p. 98). In this case, that capital is trust as it is embodied in the "public standing, reputation, and profile" of traditional media agencies (Ashuri & Pinchevski 2009, p. 145). In this perspective the current crisis of media credibility is not a surprise so much as a predictable effect of the field's dynamic. It is a crisis partially provoked by the socio-technical redistribution of aesthetic capacities. However, the liberating possibilities of this redistribution are hardly limitless. If we take Ashuri's and Pinchevski's chain of interdependent translations seriously, this shift might also subvert the position of eyewitnesses who, ultimately, owe their authority to the work of mediating second-order observers. If the apparatus of verification cannot hold up to the "current abundance and omni-presence of first-person testimonies", that crisis will probably fall back onto the technologically equipped eyewitnesses as well—unless they find new witnesses for the witness (Ristovka 2016, p. 1034).

Having discussed the witnesses and the audience, it is now important to turn our attention to the mediators as well. Whatever new forms of symbolic capital will serve as future currency for the field's social transactions, they are quite obviously no longer restricted to the genres, narratives, or the ethical standards and habitus of those mediating agencies that Ashuri and Pinchevski locate in the hegemonic centre. Again, it becomes clear that their schema stems from a broadcast structure that does not readily apply to the current constellation. Both the narrative of the technologically empowered eyewitness, as well as that of the impact-oriented strategy call into question the mediators' formerly privileged position. Nevertheless, neither the witnesses nor the audience can do without them. The mediators have changed, but not vanished. In fact, they have even multiplied.

This includes not only witnesses, who now claim former mediators' prerogatives, but also new institutionalized actors, who provide the skills and the means for distributing mediated witnessing—such as Witness, among others. Of course the more influential actors are the largely commercial platforms that provide the technological infrastructure to enable the exchange of videos and to control and exploit the data generated (Andrejevic 2009, p. 418; Kessler & Schäfer 2009, p. 285). This not only concerns the video-data and the things they make visible, but also the inevitably produced meta-data that reveal when, where and with which or whose device the footage was shot, or via which routes it has been shared and watched.

Thus, the mediators' position has not become obsolete at all, and nor have the traditional mediators (Frosh & Pinchevski 2009b, p. 11). However, their position has indeed become more complex and contested. The enforced competition between witnesses and mediators is itself an effect of a competition between traditional and new mediators. These new mediators have established themselves as important new agents in the centre of the field, and have changed its rules irrevocably. Their socio-technical protocols care less about qualitative judgements than about quantitative measures and patterns. They follow a positivist and utilitarian approach, driven by an alleged incorruptible objectivity of data rather than by journalistic impartiality. These new mediators remind us that the social epistemology of witnessing is in fact a socio-technical one that extends beyond the aesthetics and broadcasting of this footage, since the distribution of this footage crucially depends on the algorithmic processing of data in digital networks. And the new mediators pose new ethical challenges regarding surveillance, privacy and encryption, manipulation and data forensics.

At this point the question arises as to how such an unsettled field can restore a minimum of trust between old, new and newly empowered agents. And what are the role and responsibility of video witnesses in this process?

First, recapitulating the previous arguments, this responsibility mainly consists of acknowledging the contradictions that both open and limit the space for witnessing as an epistemological and political practice. So the least a responsible witness can do, is to be aware of her own Janus-faced role, which has not been resolved even by the major socio-technical changes described above.

Second, these changes exceed video-capable devices and editing platforms. Hence, video witnessing is no longer concerned merely with moving images and their soundtrack but with data and its mediating agencies. Within this sphere of data arise new ethical challenges. Confronted with these challenges, it is helpful to revisit Fiske. He reminds us that videolow's aesthetic and political authenticity is a relational capacity or even a parasitic one—exposing video-high's discursive patterns and thereby opposing the dominant power, which for Fiske, of course, is capital (Fiske 1996, p. 157). If that still holds true, and if the videolow aesthetics still account for the authority of video witnessing, then web video testimonies must also unveil their new mediators. And this means that videolow alone is not enough, but must be supplemented by something that—for lack of better terms—might be called "datalow".

Notes

1 The witnesses' fallibility is also reflected in court, where testimonies play a subordinated role compared with evidences and may be necessary to make a trial, but not sufficient (Peters 2009 [2001], p. 29; Krämer 2015, p. 149; Derrida & Stiegler 2002 [1996], p. 92).

2 The temptation of large-scale video surveillance consists not least in the promise to bypass this tricky obligation by excessive recording and storing.

3 By contrast, Krämer identifies witnessing as a basic role model for the trust-based transfer of any knowledge (Krämer 2015, p. 162). Crises in the field of witnessing would then allude vice versa to much broader social upheavals exceeding the question of media credibility.

4 The terms "tactical" and "strategic" refer to Michel de Certeau's distinction between strategies and tactics (de Certeau 1984, p. 34), which has been an important conceptual resource for various video activist groups and, in particular, gave name to the Tactical TV and Tactical Media movement (Garcia & Lovink 1997).

5 Tutorials instructing the operators to film characteristic objects, which later can easily be identified, reduplicate this aesthetic necessity on a poetological level (Mroué 2012, p. 26).

6 These witnessing texts easily escape the attention of those who worry too much about the veracity gap (Frosh 2009, p. 54), but prove right Jacques Derrida, who in the aftermath of the Rodney King video predicted that electronic and digital media would undermine the conceptual distinction between witness and testimony (Derrida & Stiegler 2002 [1996], p. 112).

7 Hito Steyerl's manifesto "In Defense of the Poor Image" can serve as a prime example of an explicitly political reading of this constellation, as it declares an audio-visual class struggle triggered by a Benjamin-inspired request for an unleashed reproduction of moving images (Steyerl 2009).

8 As an analogy to Walter Benjamin, who compares the photochemical revelation of the optical to the psychoanalytical discovery of the *id* (Benjamin 1968 [1936], p. 237), one could argue that the current media constellation unveils its social unconscious.

9 Of course, one could argue that witnessing always has been a self-referential practice (Peters 2009, p. 43). Thus, what Andén-Papadopoulos calls meta-witnessing does not mark an ontological difference in the nature of witnessing, but a moment in time when quantitative changes show qualitative effects. The more witnesses there are, the more likely they will acknowledge each other and themselves as such—and thereby extend an invitation to once again reflect on witnessing (Andén-Papadopoulos 2014, p. 765).

10 The paradigmatic incident for the interplay of these topoi is of course the (in)famous amateur recording of Rodney King getting beaten up by five LAPD-officers on 3 March 1991, that not only stimulated the Los Angeles Riots of 1992, but also several debates about the status of the audio visual witness and testimony, including the already mentioned interventions by Fiske, Derrida, and Arnheim.

11 To set the record straight, this is not meant to blame Witness for this development or criticize the organization's work from the distant view of the academic ivory tower (if such a thing existed). Quite the opposite: Witness has already raised profound ethical concerns—bringing up issues such as informed consent particularly about the rights and safety of "the people 'on film' rather than [...] those who capture images and events on video"—when at least part of the public and academic debate was still excited by the utopian idea of radical audio-visual transparency (Gregory 2010, p. 176).

References

Andén-Papadopoulos, K. (2014). Citizen camera-witnessing: Embodied political dissent in the age of "mediated mass self-communication". *New Media and Society*, 16(5), pp. 753–769. Available from: http://journals.sagepub.com/doi/10.1177/14614448134 89863 [9 May 2018].

Andrejevic, M. (2009). Exploiting YouTube: Contradictions of user-generated labor. In P. Snickars & P. Vonderau (eds), *The YouTube Reader*, pp. 406–423. Stockholm: National Library of Sweden.

Arnheim, R. (1997). The two authenticities of the photographic media. *Leonardo*, 30(1), pp. 53–55.

Ashuri, T. & Pinchevski, A. (2009). Witnessing as a field. In P. Frosh & A. Pinchevski (eds), *Media Witnessing: Testimony in the Age of Mass Communication*, pp. 133–157. Basingstoke: Palgrave Macmillan.

Benjamin, W. (1968 [1936]). The work of art in the age of mechanical reproduction. In H. Arendt (ed.), *Illuminations*, pp. 217–251. New York: Schocken Books.

Bourdieu, P. (1993). *Sociology in Question*. London: Sage.

Bourdieu, P. & Wacquant, L.J.D. (1992). *An Invitation to Reflexive Sociology*. Chicago, IL: University of Chicago Press.

de Certeau, M. (1984). *The Practice of Everyday Life*. Berkeley: University of California Press.

Derrida, J. & Stiegler, B. (2002 [1996]). *Echographies of Television: Filmed Interviews*. Cambridge, UK: Polity Press.

Fiske, J. (1996). Videotech. In N. Mirzoeff (ed.), *The Visual Culture Reader*, pp. 153–162. London and New York: Routledge.

Frosh, P. (2009). Telling presences: Witnessing, mass media, and the imagined lives of strangers. In P. Frosh & A. Pinchevski (eds), *Media Witnessing: Testimony in the Age of Mass Communication*, pp. 49–72. Basingstoke: Palgrave Macmillan.

Frosh, P. & Pinchevski, A. (2009a). Crisis-readiness and media witnessing. *The Communication Review*, 12(3), pp. 295–304.

Frosh, P. & Pinchevski, A. (2009b). Introduction: Why media witnessing? Why now? In P. Frosh & A. Pinchevski (eds), *Media Witnessing: Testimony in the Age of Mass Communication*, pp. 1–22. Basingstoke: Palgrave Macmillan.

Garcia, D. & Lovink, G. (1997). The ABC of tactical media. Available from: www.nettime.org/Lists-Archives/nettime-l-9705/msg00096.html [12 June 2018].

Garrin, P. (1992). Home(video) is where the revolution is. In J. van Bergeijk, G. van Dijk, K. Koch, & B. Raijmakers (eds), *The Next Five Minutes (N5M)*, Zapbook, Working Papers, p. 33. Amsterdam.

Gregory, S. (2010). Cameras everywhere: Ubiquitous video documentation of human rights, new forms of video advocacy, and considerations of safety, security, dignity and consent. In G. Lovink & R. Somers Miles (eds), *Video Vortex Reader II: Moving Images beyond YouTube*, pp. 268–282. Amsterdam: Institute of Network Cultures.

Holmes, B. (n.d.). Tactical television. Movement media in the nineties. Available from: www.regardingspectatorship.net/tactical-television-movement-media-in-the-nineties/ [26 April 2018].

Kessler, F. & Schäfer, M.T. (2009). Navigating YouTube: Constituting a hybrid information management system. In P. Snickars & P. Vonderau (eds), *The YouTube Reader*, pp. 275–291. Stockholm: National Library of Sweden.

Krämer, S. (2015). *Medium, Messenger, Transmission: An Approach to Media Philosophy*. Amsterdam: Amsterdam University Press.

Krautkrämer, F. (2014). Revolution uploaded. Un/Sichtbares im Handy-Dokumentarfilm. *zfm – Zeitschrift für Medienwissenschaft*, 6(11), Dokument und Dokumentarisches, pp. 113–126.

Mann, S., Nolan, J., & Wellman, B. (2003). Sousveillance: Inventing and using wearable computing devices for data collection in surveillance environments. *Surveillance & Society*, 1(3), pp. 331–355. Available from: http://wearcam.org/sousveillance.pdf [9 May 2018].

Mroué, R. (2012). The pixelated revolution. *TDR – The Drama Review*, 56(3), pp. 25–35.

Nichols, B. (1994). *Blurred Boundaries: Questions of Meaning in Contemporary Culture*. Bloomington: Indiana University Press.

Peters, J.D. (2009 [2001]). Witnessing. In P. Frosh & A. Pinchevski (eds), *Media Witnessing: Testimony in the Age of Mass Communication*, pp. 23–41. Basingstoke: Palgrave Macmillan.

Peters, J.D. (2009). An afterword: Torchlight red on sweaty faces. In P. Frosh & A. Pinchevski (eds), *Media Witnessing: Testimony in the Age of Mass Communication*, pp. 42–48, Basingstoke: Palgrave Macmillan.

Ristovka, S. (2016). Strategic witnessing in an age of video activism. *Media, Culture & Society*, 38(7), pp. 1034–1047. Available from: http://journals.sagepub.com/doi/abs/10.1177/0163443716635866 [9 May 2018].

Schmidt, S. (2011). Wissensquelle oder ethisch-politische Figur? Zur Synthese zweier Forschungsdiskurse über Zeugenschaft. In S. Schmidt, S. Krämer & R. Voges (eds), *Politik der Zeugenschaft: Zur Kritik einer Wissenspraxis*, pp. 47–66. Bielefeld: Transcript.

Schmidt, S. & Voges, R. (2011). Einleitung. In S. Schmidt, S. Krämer & R. Voges (eds), *Politik der Zeugenschaft: Zur Kritik einer Wissenspraxis*, pp. 7–20. Bielefeld: Transcript.

Sorensen, J. (1991). News with a view. In J. van Bergeijk, G. van Dijk, K. Koch, & B. Raijmakers (eds), *The Next Five Minutes (N5M)*, Zapbook, Working Papers, pp. 31–33. Amsterdam.

Steyerl, H. (2009). In defense of the poor image. *e-flux*, 10. Available from: www.e-flux.com/journal/10/61362/in-defense-of-the-poor-image/ [4 October 2018].

Thiele, M. (2010). Cellulars on celluloid: Bewegung, Aufzeichnung, Widerstände und weitere Potentiale des Mobiltelefons. Prolegomena zu einer Theorie und Genealogie portabler Medien. In M. Stingelin & M. Thiele (eds), *Portable Media: Schreibszenen in Bewegung zwischen Peripatetik und Mobiltelefon*, pp. 285–310. München: Fink.

Chapter 3

Affective images and the political trial

Jonas Bens

In January 2016, I attended a hearing at the International Criminal Court (ICC) in The Hague as part of a research project that included conducting courtroom ethnography.[1] A few months earlier, Dominic Ongwen, a former brigade commander of the Lord's Resistance Army (LRA) from Northern Uganda, had been delivered to the ICC. Ongwen is accused of committing war crimes and crimes against humanity during the armed conflict between the LRA and the Ugandan army.[2] In the early 2000s, when the conflict in Northern Uganda had reached a high-point, Dominic Ongwen was in command of LRA troops who massacred civilians in Internally Displaced Persons (IDP) camps. His charges also include pillaging, rape, sexual slavery, and the conscription and use of child soldiers. The hearing I attended that day in 2016 was the confirmation of charges hearing against Ongwen—a proceeding which concludes the pre-trial phase and after which the judges make the determination if there is sufficient evidence to commit the accused to trial. During this hearing, the prosecution presented a summary of the evidence against Dominic Ongwen.

The focal point of the prosecution's case was four specific massacres of IDP camps in Northern Uganda in 2003 and 2004. In order to prove that Ongwen was responsible for the attacks, the members of the prosecution's team presented several forms of evidence: transcripts of oral witness statements (be they from victims, fighters, soldiers or outside experts), tape recordings of intercepted radio transmissions between commanders of the Lord's Resistance Army, copies of articles published in the local and international press, audio material broadcast on local radio stations, and numerous images—photographs as well as videos. One video that was shown by the prosecution in the courtroom left a particular impression with many observers of the trial proceedings. It was shot in the early 2000s by soldiers of the Ugandan army, and shows the direct aftermath of a massacre of an IDP camp. It is little more than a minute long, and one can see burned huts (smoke is still in the air) and several dead bodies—some of which are children not older than three—terribly mutilated (Figure 3.1).

A few weeks after this hearing I went to Northern Uganda to conduct ethnographic fieldwork. Among other things, I collected impressions and feelings about the hearing from different actors. I talked with politicians, NGO representatives,

UGA-OTP-0023-0008   *Post-attack video, 21-22 May 2004*

Figure 3.1 Excerpt from the video footage the Office of the Prosecutor shown in the courtroom during the confirmation of charges hearing in the Dominic Ongwen Case on 22 January 2016.

Source: © ICC-CPI.

religious and cultural leaders, ICC employees as well as with members of victims' associations in the massacred villages. While the confirmation of charges hearing had been conducted in The Hague, it had also been broadcast in Northern Uganda at several places where LRA violence had taken place.

Such public screenings of trial proceedings are an important part of the ICC's outreach activities. Since the ICC's outreach unit for East Africa is quite small, the ICC conducted most of these outreach events in cooperation with representatives of local NGOs that assisted with putting up screens and gathering people (Bens 2019b). I asked people what they had found remarkable about the hearing, and what aspects of it in particular had moved them. For me, it was striking that my respondents from different actor groups answered this question quite differently.

There were a number of representatives of those local NGOs engaged in the public screenings, most of whom were university educated Northern Ugandans living in Gulu town, the urban centre of Northern Uganda. They quickly mentioned the video with the dead children as the moment in the trial they found most remarkable. They expressed their belief that it was one of the most impressive moments of the hearing overall. I asked them about their opinion on how the video affected the other people present during the public screenings, particularly the villagers in those places that had served as locations for

IDP camps during the conflict, and which had been looted by the LRA. To this they replied that, in their opinion, the villagers were also highly affected by that video.

I also spoke to members of the massacre survivors' associations, who live in former IDP camps in rural areas, asking similar questions about what had moved them while watching the hearing. I was surprised at first that they did not bring up the video at all. During one conversation I had, this difference in assessing the role of this video was particularly striking. When I met with one group of people from a former IDP camp that was attacked by troops under Ongwen's command, I asked them—again in the style of an open question—how they had experienced the prosecution's presentation of the evidence. One young man answered that there were aspects of it he found "not satisfactory", especially "the graphic video". All one would have been able to see were burning huts and dead children. "You could not see Dominic Ongwen on this video", nor any LRA rebels for that matter. He explained that he was sceptical of how it would be possible to prove with that video that the LRA had burned down these huts and that Ongwen had commanded the troops. In his opinion, this particular piece of evidence could not conclusively link the accused to the crime.

I found the young man's argument convincing. From a dispassionate perspective of giving testimony, the video is not very important evidence. It only proves that there was a massacre at that time and place—a fact that was never in dispute. Yet if that is so, why did the prosecution bring the video into the courtroom at all? In the course of this text, I will argue that a perspective on emotion and affect in legal proceedings opens up a space to answer this question.[3] I will discuss this issue through three questions: What is the role of image evidence in the political trial? How can we better explain this role by focusing on the affective dimension of images? Why is it that some images seem to affect some people differently than others?

Giving testimony in court: affective performance in the time machine

To understand the role of images in court proceedings, I have to make a few theoretical remarks on the role of performance in the courtroom.[4] Witnessing, testimony and the power of images can only be understood in the context of the temporal structure of the courtroom which, as I argue, functions as a time machine in which the past is re-enacted.

When visiting a court proceeding, it becomes immediately obvious that the most prominent practice there is talking. The language of the law materializes in the discourse practice of the courtroom as talk (Brenneis 1988; Levi 1990). Consequently, courtroom ethnography has traditionally focused on what people say in courtrooms, how they are saying it, and how they construct reality through talk (Conley & O'Barr 2004).

Talking means performing language. Performing language means first and foremost engaging in a bodily practice in the real world, hence "doing language" (Chomsky 1965, pp. 10–15). It means furthermore to act with language in such a way as to transform the outside world as with any other bodily practice, "doing something with language" (compare Austin 1962).[5] Finally, it means acting by way of language in a social-relational setting structured by the expectations and established aesthetic canons of a given audience (Bauman 1977; Goffman 1956; Turner 1987).

Consequently, court proceedings have been analysed as performances (Diehl et al. 2006; Reinelt 2006; Cole 2009). This perspective keeps linguistic utterances at the heart of court proceedings, while also including other dimensions such as voice, gesture, spatial arrangements, and visual regimes. In this view, images appear as an integral part of the courtroom performance.

The courtroom is an agonal *dispositif* (Vismann 2011, pp. 72–96).[6] Different courtroom actors, such as the defence and prosecution, strategically perform different versions of the facts that serve their interest. From this perspective, it appears that what is called truth finding in the courtroom is in fact a competition between several carefully scripted productions of reality and their scripters' attempts to establish their respective versions as plausible. As theorists of the performative power of the law have highlighted (especially Derrida 1989), the law usually tries to disguise its performative dimension. Since engaging in legal proceedings entails "putting up a show" in an agonal space, the version of reality that ultimately gains acceptance among judges or the jury is not the only possible version. In turn, this means that, if the law and its actors openly admit that, at the end of the day, the legal process cannot guarantee that the version they have established as the most plausible in court is also "the truth", the law's promise of delivering justice and equality can be all too easily called into question. Legal practice, much like academic practice, is characterized by this simultaneous commitment to established methods of truth-finding while obscuring the fact that these methods cannot guarantee the axiomatic truth.

That it is necessary to perform the law is a direct consequence of the courtroom's temporal structure. Court proceedings take place in a complex dissociated structure of time (Vismann 2011). In criminal trials, the time of the crime and the time of the court proceedings do not overlap. A temporal gap emerges, and the performative process of filling this gap can be described as a form of re-enactment. The legal actors strive to bring the past of the crime into the present of the court proceedings and—like theatre actors on the stage—they must do so through different performances (Schneider 2011). To perform this re-enactment, they introduce pieces of evidence. Texts, images, and objects bring the past into the courtroom. As such, the courtroom appears as an arrangement in which the past is reconstituted in the present. Not unlike a theatre in which re-enactments can take place, the courtroom functions as a time machine (Roselt & Otto 2014).

The process of witnessing is crucial for bridging the past crime to the current proceedings. Giving evidence in court is a performative act in a complex process of re-enacting the past, in which several realities compete for plausibility. The curious English expression that one must produce evidence to prove a claim already indicates how much the practice of courtroom witnessing is a constructive endeavour. Because of the dissociated temporal structure of the courtroom, such performance has the form of a re-enactment in which the testimony and pieces of evidence in various forms serve as crucial devices for running the time machine.

Actors perform in order to affect audiences. Exploring the affective dimension of courtroom performances means coming to terms with the connections that are established between all kinds of (human and non-human) bodies that are in a constant state of affecting and being affected by each other in the context of a trial. Such a perspective draws from insights provided by affect theory (Gregg & Seigworth 2010; Clough & Halley 2007; Slaby & Mühlhoff 2019). As such, it highlights that producing meaning in legal proceedings is not just a matter of rational deliberation facilitated through linguistic utterances, but also entails a myriad of other processes that are at once cognitive and affective (Bens 2018; Bens & Zenker 2019). It is necessary to explore images in their affective dimension in order to understand their role in legal performances.

Images and their performative power as evidence

Since the invention of photography, the status of photographic images as pieces of legal evidence has been disputed. But very early on they were admitted into the courtroom as objects bearing evidentiary value independently of the person who took the photograph.[7] The English word "evidence" has the Latin root *videre*, which means "to see". This already points to the relevance of visual images for the establishment of plausible versions of reality within legal proceedings (Mnookin 1998; Golan 2008). As I have argued, in the re-enactment of the trial, the witness bridges the temporal gap between past events and the current trial. When images perform in the time machine of the courtroom, audiences are able to see a past event "with their own eyes". As such, audiences not only listen to the witness's account of a person, but become witnesses themselves. Images thus have a particular impact for establishing a plausible version of the truth. From a media theory perspective, Peters points out this phenomenon of "presence-at-a-distance": "[T]he borrowed eyes and ears of the media become, however tentatively or dangerously, one's own" (Peters 2001, p. 717).

Photographic or videographic images have always been accompanied by a strong claim of authentically representing the past. Theorists of photography have strongly objected to this claim of truth and highlighted that these images are not just archives of the past in a mechanical sense (Sontag 1977; Barthes 1980, in English 1981). Rather, images are embedded in a dissociated temporal structure similar to that of the courtroom. As "spectres" (Kracauer 1963, in English 1995) or as "rests" (Derrida 1981, in English 1988) they recreate the past in the present. As such they are a crucial device in the performative re-enactment that is practised in the courtroom. Images are embedded in the same performative processes of evidence production as humans, and their performances are equally constructive.[8]

As much as photographic theory has aimed at deconstructing such claims for authenticity, empirical legal studies show clearly that photos and videos perform very differently, and often more powerfully, than human witnesses or other media, such as written testimony. One prominent example of this are studies of the impact of "gruesome evidence" on jury decisions in common law jurisdictions (Bright & Goodman-Delahunty 2006; Matsuo & Itoh 2015). These studies show that juries lean toward significantly higher sentences if the crime in question is represented in the courtroom with a graphic image. From the perspective of an ethnography of legal proceedings, the question is therefore not so much whether we can deconstruct the notion of the truth-telling image, but rather why and how images affect actors differently than do other forms of testimony.[9] To explore the performative power of images, I argue that it is crucial to come to an understanding of the objectivity and affectivity of image testimony.

The objectivity and affectivity of images

One way to describe the performative power of photos and videos in the courtroom is to say that they often seem to be more objective than other forms of testimony. To understand what that means, we must understand the term "objectivity" in its double meaning. As Daston and Galison (2007) have laid out in their ground-breaking history of objectivity, the emergence of the concept of objectivity in European thought is closely connected with the invention of the object. From this perspective it appears that objects are objective and subjects are subjective. This idea, applied to the image, means that the image's strong claim to objectivity is—on a most basic level—connected with the fact that photographic and videographic images are perceived as objects rather than as subjects.

Photographic and videographic images are objects, not subjects, in the sense that they are not conceived of as having an intentionality of their own. From a media theory perspective, such images appear to listeners as "'dumb' media". As Peters argues, "such mechanical, 'dumb' media seem to present images and sounds as they happened, without the embellishments and blind-spots that human perception and memory routinely impose" (Peters 2001, p. 708). Photos and videos can be manipulated by humans, but they are too "dumb" to deceive their audiences on their own account. As such, they have a different credibility than, for example, human witnesses who are subjects, not objects.

I argue that it is the image's objectivity (in the double sense) that differentiates images from other kinds of testimony, because it connects to its viewers and listeners in a different affective mode. Seeing an image feels different than hearing an oral witness account. Brian Massumi (1995), one of the leading figures of affect theory, has put great emphasis on differentiating affect and emotion—a theoretical move that still characterizes many strands of affect theory (for an overview of different approaches see: Wetherell 2012). Most affect and emotion scholarship does not follow Massumi's all-too strict differentiation between affect and emotion, but regards them as overlapping terms (Slaby & Röttger-Rössler 2018). Some even use both terms interchangeably (e.g. Ahmed 2004). Most approaches, however, seem to characterize affect as a rather basic phenomenon that can refer to very pre-cognitive, pre-structured relational connections between (human and non-human bodies) which can be very vague (Slaby & Mühlhoff 2019). Emotions, however, are experienced with a minimal degree of cognition and in the context of culturally grounded repertoires (von Scheve 2019).[10] It is my argument that how it feels to perceive image testimony in court is more a question of affect than emotion. In other words: I understand the perceived objectivity of the image as a performative register that is affective rather than emotional.

Listening to the oral testimony of a human witness is usually accompanied by many questions that must be cognitively processed by the listeners: Is the witness lying? How credible is he or she as a person? What might be the witness's intention and subjective motivation? Being confronted with talk in the context of truth finding demands a lot of cognitive labour. Talk will often be able to elicit emotional experiences, as emotion is highly structured in language (Bens 2018). An unmediated "being affected" by talk is frequently precluded by precisely that cognitive labour that most often accompanies human interaction.

With videos and photographs the situation is different because of their status as objects. All the questions that arise around the credibility of images in the courtroom are directed to the subjects in connection to the images, rather than to the images themselves: What are the intentions of the photographer or videographer—or the party in the trial bringing the images into the courtroom? How did the filmmaker cut the video? What did the photographer cut out of the photo? Has somebody manipulated the images? These are all questions posed to subjects producing, handling, using, or transforming the images rather than to the images themselves. Objects have no intentions. Images are able to connect to audiences in an affective register that is blocked to human witnesses, so long as the parties in the trial (who mobilize images to further their aims) manage to dissociate the object of the image from the subjects it is entangled with and to "let the image speak for itself". Whether or not such an affective connection between image evidence and its audiences is more persuasive than other kinds of images, remains an empirical question that depends on the context of a trial. But it is definitely more objective in the sense I have laid it out here.

The political trial

To understand the different reactions of my interlocutors in Northern Uganda to the graphic video shown during the Dominic Ongwen trial, we must add another dimension to the analysis: the video's embeddedness in the political trial. Most fundamentally, the term "political trial" connotes the idea that politics is made by means of the law and that political criteria migrate into the courts.[11] Already in the early literature on political trials, scholars have highlighted that international criminal proceedings are political trials per se (Kirchheimer 1961; Arendt 1963; Shklar 1964).

As I have indicated above, court proceedings usually tend to disguise their performative dimension. The insight that facts are produced in the courtroom rather than mechanically represented, is potentially putting into question whether the law can credibly keep its promise of delivering justice. The political trial is, in many respects, an exception to this rule. Başak Ertür (2015) has argued that political trials are different from regular trials in that their performative power is openly admitted. Political trials shall be performative since their purpose is precisely to change reality by playing out how justice is done. Finding the truth is not at the centre of the political trial, because the truth is, or at least shall be, already known. Determining the "if" of guilt and innocence is not at the centre of the political trial. The trial is conducted not to find the truth, but to show its audiences that the law can be enforced.

As the political trial publicly exposes its performative power, it is the broader public that becomes a central audience of the trial. Of course, potentially, every criminal trial has a public audience. But in the political trial the public audience asserts primacy, even before the audience of the judges, the jurors, or the victims. As such, political trials play a central role in processes of transitional justice (Teitel 2000, pp. 27–68). Political trials shall change the conceptions and perceptions of justice of large publics, whole societies even. I have argued elsewhere that people assess justice and legitimacy to a large degree in connection with affective and emotional appraisals and that people do not only follow a sense of justice but also their sentiments of justice (Bens 2017; Bens & Zenker 2017b, 2019). The political trial must also aim at targeting and transforming the sentiments of justice of those people, who have no personal connection to the case. For this project, the political trial needs devices to move these audiences who have not yet thought much about the issue at hand, and might therefore not be emotionally involved. It is for them that images, photos and videos, with their specific affective register of exerting performative power, are brought into the political trial. Images have the potential to affect the public in such a way as to change their sentiments of justice, even those of them who are not emotionally involved.

Affective images and the political trial

Returning to the graphic video in the Dominic Ongwen trial, we might now ask why the video evidence has affected different audiences so differently. Why were people who were not so personally involved in the case (such as the urban NGO members) so strongly affected by the video? And why, on the other hand, were deeply involved individuals, such as the villagers from the former massacre sites, so business-like about it? I believe the reason lies in the affective rather than the emotional register of the images that were performed. The connection of the images to their audiences made in this register is not made to everybody in the same way.

The villagers, many of them victims of the massacres, were not affected in a uniform way by the experience of seeing images of the dead bodies of children. Following the thoughts I have laid out in this text, I argue that they were not affected in the same way, because they were too emotionally involved. What moved them in this moment of the confirmation of charges hearing was not the horror of the violence described there, since they had been confronted with such violence numerous times before and are still confronted with its aftermath. They were beyond that. What moved them was engaging in the details of Ongwen's guilt, the complexity of the crime, and many doubts about the proceedings in which it was addressed. They were interested in what was going on and developed not just an affective but also an emotional need for understanding whether it was indeed possible to bring Ongwen to justice.

The video footage is much more a tool directed to a public audience—the imagined target group of transitional justice projects (see also Vismann 2011, p. 249). The affective video was not for the victims. It was for those more distanced from the case at hand, those without an emotional stake of their own in Dominic Ongwen and his deeds. The emotionally involved victims cognitively processed the image as evidence for Ongwen's guilt or innocence. What they quickly realized is that the video in question does not serve this purpose very well. Most more distanced public audiences are not interested in these nitty-gritty details of who, where, and when. The members of the wider public are able to let themselves be affected by these images, exactly because they are not interested in them as evidence for a specific crime. This is also not what political trials with their publicity are about. In this trial, the video emerged as a performative force to affect public audiences rather than a determinant of the accused's guilt or innocence in the narrow sense.

In a sense, the video in question served as a witness, after all, but in a much broader sense than the one I have described before. It was a witness in the sense of "media witnessing", as described by Frosh and Pinchevski (2009, p. 1): "'media witnessing' is the witnessing performed *in*, *by*, and *through* the media. It is about the systematic and ongoing reporting of the experiences and realities of distant others to mass audiences". In this sense, the gruesome video represents a paradigmatic example for the kind of witnesses prevalent in the political trial.

When public audiences allow themselves to be affected by such images, the impact is difficult to assess. Being affected may or may not lead them to a greater sense of emotional involvement. Affective experience might inscribe itself into the bodies of those who are enmeshed in it and transform their thinking and feeling in important ways. Or, the moment of affection might come and go, leaving the subject unchanged. It is one of the more important insights of affect theory to show that the way these dynamics play out is difficult to predict.

Political trials, and the actors that conduct them, aim at affecting publics. But whether they succeed in the intended way remains unclear. In this context, images remain one of the prime devices to move people from a distance, even if only for a moment.[12] Images thus play out the performative power of the political trial—a power that consists, above all, in the capacity to affect.

Acknowledgement

This article is indebted to many discussions with and feedback from my colleagues at the Affective Societies Collaborative Research Center at Freie Universität Berlin, especially Olaf Zenker, Leonie Benker, Antje Kahl, Birgitt Röttger-Rössler, Gabriel Scheidecker, Tobias Wendl and, above all, Kerstin Schankweiler and Verena Straub for organizing the workshop "Image Testimonies: Witnessing in Times of Social Media" in the course of which I was able to present a first version of this paper. Many thanks go to Tamar Blickstein for extensively commenting on a previous version of this text. The field research on which this article is based was funded by the Deutsche Forschungsgemeinschaft (DFG, German Research Foundation) – SFB 1171.

Notes

1 During my field research at the International Criminal Court in The Hague I have conducted courtroom ethnography. Anthropologists but also sociologists ethnographically investigate the courtroom in Western contexts (Bennett & Feldman 1981; Conley & O'Barr 1990; Merry 1990; Greenhouse, Yngvesson & Engel 1994; Yngvesson 1994; Scheffer 2010), as well as in non-Western or post-colonial contexts (Messick 1992; Goldman 1993; Hirsch 1998; Richland 2008).

2 For background on the conflict between the Lord's Resistance Army and the Ugandan government that endured from the mid-1980s until about 2006 in Northern Uganda see Allen (2006), Allen and Vlassenroot (2010) and Finnström (2008).

3 By taking such a perspective, this article contributes to an established body of research on law and emotion scholarship, for review articles see (Maroney 2006; Abrams & Keren 2009; Bandes & Blumenthal 2012; Bens & Zenker 2017a).

4 I have elaborated elsewhere on rethinking courtroom ethnography to the background of affective performances (Bens 2018b). Methodologically I see approaching the courtroom as a specific aspect of what I have called the ethnography of discourse practice (Bens 2019a).

5 The philosopher of language, J.L. Austin (1962) has most prominently expressed the argument that speaking is a practice with consequences, that one can do something with words. Central here is his famous distinction between constative and performative utterances. In his argumentation, it is often the case that speech acts not only describe reality (the constative utterance), but also produce and transform it (the performative utterance). Austin sees legal language as a prototypical example of the performative dimension of language, a perspective which plays a central role in the legal theory of poststructuralist philosophy (Derrida 1989; Butler 1997). What is said and done in the courtroom is not only representing the world outside of it, but it is a powerful actor in creating the structures of meaning through which it is represented.

6 The term *dispositif* is central in Michel Foucault's thinking on processes of subjectivation in institutions. He defines the term in an interview as

a thoroughly heterogeneous ensemble consisting of discourses, institutions, architectural forms, regulatory decisions, laws, administrative measures, scientific statements, philosophical, moral and philanthropic propositions—in short, the said as much as the unsaid. Such are the elements of the apparatus. The apparatus itself is the system of relations that can be established between these elements. [...] What I am trying to identify in this apparatus is precisely the nature of the connection that can exist between these heterogeneous elements. [...] Between these elements, whether discursive or non-discursive, there is a sort of interplay of shifts of position and modifications of function which can also vary very widely. [...] I understand by the term "apparatus" a [...] formation which has as its major function at a given historical moment that of responding to an urgent need. The apparatus thus has a dominant strategic function.

(Foucault 1972, pp. 194–195)

7 The German Reichsgericht for instance decided this already in 1903 (RGSt 36, p. 55). Since then, images can replace oral testimony by human witnesses when they are seen by the judge and everybody else in the courtroom (Wenskat 1988). They are allowed to speak for themselves. Video recordings and audio recordings are then often replacing the human accounts and are themselves awarded the status of witness. In common law one speaks in this context of the "silent witness" theory (Wigmore 1970, sec. 790; Robinson & Richards 2010). This is a curious expression, because these recordings are by no means silent. They have an enormous performative quality.

8 It might not be a coincidence that photographic realism, hence the idea that photographs are judged as legitimate as much as they faithfully represent reality is a judgement of taste characteristic of viewers with a lower class status—a kind of judgement of taste that is equated in Kantian aesthetics with "barbarous taste" (Bourdieu 1984, pp. 39–43). As such, the strong objection against the photograph's claim of authenticity is not least made from a specific class position and a specific regime of artistic taste.

9 Peters makes an additional point in regard to the debate on the deconstruction of the authenticity of images, which is, at heart, an epistemological debate. He points out that "the boundary between fact and fiction is an ethical one before it is an epistemological one. [...] The contrast of fact and fiction has less to do with different orders of truth than with who is hurting and when" (Peters 2001, p. 721). From the perspective of legal professionals, who are mainly concerned with the ethical implications of legitimately punishing perpetrators, the ethical question consumes the epistemological. On the ethical and political implication of witnessing generally, see Givoni (2011).

10 I am following here one of the most basic insights from social science emotion research, namely that thinking and feeling are not mutually exclusive but always entangled. One cannot experience emotion without cognitive appraisal, and intensive thinking does not preclude an emotional experience (Rosaldo 1984; Röttger-Rössler & Markowitsch 2009; Burkitt 2014).

11 There is a broad debate on the politicization of international criminal law (Leebaw 2011; Mégret 2002; Moyn 2013). Underlying this term is of course the conceptualization of a dualism of and a contradiction between law and politics—an assumption that also seems to underlie critiques of "judicialization of politics" in anthropological debates (Comaroff & Comaroff 2006). This conceptual divide between law and politics can (and maybe should) also be questioned. For the purpose of this article, however, some approaches from the analysis of political trials are useful to make sense of the performative power of the law.

12 There are many excellent social science studies pointing this out, see for example Luc Boltanski (1999), and for the case of international criminal law in Africa, Kamari Clarke (2018, ch. 3).

References

Abrams, K. & Keren, H. (2009). Who is afraid of law and the emotions? *Minnesota Law Review*, 94(6), pp. 1997–2074.

Ahmed, S. (2004). *The Cultural Politics of Emotion*. Edinburgh: Edinburgh University Press.

Allen, T. (2006). *Trial Justice: The International Criminal Court and the Lord's Resistance Army*. London: Zed Books.

Allen, T. & Vlassenroot, K. (eds) (2010). *The Lord's Resistance Army: Myth and Reality*. London: Zed Books.

Arendt, H. (1963). *Eichmann in Jerusalem: A Report on the Banality of Evil*. New York: Viking Press.

Austin, J.L. (1962). *How to Do Things with Words: The William James Lectures Delivered at Harvard University in 1955*. New York: Oxford University Press.

Bandes, S.A. & Blumenthal, J.A. (2012). Emotion and the law. *Annual Review of Law and Social Science*, 8, pp. 161–181.

Barthes, R. (1980). *La chambre claire: Note sur la photographie*. Paris: Le Seuil.

Barthes, R. (1981). *Camera Lucida: Reflections on Photography*. New York: Hill and Wang.

Bauman, R. (1977). *Verbal Art as Performance*. Rowley: Newbury House.

Bennett, W.L. & Feldman, M.S. (1981). *Reconstructing Reality in the Courtroom: Justice and Judgment in American Culture*. New Brunswick: Rutgers University Press.

Bens, J. (2017). Gerechtigkeitsgefühle und die Legitimität des Internationalen Strafgerichtshofs in Norduganda. In J. Bens & O. Zenker (eds), *Gerechtigkeitsgefühle: Zur affektiven und emotionalen Legitimität von Normen*, pp. 215–241. Bielefeld: Transcript.

Bens, J. (2018a). Sentimentalising persons and things: Creating normative arrangements of bodies through courtroom talk. *Journal of Legal Anthropology*, 2(1), pp. 72–91.

Bens, J. (2018b). The courtroom as an affective arrangement: Analysing atmospheres in courtroom ethnography. *Journal of Legal Pluralism and Unofficial Law*, 50(3).

Bens, J. (2019a). The ethnography of affect in discourse practice: Performing sentiment in the time machine. In A. Kahl (ed.), *Analyzing Affective Societies: Methods and Methodologies*. London: Routledge.

Bens, J. (2019b). Transitional justice atmospheres: The role of space and affect in the international criminal court's outreach efforts in Northern Uganda. In K. Seidel & H. Ellisie (eds), *Normative Spaces in Africa*. London: Routledge.

Bens, J. & Zenker, O. (2017a). Gerechtigkeitsgefühle: Eine Einführung. In J. Bens & O. Zenker (eds), *Gerechtigkeitsgefühle: Zur affektiven und emotionalen Legitimität von Normen*, pp. 11–36. Bielefeld: Transcript.

Bens, J. & Zenker O. (eds) (2017b). *Gerechtigkeitsgefühle: Zur affektiven und emotionalen Legitimität von Normen*. Bielefeld: Transcript.

Bens, J. & Zenker, O. (2019). Sentiment. In J. Slaby & C. von Scheve (eds), *Affective Societies: Key Concepts*. London: Routledge.

Boltanski, L. (1999). *Distant Suffering: Morality, Media and Politics*. Cambridge, UK: Cambridge University Press.

Bourdieu, P. (1984). *Distinction: A Social Critique of the Judgment of Taste*. Cambridge, MA: Harvard University Press.

Brenneis, D. (1988). Language and disputing. *Annual Review of Anthropology*, 17, pp. 221–260.

Bright, D.A. & Goodman-Delahunty, J. (2006). Gruesome evidence and emotion: Anger, blame, and jury decision-making. *Law and Human Behavior*, 30(2), pp. 183–202.

Burkitt, I. (2014). *Emotions and Social Relations*. London: Sage.

Butler, J. (1997). *Excitable Speech: A Politics of the Performative*. New York: Routledge.

Chomsky, N. (1965). *Aspects of the Theory of Syntax*. Cambridge, MA: MIT Press.

Clarke, K.M. (2018). *Affective Justice*. Durham: Duke University Press.

Clough, P.T. & Halley, J. (eds) (2007). *The Affective Turn: Theorizing the Social*. Durham: Duke University Press.

Cole, C.M. (2009). *Performing South Africa's Truth Commission: Stages of Transition*. Bloomington: Indiana University Press.

Comaroff, J. & Comaroff, J. (2006). *Law and Disorder in the Postcolony*. Chicago: University of Chicago Press.

Conley, J.M. & O'Barr, W.M. (1990). *Rules versus Relationships: The Ethnography of Legal Discourse*. Chicago: University of Chicago Press.

Conley, J.M. & O'Barr, W.M. (2004). *Just Words: Law, Language, and Power*, 2nd edn. Chicago: University of Chicago Press.

Daston, L. & Galison, P. (2007). *Objectivity*. New York: Zone Books.

Derrida, J. (1981). Les Morts de Roland Barthes. *Poétique: Revue de Théorie et d'Analyse Littéraires*, 47, pp. 262–292.

Derrida, J. (1988). The deaths of Roland Barthes. In H.J. Silverman (ed.), *Philosophy and Non-Philosophy Since Merleau-Ponty*, pp. 269–292. London: Routledge.

Derrida, J. (1989). Force de loi: Le fondement mystique de l'autorite/Force of law: The mystical foundations of authority. *Cardozo Law Review*, 11(3), pp. 920–1045.

Diehl, P., Grundwald, H., Scheffer, T., & Wulf, C. (eds) (2006). *Paragrana: Internationale Zeitschrift für historische Anthropologie*, vol. 15 (*Performanz des Rechts: Inszenierung und Diskurs*). Berlin: Akademie-Verlag.

Ertür, B. (2015). Spectacles and spectres: Political trials, performativity and sciences of sovereignty. PhD thesis, School of Law, Birkbeck, University of London.

Finnström, S. (2008). *Living With Bad Surroundings: War, History, and Everyday Moments in Northern Uganda*. Durham: Duke University Press.

Foucault, M. (1972). *Power/Knowledge: Selected Interviews and Other Writings*. New York: Pantheon Books.

Frosh, P. & Pinchevski, A. (eds) (2009). *Media Witnessing: Testimony in the Age of Mass Communication*. New York: Palgrave Macmillan.

Givoni, M. (2011). Witnessing/testimony. *Mafte'akh: Lexical Review of Political Thought*, 2, pp. 147–169.

Goffman, E. (1956). *The Presentation of Self in Everyday Life*. Edinburgh: University of Edinburgh Social Science Research Centre.

Golan, T. (2008). Visual images in the courtroom: A historical perspective. *Parallax*, 14(4), pp. 77–89.

Goldman, L. (1993). *The Culture of Coincidence: Accident and Absolute Liability in Huli*. Oxford: Clarendon.

Greenhouse, C.J., Yngvesson, B., & Engel, D.M. (1994). *Law and Community in Three American Towns*. Ithaca: Cornell University Press.

Gregg, M. & Seigworth, G.J. (eds) (2010). *The Affect Theory Reader*. Durham: Duke University Press.

Hirsch, S.F. (1998). *Pronouncing and Persevering: Gender and the Discourses of Disputing in an African Islamic Court*. Chicago: University of Chicago Press.

Kirchheimer, O. (1961). *Political Justice: The Use of Legal Procedure for Political Ends*. Princeton, NJ: Princeton University Press.

Kracauer, S. (1963). *Das Ornament der Masse: Essays*. Frankfurt am Main: Suhrkamp.

Kracauer, S. (1995). *The Mass Ornament: Weimar Essays*. Cambridge, MA: Harvard University Press.

Leebaw, B. (2011). *Judging State-Sponsored Violence, Imagining Political Change*. New York: Cambridge University Press.

Levi, J.N. (1990). *Language in the Judicial Process*. New York: Plenum Press.

Maroney, T.A. (2006). Law and emotion: A proposed taxonomy of an emerging field. *Law and Human Behavior*, 30(1), pp. 119–142.

Massumi, B. (1995). The autonomy of affect. *Cultural Critique*, 31, pp. 83–109.

Matsuo, K. & Itoh, Y. (2015). Effects of emotional testimony and gruesome photographs on mock jurors' decisions and negative emotions. *Psychiatry, Psychology and Law*, 23(1), pp. 85–101.

Mégret, F. (2002). The politics of international criminal justice. *European Journal of International Law*, 13(5), pp. 1261–1284.

Merry, S.E. (1990). *Getting Justice and Getting Even: Legal Consciousness Among Working Class Americans*. Chicago: University of Chicago Press.

Messick, B. (1992). *The Calligraphic State: Textual Domination and History in a Muslim Society*. Berkeley: University of California Press.

Mnookin, J.L. (1998). The image of truth: Photographic evidence and the power of analogy. *Yale Journal of Law and the Humanities*, 10(1), pp. 1–74.

Moyn, S. (2013). Judith Shklar versus the international criminal court. *Humanity*, 4(3), pp. 473–500.

Peters, J.D. (2001). Witnessing. *Media, Culture & Society*, 23(6), pp. 707–723.

Reinelt, J. (2006). Toward a poetics of theatre and public events: In the case of Stephen Lawrence. *The Drama Review*, 50(3), pp. 69–87.

Richland, J.B. (2008). *Arguing with Tradition: The Language of Law in Hopi Tribal Court*. Chicago: University of Chicago Press.

Robinson, E.M. & Richards, G.B. (2010). Chapter 12: Legal issues related to photographs and digital images. In E.M. Robinson (ed.), *Crime Scene Photography*. Amsterdam: Academic Press.

Rosaldo, M.Z. (1984). Toward an anthropology of self and feeling. In R.A. Shweder & R.A. LeVine (eds), *Culture Theory: Essays on Mind, Self, and Emotion*, pp. 137–149. Cambridge, UK: Cambridge University Press.

Roselt, J. & Otto, U. (2014). *Theater als Zeitmaschine: Zur performativen Praxis des Reenactments, Theater*. Bielefeld: Transcript.

Röttger-Rössler, B. & Markowitsch, H.J. (eds) (2009). *Emotions as Bio-Cultural Processes*. New York: Springer.

Scheffer, T. (2010). *International Studies in Sociology and Social Anthropology*, vol. 116 (*Adversarial Case-Making: An Ethnography of English Crown Court Procedures*). Leiden: Brill.

Schneider, R. (2011). *Performing Remains: Art and War in Times of Theatrical Reenactment*. London: Routledge.

Shklar, J.N. (1964). *Legalism: An Essay on Law, Morals and Politics*. Oxford: Oxford University Press.

Slaby, J. & Mühlhoff, R. (2019). Affect. In J. Slaby & C. von Scheve (eds), *Affective Societies: Key Concepts*. London: Routledge.

Slaby, J. & Röttger-Rössler, B. (2018). Introduction: Affect in relation. In J. Slaby & B. Röttger-Rössler (eds), *Affect in Relation: Families, Places, Technologies*. London: Routledge.

Sontag, S. (1977). *On Photography*. New York: Farrar, Straus and Giroux.

Teitel, R.G. (2000). *Transitional Justice*. Oxford: Oxford University Press.

Turner, V. (1987). *The Anthropology of Performance*. New York: PAJ Publications.

Vismann, C. (2011). *Medien der Rechtsprechung*. Frankfurt am Main: S. Fischer.

von Scheve, C. (2019). Emotion. In J. Slaby & C. von Scheve (eds), *Affective Societies: Key Concepts*. London: Routledge.

Wenskat, W. (1988). *Der richterliche Augenschein im deutschen Strafprozess*. Frankfurt am Main: Peter Lang.

Wetherell, M. (2012). *Affect and Emotion: A New Social Science Understanding*. Los Angeles: SAGE.

Wigmore, J.H. (1970). Evidence in trials at common law: §687–867. *Evidence in Trials at Common Law*, vol. 3. Boston: Little, Brown.

Yngvesson, B. (1994). *Virtuous Citizens, Disruptive Subjects: Order and Complaint in a New England Court*. New York: Routledge.

In conversation

Chapter 4

Fearless filming

Video footage from Syria since 2011

*Marianna Liosi with Guevara Namer and
Amer Matar*

This chapter is based on a conversation between curator Marianna Liosi and
Syrian filmmakers Guevara Namer and Amer Matar that took place as part of the
symposium "Image Testimonies. Witnessing in Times of Social Media" (Berlin,
July 2017). It was accompanied by a screening of mobile phone videos and
experimental films originating from Syria in the context of the uprisings since
2011. Amer Matar is a journalist, documentary filmmaker and co-founder of the
Syria Mobile Film Festival that was launched in 2013 with the aim of creating a
unique platform to encourage professional directors and amateurs to make low-
budget, creative films with a mobile phone camera. Guevara Namer is a photographer, filmmaker, producer and co-founder of DOX BOX e.V., a non-profit
organization and platform for supporting, networking and promoting documentary film professionals from the Arab world.

MARIANNA LIOSI (M. L.): Amer, the peaceful uprising against President Bashar al-
    Assad that started in March 2011 and its escalation into a full-scale war
    have also marked your activity as a filmmaker, journalist and cultural activ-
    ist. Your film "Azadi", which covers the everyday events of the riot in Qam-
    ishli, the Kurdish areas of northern Syria, was award winning at the
    Rotterdam International Film Festival in 2011. At that time, however, you
    were not able to attend its premiere as you were detained in Syria, accused
    by the government for your journalistic work. Already in 2010 you were
    aware of the urgency of using the camera as a tool of struggle and resist-
    ance, as well as the need to train other professionals and non-professionals
    to do the same. You initiated a series of workshops with filmmakers and
    citizen journalists in Syria and Turkey. What was the aim of this project?
AMER MATAR (A. M.): In the first year of the Syrian revolution, a pivotal concern
    was to film our life in Syria and introduce it to the world. It was a huge illu-
    sion, based on the assumption that if the world saw the brutal injustice of
    the authorities in my country, Syria, they would help us get rid of the dic-
    tator. I call it an illusion because the Syrians documented every minute of
    the peaceful demonstrations, the massacres and later the ruthless bombing
    of the cities, they published and posted the pictures in media and on social

media—but to no avail. With a large number of colleagues we are still documenting what our country is enduring after years of the dissipation of this illusion and the perpetuation of the massacre. We record the crimes, and the small and big events of daily existence that shape people's lives, in an attempt to write history from the perspective of Syrian society. To create space for the image that reflects the Syrian reality as perceived by the people inside and outside Syria and the ability of this image to generate a cultural, ideological and political state of awareness.

M. L.: The uprising in 2011 also marked a turning point in your work, Guevara, especially for the initiative DOX BOX that you are a part of and which is now located in Berlin. You played a pivotal role in the initiation of this project. Can you tell us more about its foundation?

GUEVARA NAMER (G. N.): Originally, DOX BOX was an annual event, initiated by the Syrian independent film production and distribution company ProAction Film. Starting in 2008, the DOX BOX International Documentary Film Festival quickly became the largest and most important documentary film festival in the Arab World. The festival not only screened films but was also establishing links between filmmakers within the documentary film industry from all over the world, aiming especially at creating a bridge between the Arab countries and Europe. Until 2011, the Festival was screening films in different cities in Syria, and its programme had a very activist nature. Despite censorship, we were able to show the Syrian audience a selection of international movies dealing with social and political issues, things that were not discussed in public in Syria. By coincidence, on 15 March 2011, the day after the Festival's closing nights, the Syrian uprising began.

M. L.: The eruption of the civil demonstrations has obviously affected DOX BOX's cultural activity. How have the format and purpose of the initiative evolved after the revolts' turmoil?

G. N.: In 2012, the festival's team published a statement on the main page of the website to declare that they would no longer organize any public events in a situation in which human rights were daily violated everywhere across the country. Nevertheless, we didn't want to stop DOX BOX's activity. Therefore, we curated an international film programme, titled "Syria Global Day", that occurred between 15 and 18 March 2012, corresponding to the first-year anniversary of the Syrian uprising. Thanks to collaborations with other festivals, film libraries, cinemas and universities all over the world, the film programme was able to travel to more than 40 cities in different countries. This first edition of "Syria Global Day" included ten documentaries by Syrian directors, such as "Step By Step" (1972) by Ossama Mohammed, and we concluded with "Turnsole" (2011), by an anonymous filmmaker. These are films that had long been forgotten by Syrians as their screening was forbidden in our country.

M. L.: Amer, with the Syria Mobile Film Festival you co-founded in 2013, you had a similar endeavour. Despite the hard security conditions, the festival aimed to show stories that Syrian directors have filmed through their mobile phone cameras. What is the Festival's mission and its main focus?

A. M.: We started preparing for the launch of the Syria Mobile Film Festival in 2013 because the mobile camera was transformed into a public tool and played a crucial role in the Arab protest movements. In defiance against the dictatorial regimes, thousands of activists and citizen journalists filmed exceptional video clips that courageously transmitted the facts from their countries. The mobile camera emerged as an essential tool in the peaceful struggle, the free expression and the artistic production. The festival sought to motivate young people from inside and outside Syria to engage in free artistic expression by empowering them with alternative cinematographic tools, as well as propagating a culture of criticism that contributes to the creation of an artistic narrative, free from the constraints of oppression and marginalization.

M. L.: Where did the Festival take place?

A. M.: The first edition started in 2014 with screenings organized in more than 16 cities and regions in Syria. Simultaneously the performance moved across several European cities and was then organized every two years. The festival basically seeks to regain the right to public space which was colonized and monopolized for decades by the repressive regimes. During the previous two editions, the festival presented four awards: best film award, best Syrian film, the jury award and the audience award. It also provided 13 production and development grants during the two editions, as well as the mobile film industry workshops. From the first to the second edition of the festival the attendance inside Syria increased from 1000 spectators in 2014 to 3000, among them 1000 women.

M. L.: Guevara, while you and DOX BOX also work with professional film-makers, you were furthermore interested in videos taken by non-professionals. Together with five other filmmakers and activists, you created the series "Citizen with a Movie Camera" between 2012 and 2013. Can you tell us more about this series?

G. N.: We organized this series as part of the second edition of "Syria Global Day" in 2013. Curated by the team of DOX BOX, this series is composed of a selection of YouTube videos uploaded by Syrian citizens in 2011 and 2012, which are organized thematically in six chapters: "Leaks", "Stories", "Dialogue", "In search of truth", "Letters" and "The moment". The documentary series was created in homage to the brave citizen journalists of the country. It was screened in more than 30 cities around the world, it was broadcast in TV channels, and it was also uploaded to online platforms and professional websites.

M. L.: At that time you had all escaped from Syria and relocated in Egypt. Why did you choose YouTube as an archive, as a source for the series?

G. N.: We started to explore YouTube in search of potentially valuable materials because we realized that, after two years of revolution, there was an enormous variety of image content circulating on YouTube, uploaded by dozens of video activists. However, due to the specific features of the digital platform itself and its internal functioning, there was no visible narrative that would link these diverse testimonies to each other. So we started surfing YouTube in search of videos shot in Syria from 2011 onwards that would mirror the ongoing conflict and tell us about its actors and the evident and tacit consequences of the war on a local and on an international level.

M. L.: What kind of images were you looking for specifically?

G. N.: We were looking for footage posted by subscribers who shot the videos themselves. We avoided reposted clips, as we were interested in tracking the original sources of the visual testimonies. For this, we had to combine our online-search with research offline. With the support of local activists, we tried to locate videos that stuck in our memory. As it turned out, it was impossible to identify the producers of the clips. The names or logos in the videos were always fake. These difficulties in locating and classifying the videos mirrored the chaotic situation that Syrians were living in. Still, we were surprised to find so much powerful footage, which had never been spotlighted before.

M. L.: What do you think were the reasons why these videos remained unknown to this point?

G. N.: It was probably due to translation problems, or because the author had not provided any clear title or context related to the images. In fact, during our research we discovered a paradox: the most searched keyword on YouTube in 2012 was "Syria"—in English. Obviously, people all over the world were looking for videos in order to understand the circumstances in Syria. As described above, there was a lot of content, but there just wasn't enough in English. Most of the uploaded clips were in Arabic, without any translation or subtitles. Therefore, although there was a huge amount of grass-root evidence filmed and spread by Syrian citizens, these materials couldn't be accessed by the international community. This might explain why, in the meantime, we were feeling as if no one was taking our struggle seriously.

M. L.: You stated that it was not possible to identify the producers of these image testimonies. Usually, the reliability of a witness is tied to his/her reliability as a person. That means that the witnesses' identity is quite important. Isn't the anonymous witness a paradox?

G. N.: During the revolution, remaining anonymous was simply a question of personal security. People with mobile phone cameras were a target for the regime. They were amongst the first ones to be killed. Sometimes their mobile phones were then taken by other activists who uploaded the footage. On the one hand, witnessing was an act of resistance and therefore a strategy to survive. On the other hand, it was endangering survival.

A. M.: Filming was forbidden in Syria, it was an indictable offence, liable to imprisonment or death. Hence, significant video clips were posted on

I still feel nervous when I hold
my phone to film in a street

Figure 4.1 Milad Amin, "Hide Your Mobile Phone", 2013, 07:21 min., film still.
Source: © Amer Matar.

YouTube and Facebook filmed by anonymous mobile owners. For example, activists and citizen-journalists fearlessly posted what was happening in their countries without security authorization. There is no director's name on the film "For whom the Bell Tolls" that we showed in our film festival because the director lives inside Syria and publishing his name may expose him to murder or detention. Despite this danger, a great number of Syrian filmmakers and activists continued shooting videos. Some of them managed to get away with it and survive, others were killed, together with tens of thousands of victims in prisons.

M. L.: What were the expectations attributed by Syrian citizens to the act of filming and sharing images online? Why did filmmakers and activists risk their lives in order to produce videos and share them with the world?

A. M.: The Syrian reality was overwhelming, like a fable. Sometimes we as Syrians could not easily understand it, so we tried to capture the reality, the "image and sound", when we thought of exporting it to the world. No one would have believed the details had it not been documented on video.

G. N.: Syrian citizens began shooting their private life and the collective sphere because they aimed to tell the truth. Censorship concerned not only the use of social media, but also of cameras and recording tools in the public space. Syrian citizens were not used to employing these devices, whether privately or socially. However, since it has become a matter of life or death, the majority of people felt the need and the urgency to shoot their daily existence under fire and share their experience with everyone. Despite the ban, citizens understood that they had nothing to lose. The act of shooting the protests, and later the war, turned into the largest statement agreed by millions of people, enacted without any pre-consensus. It's also worth mentioning that none of Al-Assad's previous massacres have ever been documented. This absence of traces encouraged people in thinking that, if they were able to produce documentations, nobody could ignore these crimes anymore, and Al-Assad would immediately stop his attacks on civilians. In this concern, the first slogan chanted by protesters at the beginning of the revolts, in March 2011 was a very old one, reciting "There will be no second Hama", in reference to Hama's massacre in 1982.

M. L.: This point is really relevant, Guevara. In fact, amateur footage disseminated by and stored in YouTube is now considered trustable evidence in trials against war crimes. Furthermore, you stress the reliance on Syrian citizens in the exposure of their horrific experiences. As if making their reality visible could automatically correspond to a substantial political changeover.

In this concern, do you think that people's beliefs have changed after seven years of conflict, in comparison with the time of the civil uprising in 2011? I mean, have you noticed any difference in the way people witness events with their smartphones, or in the way they share testimonies via social media?

G. N.: People are now disappointed and hopeless. At the beginning of the protests, they believed that the highly advanced devices available and the internet could play a role in supporting their humanitarian cause. In my view, the possibility of documenting the massacres was the main contribution given

He hid his mobile phone in his shirt's front pocket and filmed the police

Figure 4.2 Milad Amin, "Hide Your Mobile Phone", 2013, 07:21 min., film still.
Source: © Amer Matar.

by technology to people during the Syrian war. Unfortunately, citizens have later realized that the truth is different, as the technology seemed to sustain the oppressors rather than the civilians. In fact, technological developments also provided the dictator with modern methods of killing through several weapons, including chemical ones. When I find a video depicting people pleading for the world's aid, I'm shocked. I'm in pain when I think of how patient they are in still believing that someone will ever respond to their call.

A. M.: The camera turned into a public tool. Maybe the mobile phone camera will acquire a bigger role in chronicling and in the documentary film industry. In dictatorial countries it is currently an instrument of peaceful struggle. Looking at the documentary film production in the Middle East in recent years, one can sense that the "the most accurate picture is not necessarily the clearest one". Filming an exceptional event with a low-accuracy mobile phone camera is more valuable than footage of a normal event on a high-accuracy camera. This applies to the artistic element of the work.

M. L.: The Syrian community's appropriation of tools to self-represent and to narrate the war from its own perspective, without top-down mediators (mass media channels, or the regime) seems to have another relevant implication. It contributes to debates about the moral right of exposing human suffering.

G. N.: This is a big issue. I believe that the fact of documenting and showing our reality shouldn't generate questions about the fairness of its exposure or not. This is what is happening, while many other people live their daily lives. Of course, it's not a matter of blaming the viewer, but rather of being aware that we all live in the same reality, although each of us has his or her own truth. This is what documentary filmmaking aims to explore.

M. L.: Amer, the Syria Mobile Film Festival presents many documentaries that are based on footage similar to that we just talked about, collected online by filmmakers. "News Dreamers" by Ziad Adwan, for example, is composed entirely of a montage of videos found on YouTube. It is inspired by dreams that were posted by citizens on the Facebook page of the "Syrian Dreams Project". "Hide your mobile" was the first video by Milad Amin, in which he combined images he shot himself with videos from YouTube. Interestingly, one of the production grants that Syria Mobile Film Festival provides is called "Syria Tube", and addresses artists who wish to include videos from the digital archive of YouTube in their films. Why do you consider footage from YouTube so worthy for art production?

A. M.: YouTube was the refuge where Syrians stored their pictures for the world to see in the hope of changing their reality and of leaving photographed evidence for future generations to see the price we paid in the face of dictatorship and injustice. We did not own our lives nor had personal stories from before the revolution; it was all about the dictator, who represented the father and the God. Today, each one of us has a story, which he or she can narrate and photograph. Accordingly, people in Syria and in the Arab Spring countries had to film and document the chronicles of the demonstrations using small, easy-to-hide tools, like the mobile. The mobile phone camera film industry is developing continuously as a tool of defiance against dictatorships and censorship. In addition, the low cost of filming breaks the monopoly of production companies. Real creativity is not contingent upon money or the amount spent. It is determined by the imagination, and by a genuine relationship with reality.

M. L.: Guevara, with your series "Citizen with a Movie Camera", you found your own way to sort through the hyper archive that is YouTube. Despite the fact that YouTube and other social networks don't have the mission of conservation, people conceive and employ them as repositories of testimonies and different histories. However, the constant re-use by viewers of the footage online—through selection, embedding and re-contextualization—seems to be the only means to rescue videos from potential disappearance and oblivion. I'm very interested in the curatorial process behind the videos' selection and montage of this series. For instance, in the chapter "Stories", you gathered a variety of video testimonies that documented the arrest of an old man by the armed militia, a man destroying posters with portraits of Assad in a school, or the revenge of a mother slapping the killer of her son. You kept all meta-data—such as title, place and date, and number of views—and you showed them with an introductory slide. You also added comments, aiming to draw the attention of the viewer to some relevant issues, such as the act

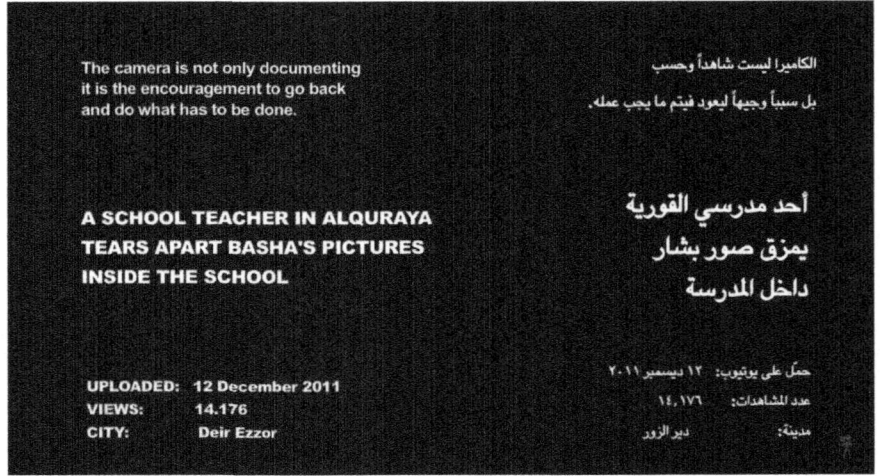

Figure 4.3 DOX BOX, introductory clip to the video "A school teacher in Alquraya tears apart Basha's pictures inside the school", 2012, from the series "Citizen with a Movie Camera" (DOX BOX).

Source: © Guevara Namer.

Figure 4.4 Anonymous Syrian citizen journalist, "A school teacher in Alquraya tears apart Basha's pictures inside the school", 2011, 6 min., film still, from the series "Citizen with a Movie Camera" (DOX BOX).

Source: © Guevara Namer.

of filming, the subjective perspective of the filmmaker, and the role of editing in the rewriting of reality and lived experience.

G. N.: Sometimes it was the narrative or the presence of certain characters that captured our attention. In other cases, we selected videos that seemed to introduce new aesthetic styles, due to the individual uses of the smartphone camera. Each video had the power to disclose an entire world. Initially we selected around 1500 clips, of which we kept only a hundred. We agreed on the final six themes during the editing but refrained from any cuts or manipulations of the videos. Furthermore, we subtitled and translated existing content already provided by the authors, adding comments from the filmmaker's points of view, and other information that could link the clips to each other.

M. L.: Watching these videos from outside of Syria, it is extremely difficult to fully understand their content, especially when accessed through YouTube, which often lacks a contextualization of the videos. In contrast, I think that through the creation of six thematic chapters, you emphasized the historical and social relevance of these videos for a global audience.

G. N.: We indeed imagined to speak to an international audience. We believed that there was a wide gap between the kind of images that were produced and who was in charge to distribute them around the world. We aimed to create a new format for watching this material since, from our perspective, making news out of this footage was unfair.

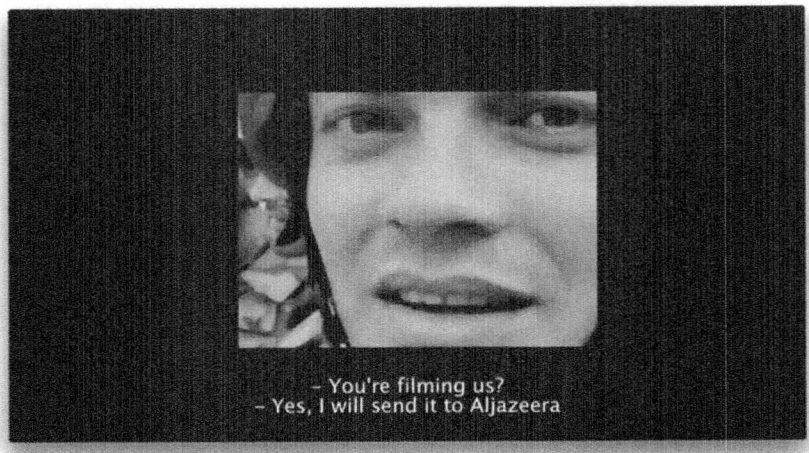

Figure 4.5 Anonymous Syrian citizen journalist, "The suicide of a pacifist demonstrator in Syria", 2011, 2:20 min., film still, from the series "Citizen with a Movie Camera" (DOX BOX).

Source: © Guevara Namer.

M. L: You mentioned the aesthetic style of the videos and refer to the witnesses as "filmmakers". Why are they filmmakers in your view?

G. N.: Let me put it like this: there is definitely a voice of filmmaking in these videos. One could even question the figure of the amateur itself. Many videos not only tried to document events but actually really tried to tell a story, like it would be the endeavour of a filmmaker.

Part II

Affective witnessing

Chapter 5

"Moroccan Lives Matter"

Practices and politics of affecting

Kerstin Schankweiler

The violent death of fishmonger Mouhcine Fikri, crushed in a garbage truck after a dispute with the police in the city of Al Hoceïma in Morocco on 28 October 2016, instigated the largest uprising in the northern Rif region and across the country since the so-called Arab Spring. The viral video of this incident not only drew widespread attention to what had taken place, but served a critical role in mobilizing and uniting people. Slogans of collectivization, such as "We are all Mouhcine Fikri", soon appeared on protest signs, indicating the sense of cohesiveness that the tragic occurrence, conveyed by the video, had triggered. "We are all"[1] has become one of the most prominent tropes of solidarity in civic protest, effectively connected to social media, images and affects. In Morocco, there were also cross-references to other social movements: "Moroccan Lives Matter" was a slogan on a protest sign a young man was holding up in a demonstration shortly after Fikri's death (Figure 5.1). It refers to the Black Lives Matter movement in the United States, which fights against racism, structural discrimination, police brutality and violence that Black Americans experience, and is especially associated with protests against police killings of black people and a series of shocking amateur videos.

What had happened on that evening of 28 October? The story goes that the police confiscated the fish Mouhcine Fikri was selling and threw it into a garbage truck. Fikri followed, jumping into the truck in order to protest or save his goods. As the garbage compactor suddenly began operating—it was not clear why—two other men, who also had jumped into the truck, were able to jump out quick enough, but not Fikri. One witness who was quoted in the local news reported that he had heard one of the police officers ask for the compactor to be activated, to scare away the people. Officials described Fikri's death as an accident (Alami 2016). On that evening, several people who were close to the truck witnessed the brutal killing of the 31-year-old. At least one person filmed the scene with his mobile phone camera. The video went viral on social media and sparked widespread protest in the country. The world climate summit in Marrakech scheduled to take place in November, shortly after the incident, brought additional global attention to the demonstrations. What began as a spontaneous uprising calling for a proper investigation of Fikri's death soon broadened to a movement, called

Figure 5.1 Mohammed Taoufik holding a protest sign "Moroccan Lives Matter", Casablanca, October 2016.

Source: courtesy of Mohammed Taoufik.

the Rif Movement or Hirak Chaabi (Popular Movement). What happened to Fikri resonates with a specific history of state-enforced marginalization and underdevelopment targeting the North-Moroccan Rif and is inscribed in a long history of police brutality, state violence, and human rights activism in Morocco (Slyomovics 2005). Although the focus of the protests was initially on structural discriminations against people in the Rif region, the political movement has become important for Morocco as a whole. Since October 2016, the protests have not ceased, even if political promises and interventions temporarily calm the situation. However, incidents of violence or detentions of social and economic rights defenders have caused the intensity of demonstrations to increase again and again, for example when the activist Nasser Zefzafi, one of the leading figures of the protest, was arrested in May 2017.

Connecting with others through images

In recent years, citizens all around the globe have been documenting police brutality and other human rights violations with their mobile phone cameras and have been circulating videos on social media. These videos constitute a distinct genre of what Kari Andén-Papadopoulos has termed "citizen camera-witnessing". She explains that

> the term refers to camera-wielding political activists and dissidents who put their lives at risk to produce incontrovertible public testimony to unjust and disastrous developments around the world, in a critical bid to mobilize global solidarity through the affective power of the visual.
> (Andén-Papadopoulos 2014, p. 754)

Andén-Papadopoulos is focusing on activists and their image practices, but the case of Fikri's death is somewhat different. People recording incidents like this often witness human rights violations and police brutality by chance, and not because they are already and necessarily involved in political movements. Stuart Allan has called this constellation "accidental journalism" (Allan 2013, p. 1). This means that people directly affected by an event, or mere bystanders might produce images spontaneously without clear intentions—be it out of voyeurism, to document their own involvement, or in order to raise awareness. On a more basic level, witnessing always entails becoming responsible to the witnessed event (Peters 2001, p. 708). Thus, people might very well become politically active as a result of becoming witnesses. For example, the eye witnesses of Fikri's death might have joined the subsequent Hirak Chaabi. But deciding to do something with the image testimonies—uploading them and sharing them—can be described as taking political action motivated by the "desire to connect with others" (Peters 2001, p. 708). While witnessing designates the act of bearing witness and of experiencing an event, testimony is a product of witnessing, a directed, motivated, and necessarily subjective account of the event (Richardson & Schankweiler 2019). The threshold to the political is crossed when acts of witnessing are rendered into testimony that can be perceived by others.

Regardless of the various contexts of their production, these videos themselves are characterized by strong affective dynamics, and they trigger affect. As Michael Richardson has put it: "Images [...] not only show but also produce intensities and provoke bodies. [They] call the viewing body into relation to them through the capacity to affect" (Richardson 2016, p. 75). And they do not only move and shake viewers to the core, they subsequently can fuel protest or other actions of dissent as well as instigate the production of further testimonies. Using the video of the death of Mouhcine Fikri and the Moroccan uprising it helped provoke, in this chapter I read media witnessing of police brutality as a practice and a politics of affecting.

"Sousveilling" police violence

The best-known recent incidents of police violence are certainly from the United States. There, image testimonies played a major role in what has become the Black Lives Matter movement.

Police officers have repeatedly killed African Americans while being recorded by the mobile phone cameras of civil bystanders, as in the case of the brutal and fatal police arrest of Eric Garner, resulting in his death; the shooting of Kajieme Powell in St. Louis; or Philando Castile's shooting to death by police during a traffic stop.[2] However, such video testimonies are as global a phenomenon as police and state violence mostly directed against marginalized groups in societies. Known examples of police violence from other contexts of the past years that became public through viral videos are the so-called "Blue Bra Girl", a woman who was brutally beaten by a group of military men at Tahrir square in Cairo during the Egyptian Revolution 2011, or the abuse of a young black man in a Paris suburb that lead to the protest movement "Justice pour Théo" (Schankweiler 2017). It is through social media that this specific culture of protest has become transnational. There is a global awareness of social movements around the world. The slogan "Moroccan Lives Matter" also indicates this, as it references the Black Lives Matter campaign and is immediately understandable as a protest against state and police violence.

There is of course also a historical tradition of image testimonies of police violence. Even before the emergence of the internet, civilians took photographs and recorded videos of police violence. The distribution of those images gave rise to public outrage and debate. A prominent example is the videotape of the beating of Rodney King by four white police officers in 1992 (Goodwin 1994). An even earlier example from New York dates from 1988 and can be found in the online archive of Tactical Media, a project focusing on practices of media activism (Kluitenberg 2011). The civilian who recorded the video was a media artist named Paul Garrin. This may explain why he had a video camera in hand during the escalating street protests, which went down in history as the Tompkins Square Park riot. The riots occurred after police started evicting homeless people from the park. Garrin documented the brutality with which the police proceeded against the demonstrators and passed the material on to television broadcasters. The pictures were broadcast nationwide and sparked a public debate. The video is blurry, shaky and dark. It was recorded in the evening hours and Garrin was attacked while he was filming. One can hardly see what is happening, yet there is an intensity to the scene. Figures move hectically, the camera is turbulent with rapid movements, and the soundtrack is characterized by chanting and yelling.

The video has been preserved as a collage, which contains the original footage, some television newscasts, in which the material was used, and a retrospective comment by the artist. At the end of the video, Garrin speaks the programmatic words:

> Video is a tool, it's a weapon, and it's a witness. […] It's kind of a reverse Big Brother. Big Brother is always the state watching the people, but if everybody has cameras, it's gonna be the people watching the state and they won't fuck with us anymore.
>
> (Garrin 1989)

In 1989, Garrin was unable to foresee that a little over two decades later, almost everybody would have a mobile camera. Today, his words seem almost visionary. Garrin's video activism marks the beginning of a sousveillance[3] movement, an observation and surveillance of the state power "from below". It also indicates that power relations are always at stake in these kinds of image testimonies.

A case of "hogra"

Let us now return to the death of Mouhcine Fikri in Al Hoceïma. The 1:22 minute video depicting the incident (Figure 5.2) is markedly different from Garrin's video of the Tompkins Square Park riot or many other examples of police brutality and

Figure 5.2 Still from the video "Horrifying moment Mouhcine Fikri is crushed by a rubbish truck", recorded on 28 October 2016 in Al Hoceïma, Morocco and uploaded on Twitter.

Source: www.dailymail.co.uk/video/news/video-1349729/Horrifying-moment-Mouhcine-Fikri-crushed-rubbish-truck.html [4 April 2017].

killing. Here, the police are not even in the image but the incident was immediately framed as "hogra". Hogra is the Maghrebinian word for arbitrary use of power by authorities and police, and the anger that the citizens feel when they are disregarded and mistreated by police and the state (Amjahid 2016).

Although the video is supposed to prove the course of the events and the police violence—that is the way it was treated in the media—we hardly see anything. The video was recorded in the evening hours and is subsequently quite dark. Light reflections, which emanate from the backlight of the garbage truck, characterize the images. The video is blurred, the camera is shaky, and the videographer comments in an excited way. The man in the video keeps saying: "Look, the poor one, look, what they are doing to him, look, look at that! They do not allow him to have an income." It seems that he is directly addressing the viewers to also become eye witnesses: "Look, what they are doing to him, look!"[4] When the garbage compactor starts operating people are completely losing their temper and cry out in panic. We hear constantly repeated shouts "Allahu akbar", "Allahu akbar", meaning "God is great" or "God is the greatest". In this context, it is used as a formula to express strong emotions, astonishment and shock. Somebody also says: "They killed him!" and in the end someone speaks (the first part of) the shahada "I bear witness that there is no god except Allah" (Ashhadu allâ ilâha illâ llâh) which is the strongest form of testimony, one of the five pillars of Islam. It is also a tradition to speak the shahada as the last sentence on the deathbed.[5] The word "shahada" actually means to testify or to bear witness and is also related to shaheed, the martyr, meaning "witness" in its literal translation. Although there is a religious connotation here, it is maybe no coincidence that bearing witness is called upon. Or rather, this act of bearing witness is connecting to the vitally important modes of religious witnessing.

Unfolding witnessing

There are several layers to the issue of witnessing and testimony in the video that can be unfolded. For analytical purposes, I will consider these layers separately, but they are in fact strongly interwoven.

The video documents Fikri's martyrdom: he becomes a blood witness, the witness par excellence (Agamben 1999; Fassin 2008). In recent years the figure of the martyr or shaheed has played a central role in civil protests against oppressive regimes in North African and Middle Eastern countries. This has led to a global circulation of martyr images. In social media as well as on the streets, Mouhcine Fikri immediately became stylized as a martyr and icon of protest and was related to Mohamed Bouazizi. Bouazizi is the Tunisian street vendor whose self-immolation is said to have instigated the revolution in Tunisia in December 2010 and helped inspire uprisings in other countries. He set himself on fire to protest against the authorities, because his goods had been confiscated, he had been publicly offended and slapped in the face by a police woman. Bouazizi's case was another example of hogra, why people linked it to Fikri's death. Tweets stated for example: "Mouhcine Fikri from now on is the Mohamed Bouazizi of Morocco". The comparison of Fikri and Bouazizi contains the hope that the case of Mouhcine Fikri might unfold similar affective dynamics and subsequent political effects as in Tunisia. A cartoon that circulated online depicted Fikri and Bouazizi as relay racers, the already burning Bouazizi passing a torch on to Fikri in the garbage truck (Figure 5.3).

As a second layer of witnessing, the people who are around the garbage truck, physically present at the event, have become eye witnesses, including the videographer. The presence of the eye witness is an essential condition for acknowledging the martyrdom of Fikri, who cannot speak and testify for himself. Without an eye witness, someone who bears witness to his death, no one would know about the blood witness. At the same time, the eye witnesses are themselves potential victims of police violence and hogra. They could as well become martyrs, just like Fikri.[6] In fact, they are not only recording the violence of this specific case, they document and feel their own repression at the same time. Beyond the scope of Fikri's death and unintended martyrdom, the eye witnesses seem to tell the audience: "This is how the police and the state are treating us! We are all garbage to them!" The solidarity with Fikri, the anticipation of "us" against "them", is expressed by the man saying: "Look what they are doing to him […]! They do not allow him to have an income."

Another layer is the video itself as a witness. In his reception-oriented reading of witnessing, Paul Frosh has theorized media witnessing and stated that "'bearing witness,' … is an act performed not by a witness but by a witnessing text" (Frosh 2006, p. 274). The relevance of the witnessing text, in this case the video, is even more obvious in times of social media and its economies of image

Figure 5.3 Cartoon by Osama Hajjaj, "The future of fish vendor Mouhcine Fikri …".
Source: © Osama Hajjaj.

testimonies, when witnesses can hardly be identified as individuals. In this case, it was not possible to find out who recorded the video.[7] We also do not see the anonymous videographer in the clip, we only hear him. He is in the blind spot behind the camera and has taken on the perspective of witnessing. (One might as well think of the camera as a witness.) Thus, the image testimony has taken on its own life, somewhat independent from the witness as an individual person.

The video, then, enables the viewers to become co-witnesses, or what might be thought of as secondary eye witnesses. Witnessing of course always entails media and mediation, as Paul Frosh and Amit Pinchevski have already pointed out: "every act of witnessing implies some kind of mediation [...], every act of mediation entails a kind of witnessing, particularly the use of technology as a surrogate for an absent audience" (Frosh & Pinchevski 2009, p. 1). At the most basic level, the human body of the witness as the central agent of witnessing is a medium in the broadest sense. More substantively, the question of mediation takes centre stage when considering that "any practice of bearing witness [...] is a mode of address" (Tait 2011, p. 1227). Witnesses always rely on other witnesses that bear witness to their testimony, as Guerin and Hallas (2007, p. 10) have highlighted. One cannot testify all by oneself. Witnessing and bearing witness are both fundamentally relational. The idea of media witnessing stresses that it is not enough to witness an event; one must give testimony that can be witnessed by others who were not present at the event. Thus, testimony describes a transformation: something that is singular, ephemeral, situational, that refers to a specific event of witnessing, becomes a generic testimony that is permanent and that enables circulation and reiteration. Witnessing Fikri's death was undeniably a most exceptional event in time and space, without comparison. But when becoming a media event of witnessing, it is no longer unique, but repeatable in other times and spaces. Frosh and Pinchevski have referred to this as the "repeatable singularity" of witnessed events, as events of witnessing (Frosh & Pinchevski 2009, p. 9). The moral and ethical implications of Fikri's death as an event of witnessing are far from being clear or understood.

Amateur aesthetics

Important in this type of citizen camera-witnessing is that these images promise to document what otherwise would not have been seen, what would remain invisible, even suppressed. This may be because journalists are simply not present as the events unfold or because official media do not cover the events, these image testimonies have the character of a leak. It is telling that the figure of the amateur has become so important in discourses around new image practices and testimonies, although the precise status of the witnesses is often not clear at all. The videographer Paul Garrin, for example, who recorded the Tompkins Square Park riot, is a video artist and cannot be labelled an "amateur" as such, but his video was marked as "amateur videotape" in news programmes. I argue that the figure of the amateur is rather linked to a certain aesthetic appeal of such videos and that it is used to construct authenticity.

I will briefly outline some aspects to the amateur appearance of the video recorded that night in Al Hoceïma. First, the bad quality. Like many images and videos made with mobile phone cameras and uploaded online, it is of low resolution, unfocused, pixelated and blurred. Hito Steyerl has theorized this specific aesthetic quality as the "poor image" that "tends towards abstraction" (Steyerl 2009). Second, the vertical format. Film and video have always been horizontal and wide, but smartphones have given rise to videos that have been shot vertically, because the phones are designed to be held vertically (Gotto 2017, p. 356). Although vertical video seems to be gaining acceptance, this mode of shooting is still seen as an amateur way of doing it, as if recording the wrong way around. YouTube, for instance, only accepted horizontal videos until the summer of 2015. That is why many mobile phone videos are still edited, and computer programs have functions to crop vertical videos into horizontal ones. The video of Fikri's death is an example of one such technique that is very common. To fill in the sides of vertical videos, it is cropped, blurred and used as background so that the video is reproduced in the back, mirroring what is seen in the front. Intended to adjust the mobile phone videos to the norm of horizontal screening, this mode of presentation has become iconic of "amateur" witnessing and its pledge of immediacy. Videos like this are increasingly used in television news, for example. In these cases, the vertical video that is framed by two vertical stripes of even greater blurriness than the video itself is what identifies it as "amateur video" and as taken from social media. The poor image here becomes even poorer. The blurriness as the main characteristic of amateur videos is exaggerated and is used to frame this video as a certain practice. Poor quality does not only signify the aesthetics of these videos, it has become the frame work of citizen camera-witnessing.

I argue, however, that the key point is not that image testimonies were taken by amateurs but that the videographers were intensely emotionally moved and involved. Their subjective, situational, political, and emotional point of view is important rather than their objective, professional, impartial look at things. This creates a strong claim to authenticity. Hito Steyerl has pointed out that digital documentary photography, as it is circulated online, often shows hardly anything except its own excitation. The specific aesthetics that I have described reflect this. The images are highly ambiguous, hardly suitable for reconstructing the events—even if this is tried again and again. Despite, or rather because of this, they are reproduced in the media as an authentic artefact of events. The question of indexicality was one of the central topoi of theories of photography from the beginning—for example in the works of Roland Barthes, Susan Sontag, or Rosalind Krauss. The assertion of truth in relation to photographic images has long been scrutinized. Yet photographs seem to continually renew their promise of authenticity. In fact, the image practices in social media have decisively contributed to renewing this promise in the digital age. Egyptian artist Lara Baladi has written about the images of Tahrir Square in Cairo that were shared world-wide in 2011:

> At the midst of the emergency, all theories about the subjectivity of photography suddenly became irrelevant. [...] Photography became objective; photography showed the truth—yes, a "truth" made up of as many truths as there were protestors in the square, but nonetheless one that had urgently to be revealed at this turning point in history.
>
> (Baladi 2013, p. 70)

Baladi is describing a paradoxical aspect of these photographs: despite all theoretical doubt about their documentary value, they nonetheless bear witness to multiple realities and bring truths into being—grounded in subjective and relational experiences. The images have a special relationship with reality, one that is primarily affective.

Affective media witnessing

The question of authenticity is less related to the depiction of a supposed reality or a referential truth than to the affective dynamics associated with the images. Bodies, things, and media enter into relations with each other, and this relationship is mainly characterized by reciprocal affecting, by an entanglement of affecting and being affected in a particular setting. Affective media witnessing accounts for both the centrality of affect and emotion to witnessing in general and the intensive relationality of the witnessed, the witness, his or her image testimony and the co-witnesses participating in the making of the testimony. I understand affect in this context as the first intense, but not clearly defined, movement between the images and different actors that brings them into a relationship with each other. As Andrew Murphie has put it: "Affects make up the relations within the temporary worlds we are constantly creating, and by which we are constantly being created. Affect involves the moment to moment question of being in the world, in all its constant change" (Murphie 2010). In the video we do not primarily witness what happened to Fikri. We rather witness the videographer (and other eyewitnesses) being affected. The intense affectivity of witnessing this incident is captured in and transmitted by the video: the panicked screams, the chants of "Allahu akbar" and the shaky camera. The video mainly communicates affectivity coming to a climax.

This is also true for many other examples where activists or bystanders take out their mobile phone cameras to record remarkable events unfolding around them, feeling not only the need that this should be documented for others not present, but also the need to share this extraordinary experience of witnessing. Thus, media witnessing of police brutality is a practice and a politics of affecting.

This observation shall by no means negate the individual content of the videos, which is not interchangeable. I rather refer to the mode in which this genre of witnessing operates. The intense affectivity of videos of police violence is central to the truth claims they can make.

> Affect enables a move to witnessing that materially imbricates the viewer. This affectivity may well be part of what enables the image to assert veracity—the very indeterminacy of affect, the non-specificity of its intensity, forges an intimate relationship between viewer and image.
>
> (Richardson 2016, p. 83)

The strong affective relationship one develops with these videos when watching them invests them with authenticity because the affective relationality is concrete, authentic and real. In these image testimonies, witnessing and affecting correlate. In other words: affect is at the core of witnessing (Richardson & Schankweiler 2019).

Witnessing an event and giving testimony have usually been two separated acts that could be far apart in time. Just think of the Holocaust survivor witnesses who often testified only years later. These testimonies were "recorded at various distances from the event" (Wieviorka 2006, p. xi). In times of citizen camera-witnessing this distance vanishes: witnessing and testifying, seeing and speaking, take place at the very same moment. The "fragility of witnessing" (Peters 2001, p. 710), which resides in the gap between experience and seeing on the one hand and witnessing and speaking on the other, seems thus reduced. The person who recorded the video on 28 October 2016, sees what is happening to Fikri, and holds and operates the camera, thus testifying for a future audience—all at the same time and in the moment of immediately being affected by what is being witnessed. He even seems to directly address the potential viewers of the video ("Look, what they are doing to him, look!"), not as if they were absent but present at the event, belonging to the group of eyewitnesses gathering around the truck.

The circulation of the images is another important part of these image practices and affective media witnessing, because the circulation organizes processes of exchanging and sharing affects. Marianna Hirsch has stressed: "In circulating my images, I can invite others to become my co-witnesses" (Hirsch 2003, pp. 78–79). The communicative structures of Web 2.0, which enable its users to share images very quickly, provides a relational structure for an affective economy of image testimonies. Because images and videos are often uploaded to social media very quickly and are available to other users in near real time, the distance in time (and place) seems to be even more minimized, with the effect of an amplification of the affective dynamics, because co-witnesses feel very close to the event. This fosters the joint political struggle against state authority and police violence, connected to larger issues of inequalities, discrimination, human rights abuses and their history in Morocco (Slyomovics 2005). Slogans such as "We are all Mouhcine Fikri" or "Moroccan Lives Matter" as well as the Rif Movement as a whole express this joint struggle. Thus, witnessing, especially when unfolding in social media, needs to be defined as a collective and relational practice with the effect of forming communities. In Sara Ahmed's terms: these images and their affective dynamics "align individuals with communities" (Ahmed 2004, p. 119). Considering this, image testimonies of police brutality always evoke a collective. They are shared to connect with others, to produce feelings of communality and solidarity, and to gather a potential affective community of political protest and dissent. Affectivity did not only play a vital role in sparking the viral circulation of the video of Fikri's death, the affective media witnessing indeed appears to have been the tipping point, the dawn of Hirak Chaabi.

Acknowledgements

This text was written within the programme of the Collaborative Research Centre 1171 Affective Societies at Freie Universität Berlin. I thank the German Research Foundation for financial support, and Mohamed Amjahid, Jonas Bens, Michael Richardson, Verena Straub, Cristiana Strava, and Tobias Wendl for discussions and suggestions.

Notes

1 For a critical perspective on the "We are all" trope see Kluger (2012).
2 See the chapter of Penelope Papailias in this volume.
3 Computer scientist and inventor Steve Mann coined the term "sousveillance", meaning inverse surveillance, as a counter to organizational surveillance. See Mann, Nolan & Wellman (2003); Bakir (2010).
4 I thank Mohammed Amjahid for the translation.
5 I thank Tom Bioly for indicating this to me.
6 Andén-Papadopoulos has already stated, that "citizen camera-witnessing [...] derives its potency from the way it reactivates the idea of martyrdom" (Andén-Papadopoulos 2014, p. 753).
7 Journalists such as Mohamed Amjahid, who know the region very well and investigated the case in Al Hoceïma, were also not able to find out.

References

Agamben, G. (1999). *Remnants of Auschwitz: The Witness and the Archive*. New York: Zone Books.
Ahmed, S. (2004). Affective economies. *Social Text 79*, 22(2), pp. 117–139.
Alami, A. (2016). Protests erupt in Morocco over fish vendor's death in garbage compactor. *New York Times*, 30 October. Available from: www.nytimes.com/2016/10/31/world/middleeast/protests-erupt-in-morocco-over-fish-vendors-death-in-garbage-compactor.html [21 March 2017].
Allan, S. (2013). *Citizen Witnessing: Revisioning Journalism In Times Of Crisis (Key Concepts In Journalism)*. Cambridge, UK: Polity Press.
Amjahid, M. (2016). Jetzt der Aufruhr? Ein Fischverkäufer wurde zermalmt, in Marokko greift Empörung um sich. *Die Zeit*, 47, 10 November, pp. 8–9.

Andén-Papadopoulos, K. (2014). Citizen camera-witnessing: Embodied political dissent in the age of "mediated mass self-communication". *New Media Society*, 16(5), pp. 753–769.

Bakir, V. (2010). *Sousveillance, Media and Strategic Political Communication: Iraq, USA, UK*. New York: Continuum.

Baladi, L. (2013). When seeing is belonging: The photography of Tahrir. In F. Ebner & C. Wicke (eds), *Cairo: Open City. New Testimonies from an Ongoing Revolution*, exh. cat., pp. 68–73. Leipzig: Spector Books.

Fassin, D. (2008). The humanitarian politics of testimony: Subjectification through trauma in the Israeli-Palestinian conflict. *Cultural Anthropology*, 23(3), pp. 531–558.

Frosh, P. (2006). Telling presences: Witnessing, mass media, and the imagined lives of strangers. *Critical Studies in Media Communication*, 23(4), pp. 265–284.

Frosh, P. & Pinchevski, A. (eds) (2009). *Media Witnessing: Testimony in the Age of Mass Communication*. New York: Palgrave Macmillan.

Garrin, P. (1989). Man with a video camera. Video, 2:27 min., Color. Available from: www.tacticalmediafiles.net/videos/4574/Man-With-a-Video-Camera [4 April 2017].

Goodwin, C. (1994). Professional vision. *American Anthropologist*, 96(3), pp. 606–633.

Gotto, L. (2017). Micro movies: Zur medialen Miniatur des Smartphone-Films. In M. Gamper & R. Mayer (eds), *Kurz & Knapp: Zur Mediengeschichte kleiner Formate vom 17. Jahrhundert bis zur Gegenwart*, pp. 349–366. Bielefeld: Transcript.

Guerin, F. & Hallas, R. (2007). *The Image and the Witness: Trauma, Memory and Visual Culture*. London: Wallflower Press.

Hirsch, M. (2003). I took pictures: September 2001 and beyond. In J. Greenberg (ed.), *Trauma at Home: After 9/11*, pp. 69–86. Lincoln, NB: University of Nebraska Press.

Kluger, J. (2012). Viewpoint: The problem with the "We Are All ..." trope. Does our chorus of empathy miss the mark? Time.com, 22 October. Available from: http://ideas.time.com/2012/10/22/the-problem-with-the-we-are-all-trope/ [19 January 2016].

Kluitenberg, E. (2011). Legacies of tactical media: The tactics of occupation. From Tompkins Square to Tahrir. *Network Notebooks 05*. Amsterdam: Institute of Network Cultures.

Mann, S., Nolan, J., & Wellman, B. (2003). Sousveillance: Inventing and using wearable computing devices for data collection in surveillance environments. *Surveillance & Society*, 1(3), pp. 331–355.

Murphie, A. (2010). Affect: A basic summary of approaches. Blog post, 30 January. Available from: www.andrewmurphie.org/blog/?p=93 [21 March 2017].

Peters, J.D. (2001). Witnessing. *Media, Culture & Society*, 23(6), pp. 707–723.

Richardson, M. (2016). *Gestures of Testimony: Torture, Trauma, and Affect in Literature*. New York: Bloomsbury.

Richardson, M. & Schankweiler, K. (2019). Affective witnessing. In J. Slaby & C. von Scheve (eds), *Affective Societies: Key Concepts*. London: Routledge.

Schankweiler, K. (2017). Reverse Big Brother: Videos von Polizeigewalt in den sozialen Medien. *kolik.film*, 27, pp. 67–72.

Slyomovics, S. (2005). *The Performance of Human Rights in Morocco*. Philadelphia, PA: University of Pennsylvania Press.

Steyerl, H. (2009). In defense of the poor image. *e-flux Journal*, 10. Available from: www.e-flux.com/journal/10/61362/in-defense-of-the-poor-image/ [7 June 2018].

Tait, S. (2011). Bearing witness, journalism and moral responsibility. *Media, Culture & Society*, 33(8), pp. 1220–1235.

Wieviorka, A. (2006). *The Era of the Witness*. Ithaca, NY: Cornell University Press.

Chapter 6

Drone's-eye view

Affective witnessing and technicities of perception

Michael Richardson

The eye of the drone captures landscapes of war and ruin, of the urban and the wild, of the beautiful and the terrible. Its vision is intimately uncanny, a technicity of perception that both escapes and extends the human. From the drone's-eye view, objects, environments and bodies flatten and bend, captured in the digital and transmitted across technical assemblages of signal, device, operator, code, relay, interface, environment and data. In this, the drone is the paradigmatic figure of emergent perception in the contemporary world, a mediating technology of anxious ambivalence that dissolves distinctions between war and domesticity, human and machine, mediation and space.

Technologies of war and vision have always been commingled as Paul Virilio (1989) has famously shown, but the drone has produced a new division between point of view and the human eye. While cinema and the military tools of vision—sights, scopes, cameras—continuously exchanged technological developments, techniques of practice and modes of aesthetics, the drone's autonomous movement and non-human perspective departs from the cinematic in important ways. Like cinema in the twentieth century, drone vision originates in the technics and defines the contemporary aesthetic of war, but it is also increasingly present in new modes of art, activism, and popular and promotional culture (Christiansen 2017; Sandvik & Jumbert 2016). Yet whatever the field in which they are encountered, drone images possess a complex, uncertain quality: natively digital and distanced in vantage-point from the machine's operator, the drone image seems almost to withdraw from our grasp. Unlike photography or cinema, drone images assert their distinction from what is possible to see with the human eye. Whereas the eyewitness, the photograph and the video have long held evidentiary authority in the courtroom and in wider culture (Felman & Laub 1992; Langbein 1977; Sontag 2003; Tagg 2009), the drone's ambivalent, contested status as an emergent technology of primarily visual perception demands that attention be paid to its particular modes of bearing witness.

Witnessing is itself an intricately knotted concept. In the simplest sense, "a witness is an observer or source possessing privileged raw, authentic proximity to facts" (Peters 2009, p. 25). Yet witnessing is also both an act and an utterance. That is, one may bear witness, but that witnessing can take the form of speech, text, image or some other mediation. For Wendy Kozol (2014, p. 6), visual witnessing is "a complex set of practices and interactions between witnesses (such as survivor-witnesses, photojournalists, and both military and nonmilitary observers), technologies that transform experiences into representation (including institutional practices of production and circulation), and viewers". In the specific context of mass media and its audiences, Paul Frosh and Amit Pinchevski described "media witnessing" as "witnessing performed *in*, *by* and *through* the media" (Frosh & Pinchevski 2009, p. 1). Permeating this—and any other—discussion of witnessing are a set of concepts potentially at odds with one another: veracity, presence, ethics, subject, object, self, other, and more. As Peters (2009, p. 24) notes, "to witness an event is to be responsible in some way to it". This responsibility is, in essence, a responsibility to communicate: to make known to others what happened. Witnessing thus has "two faces: the passive one of seeing and the active one of saying" (Peters 2009, p. 26). This doubleness signals the fragility at the heart of witnessing, which is the gap between word and event, between experience and language.

Yet as Kelly Oliver (2001) argues, witnessing is an inescapably ethico–political act, one bound up with subjectivity and subjectivation, with what it means to be human and what it means to know. Witnessing is thus a kind of flashpoint or critical juncture for a host of crucial questions about the relations between people, events, media, memory and communication. Yet what is less easy to see in this swift tour through some of the key critical thought on witnessing is that it is at least as affective as it is communicative or discursive. Whether mediated or not, first-hand or not, to bear witness is always to be affected, to be bodily encountered. It is to encounter the capacity of the body, what Spinoza called the power to affect and be affected by the world. It is this affectivity that gives witnessing its bodily force, that shifts its ethics from the abstract to the urgently embodied. Mediation can dampen, modulate, amplify and generate the affective force of witnessing, yet what does that mean when the mediating technology tends towards autonomy? When it is defined by its capacity to see and sense, to record, remember and catalogue that which its sensors capture? When it shifts the eye of the witness beyond the human? At issue here is how drone vision might enable new forms of bearing witness—and what those modes might mean for the relation of the human and the non-human.

In this chapter, I consider the drone as a technicity of perception bound up with witnessing in fluid ways irreducible to the semantic and representational content of images alone. While all drones hold the potential to bear witness, much of what follows focuses on the drone warfare of the United States because it is highly developed, widely in operation and densely documented. My contention is that the drone is entangled in affective modes of witnessing, constituted by imbrications of perception, mediation and affect. Intensive, differential and ambivalent, the drone's aesthetics of post-cinematic affect cut across the digital field, circulating on social networks and carrying with it a confusion of contents, contexts and intensities. Thus, the drone's-eye view constitutes the entry point into an emergent mode of affective witnessing, inseparable from the digital mediations of the social media age and yet uncannily other than human in its capacities of perception.

Drone apparatus

"Weapons are not just tools of destruction but also of perception," writes Paul Virilio (1989, p. 9) in *War and Cinema*. "For men at war, the function of the weapon is the function of the eye" (Virilio 1989, p. 26). For Virilio, cinema constitutes a logistics of perception in which the capacity to see is split across persons, objects, and processes. At issue here is "the philosophical question of the splitting of viewpoint, the sharing of perception of the environment between the animate (the living subject) and the inanimate (the object, the seeing machine)" (Virilio 1994, pp. 59–60). Through the technology of the drone, these logistics extend and collapse temporal and spatial zones of war and vision far beyond those described by Virilio in his work on cinema. While earlier autonomous visual technologies, such as the satellite, echo the cinematic travelling shot for Virilio, the drone more radically shifts the vantage point of the camera from direct connection to the human eye to an impossible perspective: adrift in the atmosphere, capable of switching into thermal and other sensory modes. What the military drone sees far exceeds the human eye, as evidenced by the host of analysts required to monitor its accumulated output and by the data stored for an imagined posterity in the server farms of the US national security apparatus.

This extension into an order of perception beyond the cinematic is made possible not only by advancements in logistics, but also by the concretization of new technical objects. For Gilbert Simondon, technical objects bring into being their own modes of existence, irreducible to human intention or natural process. Knowledge of their capabilities and potentials cannot be complete, except by dint of a chance alignment between science and technics (Simondon 2017, p. 39). In this sense, drones possess autonomy by the sheer fact of their technicity, as well as by design. It is their technicity, even more than the logistics within which they are bound, that defines their capacity for perception. As well as the visual in its various forms—high-definition, thermal, zoomed-in—the perception of the drone is of control signals, air pressures, wind movements, fuel or battery reserves, and much more. If Virilio's analysis of the confluence of vision and war offers a profoundly pessimistic critique, Simondon's recognition of the distinct modes of existence of technical objects provides for a more open potential in the drone. Its technicities of perception afford not only the reshaping of battlefields, but of fields of activism, art, domesticity and work. What the technical object might do is not fixed: what matters is how it functions within the social, cultural and political architectures that take up and enact its relational potentials.

Modern media technologies are emphatically relational, as Jussi Parikka demonstrates in his archaeology of what he calls insect media, or the way in which modern media technologies draw on distributed, networked and relational forms of organization from the insect world, such as the hive, swarm or web. For Parikka, technology should necessarily be understood in ethological terms as examining "the relational affording capacities of objects, processes, and agencies" (Parikka 2010, p. 79). Thus we might consider—briefly and incompletely—the assemblages that cohere around the drone: hobbyist, drone, remote control, WiFi signal, public space, aviation regulation. Or the activist, drone, control, camera, signal, contested space, security, law, media platform, political objectives. Or, on the battlefield, the pilot, the sensor operator, mission commander, flight crews, satellites, signal relays, Predator drone, Hellfire missiles, kill chains, military lawyers, rules of engagement, air force base, mission objectives, intelligence analysts, video recorders....

Each assemblage of relational actants constitutes a network of distributed agency (Latour 2005), but these networks do not exist distinct from power. We might think of these assemblages as what Michel Foucault (1980) called an apparatus, or *dispositif*: the network of discourses, institutions, objects, and so on that possess a strategic function and are located at the intersection of power and knowledge relations. Giorgio Agamben expands the concept further, using it to describe "literally anything that has in some way the capacity to capture, orient, determine, intercept, model, control, or secure the gestures, behaviors, opinions, or discourses of living being" (Agamben 2009, p. 14). For Agamben, the apparatus and the living being are distinct categories from between which the subject is produced. Thus, the same living being can be enfolded in multiple processes of subjectivation, and it is precisely this process that is at stake in the investigation of apparatuses.

Within our increasingly controlled, surveilled and enclosed contemporary moment, the military apparatuses of state power are interwoven with one another. Ian Shaw describes those collected apparatuses as the Predator Empire which "materializes a mode of state power (policing), a military strategy (predation), an archetypal technology of remote surveillance (the Predator drone), and a geographical scale (the planetary)" (Shaw 2016, p. 6). For Shaw, drones are not instruments but "geopolitical agents", reshaping the intersections of life and power (Shaw 2016, p. 6). In the apparatuses of the drone, these modes and processes are inseparable from its technicities of perception. What the drone assembles—even in its most benign and least intensive forms—are modes of seeing beyond the human that are nonetheless fundamentally concerned with the status of humans in relation to the world. For the grainy figure captured on the screen of the Predator's sensor operator, this is perceptive subjectivation in the purest sense: its specific presence within the drone's perceptive capacities is a matter of life itself. Perception as apparatus of death is crystallized in the military "kill chain" that establishes the sequence of events that leads to a fatal strike (Cockburn 2015, p. 14); a relay of human and non-human technics that produces both death and life for those within the drone's-eye view.

But the military drone is also a technology of pre-emptive power, the tip of the spear in warfare founded in perception that extends from the battlespaces of the war on terror to the surveillance of the domestic control society. Its technicity of perception not only projects power, it brings into being threats, targets, spaces and sites upon which violence will be visited. Without the drone, numerous bodies, vehicles, homes, landscapes and villages would remain outside the domain of threat, invisible to the US military superstructure. Yet the drone enfolds these bodies and places into this operative logic of threat, both actually and potentially. Drones are thus objects of what Brian Massumi calls "ontopower", a "power of emergence: a power for the serial production of variations belonging to the same power curve, or tendency" (Massumi 2015, p. 221). If Shaw's Predator Empire describes apparatuses of biopolitical enclosure, ontopower provides a way of understanding how futures as yet unrealized are brought within the domain of security. Understood in this way, it is not the Hellfire missile in which the drone's power coheres, so much as the camera, signals, satellites, screens and operators that enable its technicity of perception to produce action. And it is the echoing of this technicity in activist, artist and hobbyist drones that demands reckoning with the drone as an essential figure of the contemporary world. One crucial element of such a reckoning is asking whether, to what, and how, the drone as technicity of perception bears witness—and of what that witnessing might be composed in an age of social media.

The drone as affective witness

What the drone sees is inseparable from the assemblage within which the drone resides. "Drone vision," writes Daniel Greene (2015, p. 235), "is a globally distributed apparatus for finding, researching, fixing and killing targets of the GWOT [Global War on Terror]". For Roger Stahl, drones are a "medium for managing the visual relationship between Western centers of power and the rest of the world" (Stahl 2013, p. 659). Derek Gregory describes a scopic regime in which "new visibilities produce a special kind of intimacy that consistently privileges the view of the hunter-killer" (Gregory 2011, p. 193). Across these and other scholarly writings, drone vision emerges as the "techniques for visualizing and acting on the world specific to drone warfare", which "produce the 'smart war' discourse justifying them, and rely on it to excuse their violence" (Greene 2015, p. 234). Drone vision is what enables the domestication of drone warfare, its representation in news media, popular culture, and social media. Yet as Anthony McCosker points out, drone vision is more ambivalent than it first seems: the "new form of visuality that drone vision generates and alters is both highly technical and broadly imagined" (McCosker 2015a, p. 235). The focus in academic research on the military dimensions of drone vision tends to obscure that ambivalence, limiting its frame to the ethics of remote warfare or asymmetric vulnerability of drone pilots killing without risking their own bodies. Yet this ambivalence is inescapable once the drone is analysed transversally across multiple fields and with the locus of attention on the image itself.

Frequently flattened by its aerial vantage point, the drone camera image is decidedly non-human. Within the military domain, its clarity remains contested: from 20,000 feet, even the highest resolution lens and cleanest signal has distinct limits in clarity and an inevitable lag as the signal bounces between drone, base, satellite and command (Gregory 2011, p. 207; Pugliese 2013, p. 188). Accounts from marketers and operators frequently differ, but the images available in public can be grainy and indistinct (Figures 6.1 and 6.2). Without diminishing the distributed quality of the drone apparatus and its centrality to the materiality of drone testimony, the question remains of how these images captured by the eye of the drone coalesce what the drone-as-witness sees.

Drone images corral and compose an affective charge that works with, but is distinct from, their representational content. For all that the drone might capture within its field of view—scurrying bodies, missile strikes, devastated landscapes, architectures of the state, evacuated urban zones, wild Arctic ice-flows—it is the affect produced by its aesthetics, its visual forms, its autonomous movements, that produces intensities that raise the stakes for witnessing. Relational intensity is common to the various ways in which affect has been theorized, from the generalized force of Deleuze and Massumi to the physiological responses of Silvan

Figure 6.1 Thermal camera and aerial perspective of drone vision from a YouTube drone strike video.

Figure 6.2 Thermal camera and aerial perspective of drone vision from a YouTube drone strike video.

Tomkins to the aesthetic forms of Eugenie Brinkema. Simply put, affect is the force through which relations are composed; it is the capacity both to act and be acted upon. In an oft-cited passage, Melissa Gregg and Greg Seigworth point out that

> affect is found in those intensities that pass body to body (human, non-human, part-body, and otherwise), in those resonances that circulate about, between, and sometimes stick to bodies and worlds, and in the very passages or variations between these intensities and resonances themselves.
> (Gregg & Seigworth 2010, p. 1)

In short, then, affect is at once the stuff of relation and what relation does.

Affect is at work throughout the technicity of perception that is the drone: its distributed agency is composed of swarming relations between the human and non-human, intensities and resonances in the form of electronic signals, muscular responses or algorithmic pulsings. It is this affectivity that gathers up the differential modes of experience throughout the assemblage, from thermal imaging to the high-def camera to the buffeting of air currents, to the tensed bodies of operators and targets. Yet the form in which this affect manifests as recognizable, addressable and distributable beyond the narrow assemblage of the drone itself is in images produced by the drone's camera. Here, affect manifests in communicative and aesthetic form. Given the long, entangled history of cinema and war, it is tempting to seek to account for the affects of the drone via a cinematic reading that draws on theories of film and affect. But just as the drone itself is post-cinematic in its technicity of perception, so too is the affectivity of its images. *Post-cinematic affect* is the term Steven Shaviro uses for films and music that are, beyond anything else, "machines for generating affect" (Shaviro 2010, p. 3). For Shaviro, digital video and its associated editing effects and modulations belong to the infrastructural apparatus of our intensely networked, high-finance neoliberal world. Natively and necessarily digital, drone images are at home in that world: they are code, stored in bits and wirelessly transmitted. Whether what the image shows is what occurred is always provisional, both in the sense that tampering is always possible and that the drone's view is almost always uncannily non-human in its verticality, in its rendering of bodies as flattened, faceless, and almost limbless. Thus, the post-cinematic affectivity of the drone image is fundamental to how what the drone sees might become an act of witnessing.

Drone strike footage has become discomfortingly familiar as the technology spreads across military domains and seeps into popular culture. "Battlefield images shot through aerial cameras filter through the public mediascape", writes Stahl, "and this now iconic view through the drone's targeting system has taken its place as a major signifier of military intervention in the Barack Obama era" (Stahl 2013, p. 659). Most such footage in the public domain is in the textured greyscale of the thermal camera, white-warm bodies and vehicles framed by telemetry and targeting information, crosshairs hunting movement or fixed on their target. The narrative is always brisk: the drone watches, perhaps it flicks from thermal to regular camera, or zooms out or in, but soon enough a target is acquired. Affect accumulates in the looming certainty of the missile's launch, in the pending arrival of death. White consumes the screen, or much of it, a burst of violence that erases representation itself—death become blankness, a witnessing of erasure that is pure intensity (Figure 6.3). Rarely do bodies acquire the specificity that might demand attention to their humanity or place the spectator in some moral relationship to them (Boltanski 1999). They are blurs of heat—standing, walking, running—or hidden within vehicles or buildings. Thermal footage keeps affect in the abstract, such that its heightening resists coalescing on particular bodies but rather occurs as a relation between the temporality of the video and the certainty of the strike's arrival.

Footage of the banality of drone warfare is rare, if not impossible to find. Nothing is seen of the typically long hours of operator boredom that only occasionally congeals into the desire for action, for release of attention into kinetic violence. Drones and their operators are not only witnesses to kills, but to the battlespace, to the kill-chain, to the loss of context entailed in seeing through the

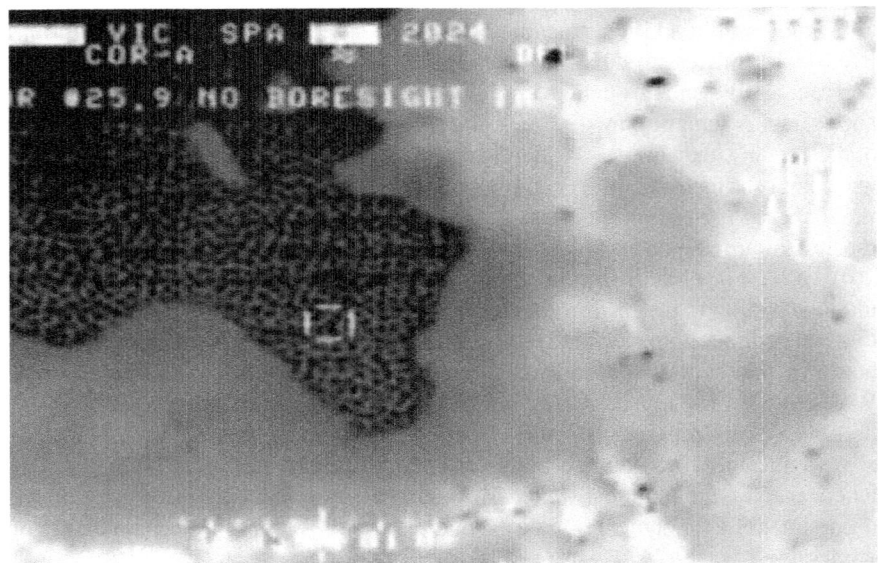

Figure 6.3 Thermal camera and aerial perspective of drone vision from a YouTube drone strike video.

eye of the drone. As one operator put it, watching war through the drone camera is like looking through a soda straw: all context vanishes (Gregory 2011, p. 193). Its angle of perception, the necessity of the height of its flight patterns, technological limitations of cameras and delays in signal relay construct very particular visibilities. These "spaces of constructed visibility are also always spaces of constructed invisibility—because they are not technical but rather techno-cultural accomplishments" (Gregory 2011, p. 193). What is witnessed in military footage is only those sequences of the most intensive affective force, in which the invisibilities necessitated by the soda straw fall away and only the amplified arrival of death waits to be digitally captured in a burst of white pixels. Here, mediation becomes vital process, defined by what Sarah Kember and Joanna Zylinska (2012) call "lifeness", to the fullest extent possible: its vitality also entails death, such that mediation becomes both the means to the end of life and its witness.

Kill videos and their affects are not encountered in a vacuum, but rather circulate in the digital sphere, on sites such as LiveLeak and YouTube. Here, they serve as reminders of the ambivalent and multiple positions of the witness: perpetrator, bystander but also victim, objectified into mere "lumps" of pixels and denied agency. The affective forcefulness of these kill videos is more than evident in the views and comments they accumulate, yet so too is the openness of affect's intensity to be channelled into differing discourses. Bearing witness can entail excitement, celebration or pleasure, as much as horror, dismay or grief. The witness, after all, can be the perpetrator as readily as he or she can be victim or bystander (Felman & Laub 1992, p. 207). Indeed, the affective economy of such videos might be better understood as one of desire rather than condemnation: on YouTube, the mediated witness can desire a far more intimate relation to the event. Yet if witnessing in the purest sense is "to put one's body on the line" (Peters 2009, p. 30), then what these commenters desire is something that stops short of direct relation to the event, a responsibility that remains mediated.

Critique of drone warfare occurs more prominently in artistic interventions that testify in some way to its violence. For example, Josh Begley's Drones+ app places drone strikes onto maps, an apparent outrage for which it was rejected 13 times by the Apple Store despite a name change to Metadata+ and the absence of any violent or offensive image (Figure 6.4). Rather than depict atrocity, his work attends to the enfolding quality of the drone apparatus and its imbrication with networked media technologies. Begley's app collapses the technological distance between the mapping function of the smartphone and the geolocated delivery of missiles to simply render death as data presented in familiar form. In doing so, Drones+/Metadata+ bears witness to the technicity of perception itself. So too do Josh Bridle's multiple works on drone warfare, of which his @dronestagram account on Instagram makes a particularly affecting intervention (Figure 6.5). Each post from the account is a Google Earth image of the site of a drone strike, buildings and landscapes still intact. Accompanying text details the strike and the deaths it caused. While not drone footage, the images echo its visual aesthetics and remind the viewer of their similarity to the mapping and satellite images that are increasingly part and parcel of everyday life. Their affectivity occurs in their aesthetic and semantic relation to drone vision, in their assertion of context and complicity.

Linguistically, the term "dronestagram" also signals the ambivalence of drone vision, its strange slippage into the domestic sphere. As it happens, Dronestagram is also the name of a photo-sharing platform for drone photography, launched in 2013, or a year after Bridle's project began. This celebratory Dronestagram—and indeed most hobbyist activity—is a reminder that the drone is often simply seeing and not witness to anything, nor under the injunction to be so. Rather, the affectivity of such drone clips is conveyed in what Anna Munster describes as "a sense of being in the midst of transmission, buoyed by a network of multiple signal flows, subject to fluctuations, transitions, instabilities" (Munster 2014, p. 154). Distributed on YouTube and elsewhere, hobbyist drone footage is more intent on communicating the liberating escape of the drone itself. This emergent fascination with drones is in part fuelled by a desire to see beyond the human, to enable precisely that technicity of perception upon which remote warfare is founded. These quotidian uses of drone vision intersect with witnessing in the capture of the extraordinary: drifting through Chernobyl, among the rusting struts of a Ferris wheel or the collapsing blocks of tight-packed Soviet apartments, the emptied city stopped in time, sliding into radioactive ruin and decay. Here the drone—suddenly, unexpectedly—becomes witness to environmental devastation and state neglect.

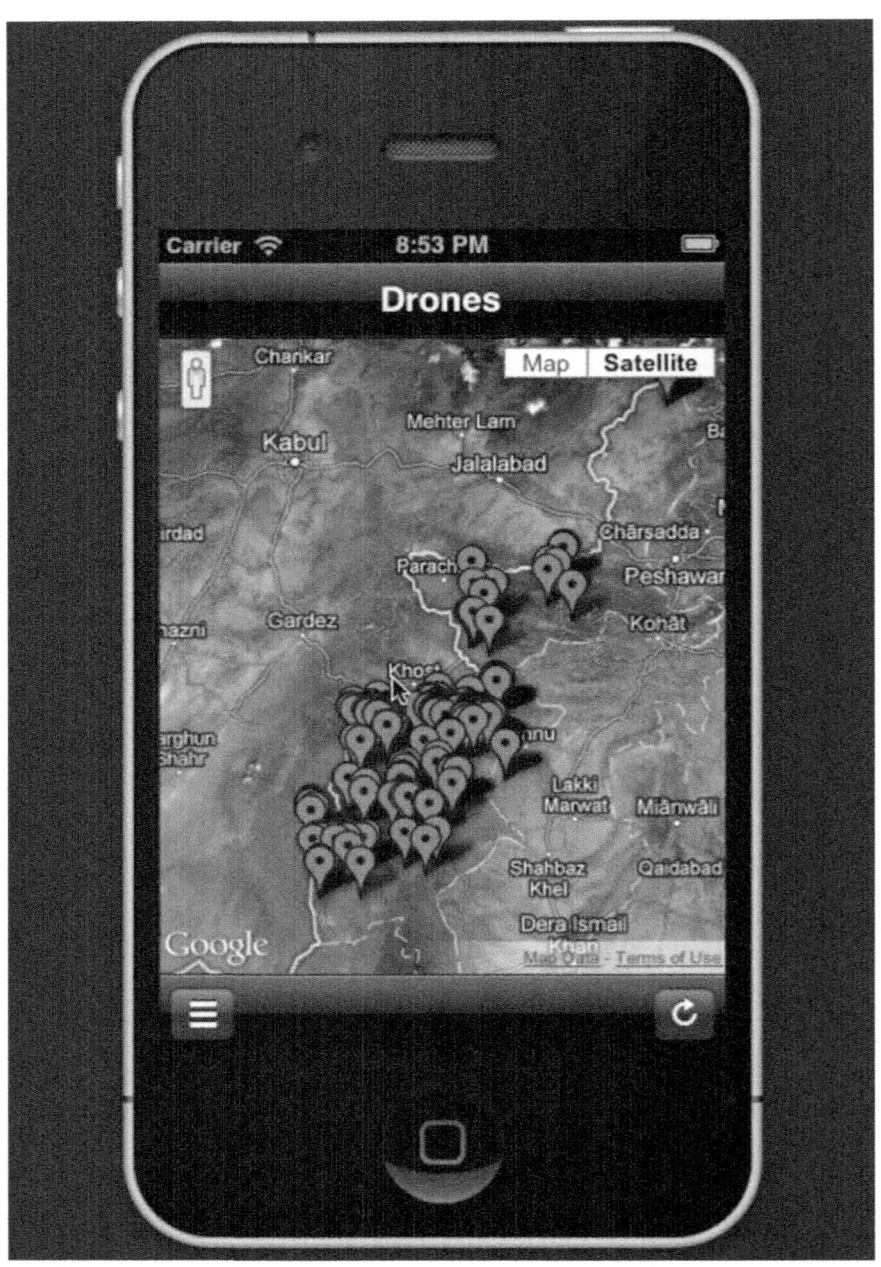

Figure 6.4 Screenshot from Josh Begley's Drones+/Metadata+ project, 2012–ongoing.

Source: © Josh Begley.

Figure 6.5 Screenshot from James Bridle's Dronestagram project, 2012–2015.

Source: © James Bridle.

This potential for the drone to enter inaccessible spaces also drives its activist appeal. Drones are increasingly tools for the exposure of state and corporate power, for revealing environmental devastation and re-imaging activist action itself by producing images of crowds, actions and police responses. Thus, the drone bears witness to bleached coral reefs, strip-mined mountaintops, devastated tar sands, polluted rivers, and more. At the Standing Rock protests against the Dakota Access Pipeline, drone footage enabled activists to track the movements of security forces and government, to see into restricted military lands. Conservation Drones, an international association, deploys drones to monitor conservation efforts and environmental violations. For protest movements in Thailand and Hong Kong, drones have enabled activists to monitor police, part of the new sousveillant assemblages made possible by mobile phones and social networks. As McCosker (2015b, p. 2) notes, the drone enables "an autonomous, motile, and indirect visuality that moves beyond the device-armed social media connected body within the protest vote." Activist drones become affect amplifiers, galvanizing cohesion via spectacular images and disrupting the visual field that might once have been dominated by the state or compliant media. "Drone video", writes McCosker (2015a, p. 14), "has a value within social networks as objects within social media systems that take vision outside of its bounded or fixed points of view". This vitality affect is what gives drone video its activist valence, its political edge.

So much of the drone's witnessing is inseparable from its natively networked nature: wirelessness is what makes them drones, after all. As Mark Andrejevic points out, "the notion of drone logic, broadly construed, unfolds the shared characteristics of distributed forms of networked data collection and response" (Andrejevic 2015, p. 22). For Andrejevic, drones are not solely unmanned aerial vehicles but any autonomous sensing device that forms part of a relational network. Approached from this angle, what the drone sees are data—and data are what it gives to the world. Thus, the drone slips easily into the sociality of the networked age, the circulation of video and still images across Facebook, YouTube and Instagram. The currency of social media is affect, not information. What is passed on in the viral is not so much semantic content as affective charge, an intensity of experience that is pleasurable or shocking (or somewhere in between) but always bodily. Drone imagery on social media bears witness within this affective relay machine. Nor can it escape the contradictions, confusions and contestations of authenticity, meaning, value, and politics that are so rife on social media.

Witnessing the predator empire

Yet this is also what makes drone imagery such a potent technicity of perception when attuned to bear witness. Its affective force—whether generated from kills, crowds or geographies—bears witness to events, but also to complex relays of affect, perception, mediation and signal that make up the very apparatuses of power today in what Shaw calls the "Predator Empire". Yet while the Predator

Empire names "the mass production of anxious, hypersecured, and highly atomized individuals", the instruments of that power are also witnesses to its workings (Shaw 2016, p. 28). If Massumi is right and the functioning of war is now founded on capacities, mechanisms and processes of perception, then the drone is one of its deadliest and most potent manifestations—and yet also an ambivalent figure of potential resistance and re-imaging. Its technicity, the entangling of bodies, technologies and processes in time and space, is an assemblage of both the affective and the material. What the drone sees is both what its camera captures and the system of networks, algorithms, signals, relays, operators, and objects that enable the drone's autonomy. Its capacity to perceive is bound up with its connectivity; its sensors are inherently networked. It is no coincidence that the drone is an emblematic figure of this age of social media, nor that its images are increasingly ubiquitous in and beyond networked spaces. From the drone's-eye view, the world is at once terrible and beautiful and strange, and its capacity to bear witness is inseparable from the affects it assembles and that manifest in all their complex, diffuse and differential force in the images that are its testimony.

References

Agamben, G. (2009). *What is an Apparatus?* Stanford, CA: Stanford University Press.
Andrejevic, M. (2015). Theorizing drones and droning theory. In A. Završnik (ed.), *Drones and Unmanned Aerial Systems*. New York: Springer.
Boltanski, L. (1999). *Distant Suffering: Morality, Media and Politics*, Cambridge, UK: Cambridge University Press.
Christiansen, S.L. (2017). *Drone Age Cinema: Action Film and Sensory Assault*. London: I.B. Tauris.
Cockburn, A. (2015). *Kill Chain: Drones and the Rise of High-tech Assassins*. New York: Verso.
Felman, S. & Laub, D. (1992). *Testimony: Crises of Witnessing in Literature, Psychoanalysis, and History*. New York: Routledge.
Foucault, M. (1980). The confession of the flesh [Interview, 1977]. In C. Gordon (ed.), *Power/Knowledge: Selected Interviews and Other Writings*, pp. 194–228. New York: Pantheon Books.
Frosh, P. & Pinchevski, A. (2009). Introduction: Why media witnessing? Why now? In P. Frosh & A. Pinchevski (eds), *Media Witnessing: Testimony in the Age of Mass Communication*, pp. 1–19. Basingstoke: Palgrave Macmillan.
Greene, D. (2015). Drone vision. *Surveillance & Society*, 13(2), pp. 233–249.
Gregg, M. & Seigworth, G.G. (2010). An inventory of shimmers. In M. Gregg & G.G. Seigworth (eds), *The Affect Theory Reader*, pp. 1–25. Durham: Duke University Press.
Gregory, D. (2011). From a view to a kill: Drones and late modern war. *Theory, Culture & Society*, 28(7/8), pp. 188–215.
Kember, S. & Zylinska, J. (2012). *Life after New Media: Mediation as a Vital Process*. Cambridge, MA: MIT Press.
Kozol, W. (2014). *Distant Wars Visible: The Ambivalence of Witnessing*. Minneapolis: University of Minnesota Press.

Langbein, J. (1977). *Torture and the Law of Proof*. Chicago: University of Chicago Press.

Latour, B. (2005). *Reassembling the Social an Introduction to Actor-Network-Theory*. Oxford, UK: Oxford University Press.

Massumi, B. (2015). *Ontopower: War, Powers, and the State of Perception*. Durham: Duke University Press.

McCosker, A. (2015a). Drone media: Unruly systems, radical empiricism and camera consciousness. *Culture Machine*, 16. Available from: www.culturemachine.net/index. php/cm/article/viewArticle/591 [26 April 2018].

McCosker, A. (2015b). Drone vision, zones of protest, and the new camera consciousness. *Media Fields Journal*, 9. Available from: http://mediafieldsjournal.org/drone-vision-zones-of-protest/2015/8/21/drone-vision-zones-of-protest-and-the-new-camera-consciousne.html [26 April 2018].

Munster, A. (2014). Transmateriality: Toward an energetics of signal in contemporary mediatic assemblages. *Cultural Studies Review*, 20(1), pp. 150–167.

Oliver, K. (2001). *Witnessing: Beyond Recognition*. Minneapolis: University of Minnesota Press.

Parikka, J. (2010). *Insect Media: An Archaeology of Animals and Technology*. Minneapolis: University of Minnesota Press.

Peters, J.D. (2009). Witnessing. In P. Frosh & A. Pinchevski (eds), *Media Witnessing: Testimony in the Age of Mass Communication*, pp. 23–41. Basingstoke: Palgrave Macmillan.

Pugliese, J. (2013). *State Violence and the Execution of Law: Biopolitical Caesurae of Torture, Black Sites, Drones*. New York: Routledge.

Sandvik, K.B. & Jumbert, M.G. (2016). *The Good Drone*. New York: Routledge.

Shaviro, S. (2010). *Post Cinematic Affect*. USA: Zero Books.

Shaw, I.G.R. (2016). *Predator Empire: Drone Warfare and Full Spectrum Dominance*. Minneapolis: University of Minnesota Press.

Simondon, G. (2017). *On the Mode of Existence of Technical Objects*. Minneapolis: Univocal Publishing.

Sontag, S. (2003). *Regarding the Pain of Others*. London: Penguin Books.

Stahl, R. (2013). What the drone saw: The cultural optics of the unmanned war. *Australian Journal of International Affairs*, 67(5), pp. 659–674.

Tagg, J. (2009). *The Disciplinary Frame: Photographic Truths and the Capture of Meaning*. Minneapolis: University of Minnesota Press.

Virilio, P. (1989). *War and Cinema: The Logistics of Perception*. New York: Verso.

Virilio, P. (1994). *The Vision Machine*. Bloomington: Indiana University Press.

Part III

Social media practices

Chapter 7

Photographic witnessing, the occupation and Palestinian politics

Simon Faulkner

Introduction

This chapter considers the value Palestinians ascribe to photography in relation to their resistance to the Israeli occupation. The chapter does not, however, discuss specific photographic images depicting aspects of the occupation. Rather it considers Palestinian representations of photography as a medium used to witness the occupation and of photographers as witnesses. This discussion is informed by Lisa Gitelman's conception of a medium as involving the combination of media technology with socially accepted ideas about what that technology does. In her words, media are "socially realized structures of communication" (Gitelman 2006, p. 7). Photography will be understood to involve the interrelation of photographic technologies that enable the capture and transportation of appearances (Berger & Mohr 1982, p. 92), with shared beliefs about what photographs are and do. Thought about in these terms, what will be termed the photographic witnessing of the occupation will be approached as both the practical matter of photographers using cameras to produce photographic images of this situation and the mobilization of certain ideas about the veracity of photographic images. The argument will be that, in the context of Palestinian struggle against the occupation, the role and meaning of photography as a veracious medium is defined in terms of a moral and political imperative to bear witness to acts of Israeli state violence. The Israeli occupation is a heavily mediated political situation. Part of this mediation involves the production of large numbers of photographic images for quite different purposes (for the commercial news industry, or for human rights and other kinds of activism). Rather than focus on these differences, the concern will be to consider the way that photographs of the occupation have been given meaning in terms of a generic conception of photographic witnessing that is part of Palestinian political culture. This means that a photographer can take pictures of the events of the occupation for largely commercial reasons and still be able to gain a kind of kudos and status in relation to the idea that photographing this subject is a moral and politically meaningful endeavour.

In the first part of the chapter, the interrelated subjects of photographic witnessing, the occupation, and Palestinian politics will be considered in general terms, starting with the example of a demonstration in 2006 in the Palestinian village of Bil'in that involved the use of props that represented photographers as an important element of contemporary Palestinian struggle. The second part of the chapter focuses on the self-images of Palestinian photojournalists working in the West Bank, as evidenced through images of themselves that they upload to their Facebook accounts. This movement from a general discussion, organized around the example of the Bil'in demonstration, to a discussion of images of Palestinian journalists is intended to provide different indications of how photographic practices and political virtue have become entwined within the culture of Palestinian resistance. This discussion is also aimed at suggesting a way of exploring photographic witnessing in the context of the Israeli occupation that is not about the political efficacy of that witnessing, but more about what witnessing means in a cultural sense.

Photographic witnessing and the Israeli occupation

On 9 June 2006, activists in the Palestinian village of Bil'in, which is near Ramallah in the occupied West Bank, created a hand-drawn banner that included a depiction of a camera for one of their weekly demonstrations against the construction of a section of the West Bank Barrier on village land. A photograph (Figure 7.1) by the Israeli activist photographer Oren Ziv shows the making of this banner on the day of the demonstration.[1]

Figure 7.1 Oren Ziv/Activestills, photograph of demonstrators creating a banner, Bil'in, West Bank, 9 June 2006.

Source: © Oren Ziv.

The camera on the banner is highly enlarged and rendered as an isolated object on a white background. Below it is the slogan, in English: "Their eyes won't stop showing the Israeli soldiers crimes". The banner represents a high degree of faith in photographic witnessing as a practice. The slogan expresses a sense of certainty that the violent acts of the Israeli military are crimes, but equally it expresses a certainty that the camera has the capacity to show these crimes. The banner is also testament to what the village activists perceived to be the invaluable role in their struggle played by the photographers who have documented their demonstrations (Maimon & Grinbaum 2016, p. 120). This is something further affirmed by the trophies, constructed by village activists from spent Israeli teargas canisters and grenades, that were awarded to certain photographers and video-activists in 2015, on the tenth anniversary of the beginning of the struggle in Bil'in.[2]

This belief in the value of photographic mediation, as a means of testifying to the reality of the occupation, is longer-standing and appears to have been particularly strong during the first Palestinian Intifada ("shaking off") in the late 1980s and early 1990s. Although the Intifada was primarily organized in terms of non-cooperation with Israeli governance in the occupied territories, Palestinians were also highly aware of the international mediation of their uprising. This is shown, for example, in the North American writer Norman Finkelstein's account of time spent in the West Bank during the Intifada, in which he recounts visiting the village of Beit Sahour, near Bethlehem, with a photographer friend to see a confrontation between stone-throwing local youth and the Israeli army:

> The Beit Sahour villagers in the side street abutting the makeshift stone barricade motioned us inside their homes. They wanted my photographer friend, especially, to have the best possible view of the action. Media consciousness was very high in the occupied territories. The success of the Intifada, everyone seemed convinced, would hinge crucially on world opinion. With whomever I talked, the first question was invariably what the people in the United States were thinking about the uprising. The apparent belief was that, if the truth were known, outside pressure would be brought to bear on Israel.
>
> (Finkelstein 1996, p. 4)

Finkelstein's account suggests that Palestinian resistance in this instance was strongly about being seen. Although political conditions have changed, as have the strategies and technologies used to gain the world's attention to the Palestinian situation, this perceived need to be seen by international audiences has in fact been relatively consistent within Palestinian political culture since the late 1960s. The Palestinian film-maker Azza El-Hassan has suggested that the belief amongst Palestinians that showing the occupation to "the world" will effect political change amounts to a "national illusion" (El-Hassan 2002; Hochberg 2015, p. 116). Nevertheless, this "illusion" has driven and given meaning to a good deal of Palestinian struggle. As Amahl A. Bishara has noted in relation to more recent demonstrations against the occupation, Palestinian activists "perform for audiences they do not know well and will likely never meet" (Bishara 2013, p. 169). This understanding that Palestinians perform political actions that they hope will be mediated to distant spectators, can be applied to the kind of confrontation discussed by Finkelstein, but it applies equally to more conventional forms of demonstration and to instances where Palestinians display the violence of the occupation inflicted on their own bodies to the camera (Collins 2004, p. 67). During the first Intifada, the photographers producing images of the occupation and resistance to it were largely international and Israeli. Since the beginning of the second Intifada in late 2000, a number of Palestinian photojournalists reporting the occupation have also established themselves. This emergence of Palestinian photojournalism, combined with the use of digital cameras and other digital technologies, has meant that the desire to be witnessed is now entwined with an ability on the part of Palestinians themselves to engage in different kinds of photographic witnessing.

The value of photographic witnessing in relation to the occupation, has been addressed in academic texts over the last decade. Although she does not use the term "witnessing", Ariella Azoulay has argued in her well-known book, *The Civil Contract of Photography* (Azoulay 2008a), that the viewing by Israelis of photographic images of Palestinian suffering can generate alternative civil relations between the photographed person and the spectator that can work against the structural distinction between Israeli citizens and Palestinian non-citizens. In contrast to this, in her book *Visual Occupations*, Gil Hochberg has responded to the surfeit of documentary and photojournalistic images of the violent effects of the occupation, by observing that photographic eye witnessing appears to have done little for Palestinians in concrete political terms. These two accounts of the photographic witnessing of the occupation are consequently quite different in character. One involves the philosophical imagining of a civil role for photography, while the other challenges the primacy of visual witnessing as a form of counter-visuality, on the basis that it appears to have little practical effect (Hochberg 2015, p. 31). Azoulay is surely correct when she suggests that Palestinians who show their injuries to the camera lens imagine that the resulting images might be seen by sympathetic spectators (Azoulay 2008a, p. 18). However, her theoretical approach does not examine the concrete relations between the actions taken by people in front of the camera, resultant images, and spectators. Nor does she consider the gaps between the expectations of photographed persons and the actual effects resulting from photographic witnessing. Hochberg, on the other hand, suggests that photographic witnessing might do more harm than good, meaning that "the problem regarding the visibility of Palestinian suffering is no longer that we are unable to see it [...] but rather that it has become almost the only thing we see" (Hochberg 2015, pp. 119–120). From this perspective, visual testimonies of Israeli violence and Palestinian suffering seem to have produced a stereotypical victimhood that occludes Palestinian political agency.

What both Azoulay and Hochberg do not address in a substantive way is the role of photographic witnessing within Palestinian political culture. Azoulay emphasizes the role of Palestinians as agents who present themselves to be photographed, while Hochberg notes that Palestinians are often amongst those who currently produce photographic testimonies about the occupation (Hochberg 2015, pp. 31, 116). But neither take these considerations further to think about what political needs are fulfilled and meanings created for Palestinians when they partake in witnessing, either as the witnessed person or as those wielding cameras. It is probably the case that the contemporary emphasis on the witnessing potential of the photographic image is partly the consequence of a crisis of Palestinian politics brought about by the overall failure of the first Intifada and the political compromises of the Oslo process during the 1990s (Allen 2009, 2013; Hochberg 2015, p. 115). Lori Allen in particular has argued that this political crisis has enhanced the ascendancy of forms of visual testimony, which came to stand-in for more substantive forms of political organization and action (Allen 2009). Yet this association of photographic witnessing with political failure affirms, rather than undermines, the argument that such visual practices have become increasingly significant to Palestinian politics. It seems important, therefore, not only to be able to criticize witnessing practices as a relatively weak and perhaps counter-productive form of political practice, but also to find ways to gain a richer understanding of how Palestinians have enacted witnessing as a form of resistance under challenging political conditions and through this, explore how such practices have enabled the cultivation of particular political identities.

This last point leads us back to the drawing of the camera on the banner in Bil'in, which was combined, not only with the English language slogan, but also with a drawing of a disembodied arm and hand making a victory sign of the kind ubiquitous within images relating to Palestinian resistance, and an image of another arm that appears to be holding some sort of weapon, or perhaps a pen to denote written journalism. Consequently, the camera is linked to at least one explicit symbol of Palestinian resistance and as such is framed as a figure of Palestinian political struggle. Another photograph by Oren Ziv shows the banner in use during the demonstration (Figure 7.2). A mock pentagonal martyr's memorial, constructed from white cardboard, is also shown being carried behind the banner. On its sides were written in English and Arabic the names of five journalists and photojournalists killed during the second Intifada. Images of these dead media workers were also attached to the top of the memorial. The text visible on the front side of the memorial states, "The Martyr: James, British, killed in Rafah", referring to the British documentary cameraman James Miller, who was killed by Israeli forces in Gaza in May 2003, while making the film *Death in Gaza* (2004).[3] The conjunction of the banner and the memorial in Ziv's photograph, suggests that this particular demonstration was themed around the figures of the journalist and the photojournalist. This combination of the banner and the memorial brings together two key concepts fundamental to the cultural

Figure 7.2 Oren Ziv/Activestills, photograph of demonstrators carrying a banner and mock martyrs' memorial, Bil'in, West Bank, 9 June 2006.

Source: © Oren Ziv.

construction of the photojournalist in the Palestinian context. The first concept being the idea, already discussed, that photography is a medium that can straight-forwardly show the violence of the occupation, while the second is the under-standing that photographers take risks and face dangers, up to and including death, to engage in the practice of photographic witnessing. Defined in these terms, photojournalists, especially when Palestinian, are not perceived to be third-party observers who represent the occupation from a position of disinter-estedness. On the contrary, photojournalists, by virtue of their struggle for the truth, are understood to be thoroughly implicated with wider political resistance to Israeli domination (Bishara 2013, p. 158). The slogan on the banner, "Their eyes won't stop showing the Israeli soldiers crimes", itself suggests commitment to a cause that is unending in a way comparable to broader conceptions of the unwavering and steadfast nature of Palestinian resistance. What this means is that the "gruelling" labour of photojournalistic work in the occupied territories (Bishara 2013, p. 2) is invested with moral and political import that goes well beyond its professional and news-related meanings. This construction of the photojournalist, as someone who struggles and takes risks to bear witness, fits with the international understanding of witnessing, described by Michal Givoni as the "heroic notion of witnessing", that portrays it as "a risky attempt to docu-ment and make known a wrong that is otherwise bound to be concealed, denied, or forgotten, so as to infuse the cause of its victims with the power of facts" (Givoni 2016, p. 6). Yet this generic construction of witnessing is inflected in the Palestinian context by specific concerns arising from the conditions of life and resistance under occupation. This means that the photojournalist killed while at work is not simply an unfortunate victim of the risks of this profession, but a martyr for the cause (Bishara 2013, p. 158).

Palestinian photojournalists, witnessing and Facebook

In her discussion of the witness as an actively produced moral and political subject, Givoni notes that witnesses are people who are meant to perform the "arduous trial" of becoming a witness and at the same time put this performance "on display" (Givoni 2016, p. 12). A specific example of this relationship between witnessing and the self-presentation of this role can be found in the way that Palestinian photojournalists have used images of themselves, engaged in their photographic work, as iconic markers of the political aspects of their identities as photographic witnesses. The rest of this chapter will focus on the use of such images on the professional and personal Facebook pages of a number of Palestinian photojournalists as a way of continuing the discussion of the political significance of photographic witnessing in the context of the occupation. These images often focus on the challenges and dangers specific to working as a Palestinian photojournalist within the occupied territories. The photojournalists often travel and work together, especially when photographing confrontations between Palestinians and the Israeli military, as being in a group enables a higher degree of visibility and protection from the Israeli army who, in theory, are not meant to target journalists (Bishara 2013, pp. 93–96, 243). This situation also provides opportunities for photojournalists to become the subjects of images taken by other photographers. Such images can be distributed in the same way as other news images, but they also become part of a more socially-oriented visual economy in which images are shared within photojournalistic peer-networks. This exchange of images of each other between Palestinian photojournalists precedes the development and popularization of digital cameras and social media (Bishara, 2013, p. 145). However, the adoption of digital technologies seems to have intensified this practice, especially because social media platforms provide Palestinian photographers with readymade opportunities to display these images of their struggles to bear witness.

Before addressing the use of these images on Facebook, it is useful to discuss further the emergence of Palestinian photojournalism. There exists a well-established photojournalistic infrastructure of picture agencies and wires, centred on Jerusalem, that employs international, Israeli and Palestinian photographers who document both the exceptional and regular events of the occupation. Over the last decade, such events have included weekly demonstrations against settlement expansion and the West Bank Barrier in multiple locations on the West

Bank, mostly within specific villages such as Bil'in. These demonstrations have constituted a relatively small-scale and fragmented resurgence of unarmed "popular struggle" after the second Intifada (Darweish & Rigby 2015). The closure of the occupied territories during the second Intifada produced a greater need on the part of international news organizations for locally-based Palestinian photographers, who could cover events in areas inaccessible to international or Israeli photojournalists (Bishara 2013, p. 176). Many of the more senior and established Palestinian photojournalists currently working as staff at agencies and wires began work during this period. Younger photographers, who followed their lead, generally work as "stringers" or freelancers for the same international organizations, although they also work for local Israeli and Palestinian picture agencies, such as Flash 90 and APA Images. In more recent years, a number of Palestinian photographers have also emerged who document demonstrations in the West Bank with the aim of circulating their images on social media (Bizawe 2014; Brown 2014).

The situation of Palestinian photojournalists differs from international and Israeli photographers working in the West Bank, insofar as they are much more likely to be arrested, hurt and even killed by the Israeli army while photographing demonstrations against the occupation (Bishara 2013, pp. 93–96). Palestinian journalists in general can also have a different relationship to dominant international notions of journalistic "disinterestedness" that, in Bishara's words, are meant to "separate between the politics journalists cover and the lives they live" (Bishara 2013, p. 109). Living and working under the occupation can make it difficult for Palestinian journalists to separate their professional activity from the conditions of their everyday lives and from the wider political struggles arising from the occupation. This does not necessarily cause a contradiction between "objective" reporting and their sense of responsibility to report the injustices of the occupation. Indeed, as already discussed, wider Palestinian ideas about photographic witnessing strongly link the assumed capacity of photography for veracity or objectivity to the role it is imagined to have within the national struggle. Nonetheless, these photographers can be pulled between the competing commitments of professional journalism and membership of a highly politicized community (Bishara 2013, p. 124). This pull between the dominant professional discourses of international photojournalism and Palestinian national politics is of particular interest when it comes to Palestinian photographers using social media, where the platforms, unlike news production companies, allow for the expression of political commitments.

Palestinian photographers express such political commitments on Facebook through the use of "Profile Pictures" and "Cover Photos" as well as through the posting of images, texts, and links on the platform's "Timeline". The discussion presented here will focus on the use of images of photojournalists engaging in their photographic work as Facebook Cover Photos. Such images are interesting because they are often visible for much longer than images posted on the Timeline and also because account holders use these images to frame their platform-based identities. The photographers to be discussed here occupy different positions in relation to the photojournalism industry. Some are staff at news organizations, while others are freelancers, activists, or both. Yet their use of photographs of themselves involved in confrontations with Israeli soldiers, or experiencing other aspects of the violence of the occupation regime as Cover Photos is similar. This suggests that many Palestinian photojournalists experience similar conditions of harassment and violence when working. Yet, it also suggests that such images have a similar value for all of these photographers, despite their differing degrees of professionalization. Many of these images depict an oppositional relationship between the photographer and Israeli soldiers. This kind of oppositional scene has been recurrent within the visual representation of the occupation since at least the 1980s, if not before (Azoulay 2008b). In this sense, the victimization of photojournalists, as represented in the images under discussion, replays imagery that is already strongly embedded within the photographic archive relating to the occupation. This is particularly the case with images of photojournalists being arrested, which resonate with a longer history of the depiction of Israeli soldiers arresting Palestinians, especially during the first Intifada. For example, a Cover Photo used by the freelance photographer Shadi Hatem in 2016, shows him being held in a headlock by an Israeli soldier as he is being detained. Earlier Cover Photos show him being intercepted by soldiers or carried forcibly into an Israeli army jeep. This is also the case with the older Nablus-based Reuters stringer Abed Omar Qusini, who used a Cover Photo showing him being detained by a soldier while another photographer takes a picture of this event. A different kind of image, with a similar theme, has also functioned as the Cover Photo for the Reuters' staff photographer Ammar Awad for nearly five years. Figure 7.3 shows a group of Palestinian children taking part in a demonstration against restrictions on press freedom in Ramallah, for which the Palestinian Authority printed large images of Palestinian journalists and photojournalists being arrested by the Israeli army. In the image, two girls are holding a large print of a photograph of Awad being arrested by three Israeli soldiers at a demonstration in Bil'in in 2007.

Another recurrent motif involves photojournalists arguing with soldiers, presumably after the soldiers have tried to stop them photographing, or when the soldiers are in the process of arresting the photographers. This motif has been used by Shadi Hatem and by the young Ramallah-based freelancer Ahmad Talat Hassan (Figure 7.4). The argument motif is also repeatedly present amongst the Cover Photos used by the Bil'in-based activist photographer Hamdi Abu Rahma. In contrast to the images of photojournalists actually being arrested, which frame Palestinian photographers as subject to Israeli military power, these images of Abu Rahma remonstrating with Israeli soldiers present him as an antagonist within a political struggle. The photographer is shown speaking back to the "petty sovereigns" (Butler 2004, p. 56) of the occupation. Abu Rahma's Cover Photos present him as an active participant in a political and somewhat militarized contest, within which the camera is understood as a kind of weapon. This is made more explicit by another Cover Photo that shows

Figure 7.3 Amar Awad, photograph of Palestinian children taking part in a demonstration against restrictions on press freedom in Ramallah in the West Bank in 2012. The children carry a large photograph of Israeli soldiers detaining the photojournalist Amar Awad at a demonstration in Bil'in in 2007. Used as a Facebook Cover Photo by Amar Awad.

Source: © Amar Awad.

him and two other Palestinian photographers arguing with four Israel soldiers. A text written by Abu Rahma to accompany and describe this image, reads: "camera, gun, camera, gun, gun, camera, gun … and who will win?" This setting up of the camera against the gun as a different kind of weapon is made even more explicit through Abu Rahma's use of a graphic image as a Cover Photo that depicts a soldier pointing a rifle at a photographer who points a camera back at him.

Other recurrent images used as Cover Photos are those that depict Palestinian photojournalists experiencing adverse conditions arising from the events they photograph, or purposely inflicted upon them by Israeli forces. The photojournalist affected by or within tear gas is a particularly striking motif, used, for example, by Ashraf Amra, a freelancer who works for APA Images, and also by the Associated Press stringer Madji Mohammed. Hamdi Abu Rahma also used a more performative image of himself wearing a gas mask with tear gas around him, while Abed Omar Qusini used a photograph of himself about to be engulfed by a cloud of gas. Similar to such images of photojournalists facing hardships

Figure 7.4 Nidal Eshtayeh, photograph of photojournalist Ahmad Talat Hasan arguing with Israeli soldiers, location unknown, 2017.

Source: © Nidal Eshtayeh.

while they work, are images of injured photographers. For example, the Anadolu Agency staff photographer Issam Rimawi has used an image of himself holding up his injured arm, perhaps hit by a gas canister, to be inspected by the Agence France-Presse photographer Abbas Momani. Like the images of photojournalists being arrested, these images separate photographers out as a particular kind of agent, while also representing them as being in a similar position to any Palestinian exposed to Israeli military violence within protest situations.

What should be made of the use of these different photographic images as Facebook Cover Photos? Are we to take them as simply illustrative of the experiences of particular photographers, or do they have a more generic significance relating to the role of Palestinian photographers as politically interested witnesses to struggles between Palestinian communities and the Israeli military? One point of reference when considering these questions is the international tendency to represent photojournalists in a romantic light, as adventurers and risk-takers in search of striking news images. As Beth E. Wilson has recently shown, the romanticized figure of the photojournalist was largely a corporate creation produced by organizations such as *Life* magazine during and after the Second World War (Wilson 2016). There is something of this romantic construction of the photojournalist in the Cover Photos used by the Palestinian photographers under discussion here. Yet, with reference back to the earlier discussion of the political value of photographic witnessing in the occupied territories, the romanticism involved in these specific images also invokes a history of generally masculinized resistance to colonization and occupation that is particular to the Palestinian situation. One might think of other figures who have constituted the iconography of Palestinian national resistance: the guerrilla fighter, or fedeyeen ("one who risks his life voluntarily"), or the figure of the child throwing stones at Israeli soldiers (Khalili 2007; Kimmerling & Migdal 2003, p. 243). The risk-taking, arrested, gassed, or injured Palestinian photojournalist, as represented in the Cover Photos discussed so far, is not the same as these other figures, but nonetheless, carries something of their meaning. Thus, in response to Ashraf Amra's use of the image of him suffering from exposure to teargas, one respondent described him as a "fighter", while in response to one of Shadi Hatem's Cover Photos, another respondent calls him a "warrior". Through these terms, photographing the occupation is equated to other forms of resistance to the Israeli military. As already pointed out in relation to the banner and mock memorial used in the demonstration in Bil'in, photojournalism is reframed as something that is not just reportage, or professional work, but also a form of struggle. This is most clear in the self-presentation of social-media oriented activist photographers such as Hamdi Abu Rahma, but it is also implied through the use of particular Cover Photos by other photographers. As Bishara observes: "Palestinian photojournalists who put themselves in the line of fire, or in the cloud of tear gas, are assuming embodied political stances that have undeniable moral significance in Palestinian society" (Bishara 2013, p. 158). The Cover Photos under discussion depict these "embodied political stances", transforming them into iconic scenarios that locate photojournalistic identity in terms of a struggle to witness the truth under adverse conditions. These adverse conditions are part of the occupation, meaning that the very struggle to bear witness has a value as resistance in and for itself. This struggle is not merely thought about as work, even by those photographers most involved with the commercial production of news images, but also as a heavy responsibility, or in Ahmad Talat Hasan's words as a "sacred mission". He uses this phrase in a post on his Facebook Timeline that reports on him being wounded in the leg while photographing a demonstration in the village of Kafr Qaddum near Nablus in 2015. This post was illustrated by three images: one a photograph of the injured Hasan being carried from the demonstration, one a photograph of his bandaged leg, and the third an X-ray of the leg. These different documents of his wounding affirm the implied relationship between the "mission" of the photojournalist and self-sacrifice, at least in terms of pain and hardship. In these terms, these images and the Cover Photos already discussed constitute a genre of imagery that frames the work of photographers within their own subcultural social-media context and for other Palestinians following them on Facebook as a specific manifestation of resistance.

Conclusion

The aim of this chapter has been to suggest that there is a need to address the use of photographic witnessing as part of Palestinian political culture, and to explore the value and meanings ascribed to these practices aside from their practical impact. The chapter has dealt with this subject in terms of examples of the cultural construction of the photographer as someone who takes risks and makes sacrifices (including martyrdom) to witness the truth of the occupation. The framing of the photographer as someone who is a potential and sometimes actual martyr entails a particular manifestation of the etymological relationship between the martyr and the witness, the person who sacrifices their life being the ultimate witness (Schankweiler & Straub 2016). The discussion has also considered the reiteration of this cultural construction of the photographer by Palestinian photographers themselves, through their use of images of themselves being arrested or facing adverse conditions while undertaking photographic work. This use of such images as Cover Photos on Facebook involves an investment in self-images congruent with long established romantic representations of the photojournalist that are also inflected with meanings relating to Palestinian nationalism that makes the mythic heroism of the photographer analogous to other masculine figures of Palestinian struggle.

Palestinian photojournalists think of photographs as visual documents that can make the violence of the occupation visible to others, yet, their commitment to the imagined political power of photography is not dependent on any certainty about its political effects. Rather, this commitment to the perceived veracity of photography is largely a matter of a socially embedded "faith" in the value of photographic witnessing (El-Hassan 2002) and should be approached as such. As Hochberg has argued, there are clearly problems in political terms with having too much faith in the power of images to alleviate and change abject political conditions, but still, it is important to understand how such a faith has arisen and how it works. With this in mind, the chapter has suggested a more cultural approach to thinking about photographic witnessing in relation to Palestinian political struggle. This specific context also suggests the need to adapt critical distinctions between professional photographic and citizen-witnessing. This is not only necessary because the situation of Palestinians living under occupation in the West Bank is one that denies them formal citizenship, meaning that their position as "citizens" is an aspirational rather than formal one, but also because the practices of the Palestinian photographers discussed often involve complex and sometimes contradictory relationships between their professional roles within photojournalism and their situation as people living under occupation. Under such conditions, social media appears to have offered such photographers virtual contexts within which to present themselves in more political terms, allowing differing degrees of intersection between their professional practices and their embeddedness in a politically saturated situation.

Notes

1 Photographs of the banner were found in the Activestills online archive, which is part of their website: http://activestills.org/archive.php [26 February 2018].
2 One of these trophies was shown to me in 2015 by the Israeli artist and video-activist David Reeb.
3 The other four journalists and photojournalists recorded on this mock memorial were: the Palestinian cameraman Nazih Datwazeh, killed in Nablus in April 2003; the Palestinian journalist Issam Hamza Al Tilawi, killed in Ramallah in September 2002; the Palestinian journalist Imad Abu Zahra, killed in Jenin in July 2002; the Italian photojournalist Raffaele Ciriello, killed in Ramallah in March 2002. For further information about this aspect of the demonstration on 9 June 2006, see Jacob Katriel's blog: http://jacob-katriel.tripod.com/id15.html [6 February 2018].

References

Allen, L. (2009). Martyr bodies in the media: Human rights, aesthetics, and the politics of immediation in the Palestinian Intifada. *American Ethnologist*, 36(1), pp. 161–180.
Allen, L. (2013). *The Rise and Fall of Human Rights: Cynicism and Politics in Occupied Palestine*. Stanford, CA: Stanford University Press.
Azoulay, A. (2008a). *The Civil Contract of Photography*. New York: Zone Books.
Azoulay, A. (2008b). *Act of State: Photographed History of the Occupation 1967–2007*. Tel Aviv: Etgar (Hebrew).
Berger, J. & Mohr, J. (1982). *Another Way of Telling*. London: Writers and Readers Publishing.
Bishara, A.A. (2013). *Back Stories: U. S. News Production and Palestinian Politics*. Stanford, CA: Stanford University Press.
Bizawe, E.S. (2014). Gaza war images you won't see on Israeli TV. *Haaretz*. Available from: www.haaretz.com/israel-news/culture/leisure/.premium-1.608931 [11 May 2018].
Brown, L. (2014). Photojournalism in the Palestinian territories. *Open Democracy*. Available from: www.opendemocracy.net/north-africa-west-asia/liam-brown/photojournalism-in-palestinian-territories [11 May 2018].
Butler, J. (2004). *Precarious Life: The Powers of Mourning and Violence*. London and New York: Verso.
Collins, J. (2004). *Occupied by Memory: The Intifada Generation and the Palestinian State of Emergency*. New York: New York University Press.
Darweish, M. & Rigby, A. (2015). *Popular Protest in Palestine: The Uncertain Future of Unarmed Resistance*. London: Pluto Press.
El-Hassan, A. (2002). Art and war. *Ars Electronica*. Available from: http://90.146.8.18/en/archives/festival_archive/festival_catalogs/festival_artikel.asp?iProjectID=11789 [10 May 2018].
Finkelstein, N.G. (1996). *The Rise and Fall of Palestine: A Personal Account of the Intifada Years*. Minneapolis and London: University of Minnesota Press.
Gitelman, L. (2006). *Always Already New: Media, History, and the Data of Culture*. Cambridge, MA and London: MIT Press.
Givoni, M. (2016). *The Care of the Witness: A Contemporary History of Testimony in Crises*. New York: Cambridge University Press.
Hochberg, G.Z. (2015). *Visual Occupations: Violence and Visibility in a Conflict Zone*. Durham and London: Duke University Press.

Khalili, L. (2007). *Heroes and Martyrs of Palestine: The Politics of National Commemoration.* Cambridge, UK: Cambridge University Press.

Kimmerling, B. & Migdal, J.S. (2003). *The Palestinian People: A History.* Cambridge, MA and London: Harvard University Press.

Maimon, V. & Grinbaum, S. (eds) (2016). *Activestills: Photography as Protest in Palestine/Israel.* London: Pluto Press.

Schankweiler, K. & Straub, V. (2016). Shaheed. *Aesthetics of Resistance, Pictorial Glossary, The Nomos of Images.* Available from: https://nomoi.hypotheses.org/824 [10 May 2018].

Wilson, B.E. (2016). The corporate creation of the photojournalist: Life magazine and Margaret Bourke-White in World War II. *Journal of War and Culture Studies*, 9(2), pp. 133–150.

Chapter 8

Witnessing to survive

Selfie videos, live mobile witnessing and black necropolitics

Penelope Papailias

On 16 June 2017, Minnesota police officer Jeronimo Yanez was acquitted of charges of manslaughter and reckless discharge of a firearm in the 6 July 2016 shooting of Philando Castile, a 32-year-old elementary school cafeteria supervisor. Castile's dying moments, documented by his girlfriend, 27-year-old Diamond "Lavish" Reynolds, via Facebook Live became a flashpoint for protest against racialized police violence, as well as for debate on the politics and ethics of witnessing on social media platforms. Reynolds had not only filmed the shooting's aftermath, but also narrated with remarkable poise the events leading up to it, alternately addressing her expiring boyfriend, the policeman who had just shot him seven times, God, her four-year-old daughter, her Facebook friends and eventually millions of unrelated viewers.

Shortly after Castile's death, vigils were staged in front of the Minnesota Capitol and at the intersection where the shooting occurred (Figure 8.1). As rhizomatic networks of screens linked up to other scenes of violent black deaths, peaceful demonstrations and retaliatory violence spread to cities around the country. The incident prompted statements by government officials such as the Minnesota governor and President Obama, who spoke out against structural racism and police violence, as well as policy clarifications by Facebook after Reynolds' video was briefly (and controversially) made unavailable.

In contesting racial profiling, police violence, white supremacy and black hyperincarceration, the Black Lives Matter movement has both drawn on and expanded the public visibility of besieged, terrified, defiant, angry, dying and dead black bodies on social media platforms. Amidst a plethora of related image testimony produced from various locations, distances, ideologies and agencies (police dashcams and body cameras, helicopters, drones, citizen cell phone cameras), Reynolds' video stands out because of the deployment of mobile witnessing technology, not from the perspective of an accidental witness, activist, agent (or voyeur) of violence, but from within the event—and through the body—of a (near) victim.

Acts of witnessing such as Reynolds' illuminate the political and ethical potentialities—and limitations—of a new mode of networked and live mobile witnessing to engage with contemporary black necropolitics. In this chapter, I begin by situating Reynolds' "sousveillant" act of turning the camera back on

Figure 8.1 Protest march in St. Paul, Minnesota, in response to the Philando Castile shooting, 7 July 2016.

Source: by Fibonacci Blue from Minnesota, USA [CC BY 2.0 (http://creativecommons. org/licenses/by/2.0)], via Wikimedia Commons.

the police in relation to the historical legacy and embodied experience of black (im)mobilities and anti-black surveillance in the USA, thus problematizing colorblind theorizing of mobile witnessing and selfie participatory journalism. I then consider how black death becomes the site in which the "live" function of social media platforms harnesses temporal contingency to illuminate the crisis of the everyday for the dispossessed, as well as how this visibility is being framed and curtailed through a neoliberal discourse on responsible streaming. Finally, I explore selfie witnessing as a gestural and connective performance, placing ethical demands on mediated witnesses while exposing sovereign violence in a startling way.

Black mobile witnessing

In violent encounters between police and African-Americans, the use of live streaming technologies incorporating front-facing networked smartphone cameras have both extended and complicated contemporary discussions of black (im)mobilities and mobile witnessing.

Castile's death clearly demonstrates the restrictions on, and policing of, black (auto)mobilities and their intersection with the scopic regimes of American "gunscapes" (Nicholson 2016). The tongue-in-cheek term "Driving While Black" (like its variants "Walking While Black" or "Driving While Indian") underscores the pervasive racialization of movement often elided in mobility studies that assume an unfettered white subject (Nicholson & Sheller 2016). With its roots in the tracking of freed slaves, contemporary forms of racial profiling, through a regime of repetitive traffic stops and charges for minor violations, systematically impede black movement, especially into white suburban space. Statistics that emerged after Castile's death reveal that although blacks make up only 7 percent of the population of Falcon Heights, the predominantly white suburb of St. Paul on the border of which Castile and Reynolds were driving, they were involved in almost half the traffic arrests (Vezner & Horner 2016).

The day Castile was pulled over for driving a car with a broken taillight could not have been more ordinary. He and Reynolds had worked that morning and just come from dropping off groceries at home and Castile's sister at her house. It was also ordinary because Castile was pulled over for yet another traffic infraction: his 46th in 14 years. As reporters who reviewed his driving record note: "Basically, Philando Castile was stopped from the very moment he got his license, through the moment of his death. That was his last stop" (Peralta & Corley 2016). He was only pulled over six times for possible violations visible from outside the car (a suspended license, for instance, can only be determined after a stop). Even though most charges against Castile were dismissed, he still found himself caught up in a cycle of fines that compromised his ability to operate a car legally.

Although it turned out Castile's taillight was not broken, a scanner traffic audio clip surfaced after the shooting pointing to a second justification for the stop, this time involving blatant racial profiling: Castile's "wide-set nose" linked him potentially to a local burglary. That Castile was shot reaching for his ID in response to the officer's command to identify himself, but that this gesture could be interpreted as his reaching for a gun, demonstrates the contradictions involved in conflating traffic violations with criminal charges. Suspected felons should be ordered to get out of their cars with their hands up, not hand over documents from inside their cars. When asked for his ID, Castile stated (as required by law) that he was carrying a licensed firearm. In police dashcam video released to the public after Yanez's acquittal (PoliceActivity 2017), the officer says, "I told him not to reach for it" (the vague pronoun "it" accommodating either gun or wallet) (Figure 8.2). Reynolds, by contrast, spoke back to the officer with precise language: "You told him to get his ID." Slippage from one potential infraction to

Police Dashcam Footage Of Philando Castile Fatal Shooting

923,533 views

Figure 8.2 Screen grab from police dashcam video of Officer Yanez shooting at Castile, after yelling at him: "Don't pull it out!", 6 July 2016.
Source: video uploaded to YouTube (PoliceActivity 2017).

another, of course, is typical of how legality is used to justify violence at moments of crisis (Benjamin 1976). That this kind of lethal "protection" of citizens is the basic principle of necropolitical state racism is captured in Reynolds' enraged comments in a later interview: "… these police are not here to protect and serve us, they are here to assassinate us—they are here to kill us—because we are black" (Mott 2016).

Guns, like automobiles, a key signifier of American autonomy, virility and whiteness, also act as a "mobile technology of race" when deployed in road-scapes, honing a one-directional, non-reciprocal gaze on potential black targets (Nicholson 2016). Castile ultimately was denied the right to bear arms for protection, let alone for vigilantism of the sort engaged in by white "defenders" of gated communities or the US–Mexico border. Instead, Castile's possession of a weapon criminalized him, "justifying" police force as "self-defense". Recent shooting deaths of unarmed black men and boys holding objects from toy guns to candy bars suggest how white fear weaponizes any embodied black movement (Nicholson 2016, pp. 556–558).

What happens, then, when a black woman wields a networked video streaming device in such a symbolically and literally loaded context? Of course, the camera—like the gun, but also with the gun—is itself a mobile technology of racial and sexual framing, part of a scopic regime of violent visualization (Feldman 2000), historically linked to broader media systems and structures of political and economic surveillance and power. The equipping of police officers with body cameras in the name of greater accountability, aside from generating controversies over privacy and reports of malfunction and misuse (cameras fallen off, not turned on), shockingly further identifies objectivity with the viewpoint of the officer, whose body is behind the camera and outside the image. By contrast, "black luminosity" historically has foregrounded the black body as a target: lantern laws in colonial New York City required blacks to carry a lantern or lit candle at night making themselves visible to panoptic white tracking (Browne 2015, pp. 153–155).

In turning camera against gun, Reynolds disjoins the scopic overlap of police gun and camera, jarring media viewers' habituated in-sight into these scenes of death, while also drawing attention to the limits of the (black) witnessing body through filmic gaps, abrupt montage and awkward angles. Rather than assuming the embodied vision of the policeman-shooter, mediated witnesses are "forced" to take Reynolds' position and face the policeman's gun pointed at them through Castile's bleeding body; later, through Reynolds' embodied viewpoint, they experience having "their daughter" taken from them and located behind the pointed gun, on the side of the police (Figure 8.3). While images produced in the context of violent visualization (i.e. Abu Ghraib torture, Rodney King) can be read critically and ethically to condemn the violence of which they are a trace,

Figure 8.3 Officers on pavement, aiming at Reynolds while holding her daughter, 6 July 2016.

Source: screen grab from Reynolds' Facebook Live video (Right Now News 2016).

the violence that produced them remains engrained and normalized within the images in a way that can be hard to defuse. The shock of Reynolds' testimony lies in placing the viewer in the scopic position of the victim rather than the victimizer.

Reynolds' act of testimony clearly demonstrates how networked mobile image technologies contribute to the emergence of new visual idioms and ethical discourses of mobile witnessing that interrupt and reshape "cultures of record": new authenticities are produced by "traversing binaries such as the private and the public, the body and the machine, the material and the virtual, the journalist and the citizen" (Reading 2009, p. 63). An enhanced physicality, even bloodiness, distinguishes these image testimonies, as the "martyrdom" of the recording body has emerged as grounds for truth claims regarding the violence of the murderous state (Andén-Papadopoulos 2014, p. 754). Selfies in particular have emerged as a newly persuasive form of witnessing events and "participatory journalism," or journalism with a "point of view" (Koliska & Roberts 2015).

Often, the witnessing texts that gain prominence in mainstream media (and come to be analyzed in media studies) are produced by "First World" bodies (commuters, tourists) moving through public space and unexpectedly caught up in a catastrophe (terrorist attack, extreme weather phenomenon). Other times activists deliberately assume the role of "citizen camera-witnesses," putting their bodies on the line to document state violence with the aim of mobilizing publics through the evidential and affective power of images (Andén-Papadopoulos 2014, p. 754). In Reynolds' case, as opposed to those of bystanders-turned-victims or activist citizen-cameras, a body has not been accidentally or strategically placed in a position to witness. In contrast to more socially privileged subjects who normally move effortlessly through public space at home (and abroad) and only exceptionally find themselves "on the run," her body was already (and always) in danger, hunted and restless. Reynolds did not start recording her boyfriend's shooting as an activist, but because she had been activated within a broader culture of witnessing in the context of agonistic practices of visualization associated with the Black Lives Matter movement and her personal experience of violence and injustice. Indeed, in interviews Reynolds noted that this was not the first time that she had documented interactions with the police.

Furthermore, given the pre-emptive criminalization of black bodily mobility, there is no pretense of an objective, disembodied "God's eye" view in Reynolds' video. Like Castile, she cannot risk moving her arms and hands (in this case to film). In the beginning of the video, we hear her being warned twice: "Ma'am, keep your hands where they are." Handcuffed at the end of the video, her phone on the floor, her face is projected at an eerie angle (Figure 8.4). In the middle of the video, as she is being taken from the car, we see fixed images of the sky and distant audio. While the acrobatic moves of selfie taking are often mocked, Reynolds' reckless stretch to document, as I will discuss in greater detail below, powerfully conveys the fact that while filming she was not (yet) a survivor, certainly not a bystander, but still potentially a victim.

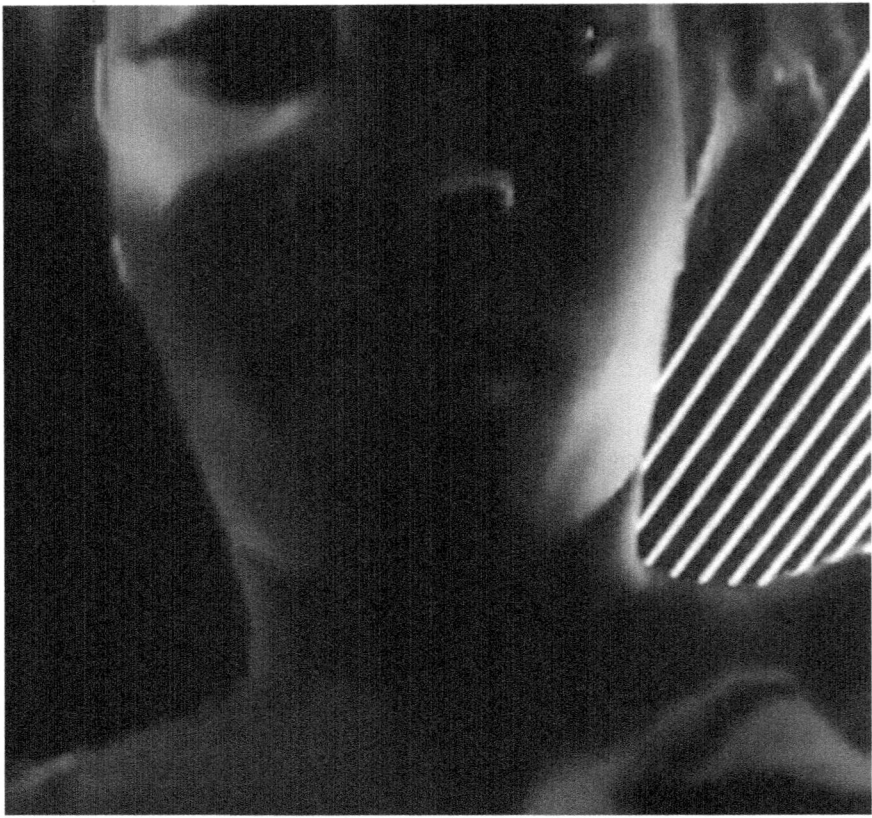

Figure 8.4 Reynolds witnessing handcuffed in the back of a police car, 6 July 2016.

Source: screen grab from Reynolds' Facebook Live video (Right Now News 2016).

Undoubtedly, the unprecedented access of "ordinary people" to a mass audience and the speed of transmission making possible alternative views on an unfolding event, as well as the intimacy and authenticity of the embodied, first-person perspective enabled by social media platforms, digital networks and smartphone technologies, have disrupted mainstream news accounts of controversial events. Nonetheless, it would be a mistake to overemphasize, or solely point to, the role of technology in the emergence of mobile witnessing and tactics of counter-surveillance to state and corporate violence. Given the long US history of racialized surveillance, "dark sousveillance" (Browne 2015), namely subversive anti-black surveillance (from "looking back" at the master to escape routes inscribed in Negro spirituals), has shaped an "oppositional imaginary that actively resists and opposes the state's surveillant gaze" (Fischer &

Mohrman 2016). Reynolds' image testimony also has a place in this technopolitical tradition.

That Reynolds risked her life to livestream demonstrates her faith in social media platforms as a means to circumvent—but also access—mainstream news media and official institutions of justice. She invites "everybody that's tuned in," from friends and family and the larger black community to a national and global public, to witness and adjudicate this injury. Yet, a deep ambivalence surrounds the fact that mobile witnessing as a tactic of exposure, access and control of images of deadly violence directed at black bodies has been unfolding on corporate social media platforms. This uneasiness is evident in the conflicted responses to the shocking images produced in this media format and the regulatory policies instituted in the aftermath of the incident.

Livestream and the emergency of the everyday

At the million view mark, Reynolds' nearly ten-minute video, which she had posted beneath the one-word message "Police," suddenly became unavailable (Right Now News 2016). Facebook later alleged there had been a "technical glitch," while Reynolds claimed that the police "took over my Facebook." An hour later, the video was reuploaded, but with an admonitory black screen ("Warning – Graphic Video. Videos that contain graphic content can shock, offend and upset. Are you sure you want to see this?") and restricted to viewers over 18 years old (Figure 8.5). Two days after the shooting, Facebook issued a clarification regarding appropriate uses of the Facebook Live function, which the day after Castile's death was used to stream the shooting of five police officers in Dallas during protests over the Castile shooting, but also that of Alton Sterling on 6 July in Louisiana (Isaac & Ember 2016). Many viewed the temporary removal of Reynolds' video as censorship, thus raising urgent questions about Facebook's role as a platform for citizen journalism involving the production and dissemination of video footage with explicit and controversial content.

Facebook Live, of course, was conceived with other bodies and lives in mind than those of Philando Castile and Diamond Reynolds: namely, those of a white middle-class suburbia of leisure, consumption, pleasure and mobility (both physical and social). Indeed, until Reynolds' video, the most viewed Facebook Live video was made by white "stay-at-home mom" Candace Payne. The video consists of Payne, wearing the mask of the hirsute Star Wars character Chewbacca, sitting in her car in the parking lot of a shopping mall and laughing hysterically at herself—as reflected in the screen of her cell phone. Payne did not come under police scrutiny for her prank (eerily reminiscent of blackface), but instead landed on the talk show circuit, while her family was awarded thousands of dollars in scholarship money.

In introducing the Live feature, Facebook was clearly aiming to profit by co-opting televisual live broadcasting (and its ad revenue), using gratis user-generated content and reaping the added value of intimacy and authenticity

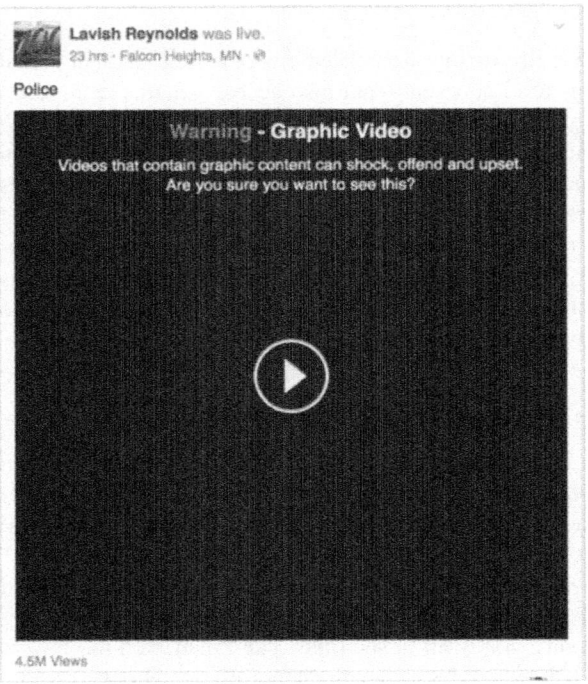

Figure 8.5 Diamond Reynolds' reinstated Facebook Live video.

associated with personalized feeds. The format's potential for enabling sousveillant acts of witnessing violence, but also for "streaming trouble" (Kulwin 2017) and thus augmenting the intensity of acts of violence, apparently was not anticipated by the company. Instead, promotions for Facebook Live imagined users live streaming events such as birthday parties for distant relatives or behind-the-scenes post-game action in the locker room. To build up interest, celebrities were paid to use Facebook Live before the feature was available to regular users, while news outlets such as Buzzfeed, but also the *New York Times*, were paid to produce content, testifying to the ongoing "mainstreaming" of livestream (Perez 2015). Much like its televisual counterpart, Facebook Live was conceived as schedulable ("lobbies" were created for followers to gather before "broadcasts"), archivable ("Lavish Reynolds was live") and rerunnable ("live" cooking "shows" were proposed as an ideal genre).

Media events such as Castile's livestreamed death, thus, inaugurated a new technopolitical modality centered on radical contingency and the startling collision with death, as well as productive of archives of state murder. Rather than simply confirming pre-existing ways of seeing, knowing and acting, "black death contributes to the birth of a new technological and industrial condition: live feed video" (Juhasz 2016). As Benjamin (1968, p. 257) has memorably observed: "The tradition of the oppressed teaches us that the 'state of emergency' in which we live is not the exception but the rule." From this perspective, the live media event both results from and exposes the emergency of the everyday for precarious subjects.

Despite the scriptability of spontaneity, the promise of the truly fortuitous "live" event can be traced back to earlier audiovisual technologies of documentation and transmission, such as photography and film and, later, radio and television (Doane 1990, 2002). The "live," as the uncontainable break with hegemonic media discourses, appears to provide unmediated access to the "real" (through death), circumventing the mediating filter of historical expertise and judicial opinion, thus enabling viewers, however distant from the scene, to be arbiters of truth and social justice (Barthes 1981, p. 80; Matsuda 1996, p. 171). The utopia of an unmediated (colorblind) public sphere, however, paradoxically rests on the simultaneous investment in, and erasure, of technologies of mediation that anthropologist William Mazzarella (2006) has aptly termed "(im)mediation." Even though explicitly posited as an alternative to platform capitalism, the American Civil Liberties Union app "Mobile Justice" (www.mobilejusticeca.org/), which enables users to directly submit smartphone videos to the ACLU, operates on a similar principle of transparency within-but-despite media.

This faith in the platform as a direct conduit to a witnessing public is evident throughout Reynolds' image testimony. Handcuffed in the back of a police car toward the end of the video, Reynolds points the camera at Yanez, identifying and accusing the shooter through her use of deictic language and positioning of the camera: "That's the police officer over there that did it with the black on." In an interview following her release from custody, she explains her decision to stream the shooting's aftermath thus:

> I wanted everyone in the world to know that no matter how much the police tamper with evidence, how much they stick together, no matter how they manipulate our minds to believe what they want, I wanted to put it on Facebook and go viral so that the people could see. I wanted the people to determine who was right and who was wrong. I want the people to be the testimonies here. All of us saw with our eyes—the only thing you guys didn't see is when he shot, and if I would've moved while that gun was out, he would've shot me too.
>
> (Mott 2016)

Reynolds explicitly defines her action as an attempt to counter dominant regimes of evidence (police "tamper with evidence" and "stick together") through mediated witnessing ("I want the people to be the testimonies here," "all of us saw with our eyes"). Live witnessing theoretically guarantees that footage cannot be tampered with since it has already been launched into the world, while also mobilizing others to the scene (in the video, Reynolds summons Castile's sister to come back). Facebook, of course, also advocates for the platform's "disappearance" by persistently distinguishing the supposed neutrality of technological infrastructure or "tools" from the content it hosts. Pressed about Facebook's editorial policies in August 2016, founder and CEO Mark Zuckerberg stated: "We are a technology company. We're not a media company.... We don't produce any of the content" (Gilbert 2016).

Yet, the same technologies that appear to provide a means of circumventing corporate and state control of course make users visible to state scrutiny, inscribing them in corporate platforms and databases that filter, track and profit from their every move online. Hardly democratic and open, censorship and algorithmic control determine what can be seen. Just two days after the killing of Castile, under mounting public pressure, Facebook updated its policy on live video streaming, ultimately preserving the company's right to remove and curate content:

> One of the most sensitive situations involves people sharing violent or graphic images of events taking place in the real world. In those situations, context and degree are everything. For instance, if a person witnessed a shooting, and used Facebook Live to raise awareness or find the shooter, we would allow it. However, if someone shared the same video to mock the victim or celebrate the shooting, we would remove the video.
> (https://newsroom.fb.com/news/h/community-standards-and-facebook-live/,
> 8 July 2016)

Facebook's policy statement assumes that violence is something inherently visible that can be objectively perceived and assessed. Yet, the visual field is hardly neutral. So many image testimonies are by-products of violent and racialized visualization (via body cams, dashcams, drones) and thus imprinted with those violent framings (Feldman 2000). Given the criminalization of black mobility, it is dismaying, but no longer surprising, that images that seem to clearly incriminate police aggression are re-viewed in case after case as evidence locating the initial threat in the male black body, rendering the transparency of visual testimony highly dubious (Butler 1993).

Moreover, these guidelines presume a neoliberal subject who will be "responsible" in sharing content, thus abdicating the platform's own responsibility for the "standards" of public discourse (Fischer & Mohrman 2016): a position that became highly controversial during the 2016 US elections in regard to "fake news" and "filter bubbles." A graphic on Facebook's Community Standards page depicting three citizens against the backdrop of a police shield promotes this outsourcing of policing to the community, while normalizing peer-to-peer surveillance of the everyday. In the context of neoliberal "responsible streaming," Reynolds' live feed video could be deemed unhelpful and rash, a needless infliction of graphic images of violence on other social media users, rather than a necessary and timely exposure of police violence, white paranoia and white panic (Fischer & Mohrman 2016).

From lynching spectacle to selfie reflexivity

Facebook's regulation of the live function on its platform comes at a critical moment in which debates about the circulation of images of the dead bodies of dispossessed subjects have led to a pushback on social media "oversharing" and "obsessive" public mourning that works against the exposure of contemporary necropolitics (Papailias 2018). Examining the corporeal, intersubjective, affective and performative attributes of selfies and their communicative and ethical dimensions, however, enables us to shift emphasis from particular images or videos that "should" (or "should not") be seen to "network performances and speech acts between different parties" that constitute scene(s) of witnessing unfolding in multiple temporalities (Reading 2009, p. 72).

For some, the massive circulation of Reynolds' video "viralized" black death, reinscribing violence against vulnerable subjects (Juhasz 2016). Earlier scenes of black death, such as that of 17-year-old Trayvon Martin in 2012, demonstrate the humiliating spectacularization of black bodies in the social media context, as the emergence of a "trayvoning" meme saw white users "playing dead" and imitating the pose of his corpse as a new kind of blackface. This dissemination continues a history of voyeuristic participation in the reproduction and augmentation of grotesque spectacles of suffering that recalls lynching photography and postcards (Noble 2014). In this view, rather than bearing witness to atrocity and, thus, limiting racial violence and gun proliferation, massively circulating Reynolds' video ironically buttressed the case for legal protection of white paranoia.

Others counter that the visibility of black death (and of white fear of blackness), as well as the public mourning of supposedly ungrievable, disposable bodies, is precisely what has sparked contemporary national discussions and open condemnation of racial profiling and police violence, enabling dynamic new forms of activism to emerge (Figure 8.6). Indeed, the Black Lives Matter movement began out of a conversation on Facebook following Martin's death, then morphed into a hashtag after his killer's acquittal. The emblematic hashtag #staywoke is indicative of an "eyes open" approach to witnessing violence and social injustice that emphasizes actively watching, rather than simply seeing— and certainly not turning away.

In contrast to these kinds of "debates" about moral spectatorship, a relational approach to image testimonies treats them as traces of networked performances and speech acts among various witnesses differently placed in time and space. The selfie's production in a "circuit of corporeal social energy" and as a result of "kinesthetic sociability" (Frosh 2015) might provide a key for a performative model of witnessing that neither assumes a priori political positions on the ethics of witnessing violent deaths, nor centers analysis on decontextualized images understood as having (or not having) the intrinsic power to mobilize mediated witnesses. Even though selfies are more often discussed in relation to still images, live mobile witnessing has a distinctively selfie dimension as users address the screen of the mobile phone when they "go live." Selfies privilege

Figure 8.6 Memorial painting of Castile on phonebooth in Brooklyn, 8 July 2017.

Source: photo courtesy of Karen Strassler.

spatiality over temporality as the time between the event and its viewing appears less significant than the distance between "mutually connected but perpetually shifting" bodies (Frosh 2015, p. 1609). From this perspective, Reynolds' video is not so much an indexical documentation of Castile's death, as the trace of multiple lexical and visual lines of address to visible and invisible, metaphysical and material bodies. Each line denotes a different social relation and responsibility toward the event. The restless darting of Reynolds' head back and forth throughout the video (in contrast to her immobilized and bound hands) reflects the impossibility of a singular point of address.

At the same time, live witnessing is also about keeping the channel of communication open in the present, about surviving through temporal co-presence with others. At the beginning of the video when Reynolds says "Stay with me," she appeals to Castile to stay alive, but her words could also be addressed to viewers of the video, as an entreaty for them to keep her alive, whether through the accountability forced on the police through exposure, or via mobilization at the scene. At the end of the video, Reynolds' four-year-old daughter poignantly reverses generational roles by witnessing her mother's suffering. At her mother's sudden breakdown of composure ("I can't really do shit because they have me handcuffed" and "I can't believe they just did this I'm fucking, fucking ... fuck!"), the little girl comforts her: "It's OK mommy.... It's OK, I'm right here with you."

Citizens (and those excluded or on the margins of citizenship) have increasingly mobilized selfies as acts of citizenship and modes of interpellation into critical events and, more generally, into public discourse that create an effect, however illusory, of public intimacy (Kuntsman 2017). The selfie "says not only 'see this, here, now,' but also 'see me showing you me'" (Frosh 2015, p. 1610). For the viewer, Reynolds' body serves as a conduit into the scene of witnessing that shifts our attention from the dying victim to the surviving witness as an almost victim. Given that in the selfie, the "body is both the platform and the limitation of this new kind of self-depiction" (Frosh 2015, p. 1613), the jarring aesthetics of Reynolds' hand-camera assemblage make tangible the severely constrained and dangerous conditions of black (im)mobility ("If I would've moved while that gun was out, he would've shot me too"). Selfies, by extension, interpellate mediated witnesses into the scene less as "close viewers," than as "near misses," with important consequences for their sense of responsibility (Papailias 2016, p. 441).

A last important point regarding the selfie is the interpellation of the photographing/videoing body within the screen along with filmed subjects. "Com-posing" a selfie occurs in real-time as an unpredictable, dynamic and emerging assemblage: this "field of embodied inhabitation" (Frosh 2015, p. 1612) is a processual event potentially transformed by the act of filming. Reynolds indeed might have been shot while filming. In traditional photographic technology, the camera operates as "a barrier between the visible photographed spaces and undepicted locations of photographing and viewing" (Frosh 2015, p. 1611). Reynolds' live video is shocking not only in turning the camera on the police, who are usually behind the camera, but also in creating a visual composition that (terrifyingly) includes the police in her familial everyday (inside the car shooting her boyfriend with her daughter in the backseat). As an act of witnessing, her selfie video thus composes social relations: in this case, bringing into visibility sovereign violence along with black death.

Epilogue

This chapter has focused on the significance of live mobile witnessing and selfie videos to the exposure and witnessing of deadly violence against black bodies in the contemporary US. After the not-guilty verdict for police officer Yanez, one might conclude that despite the daring and novelty of Reynolds' image testimony, nothing changes in the final analysis. As warranted as this pessimism might be, I still think it is important to hold on to the panic this video's circulation briefly posed for platform capitalism. The contingency of the viral created a real state of emergency breaking through routinized and normalized racial profiling and derailing habituated structures of representation of scenes of black death. Second, thinking about the status of the body as platform and limit in a selfie video, but also in the black experience of compromised mobility, suggests how in "times of social media" witnessing operates as a performative interaction of bodies and gazes, as an intersubjective and intimate gesture of framing and com-posing the self with others, as a means of imagining the reversibility of a situation and of engaging the affective power of the image and, finally, as a kind of observant-participation in events that shows survival to be less the precondition of witnessing than its outcome.

References

Andén-Papadopoulos, K. (2014). Citizen camera-witnessing: Embodied political dissent in the age of "mediated mass self-communication". *New Media & Society*, 16(5), pp. 753–769.

Barthes, R. (1981). *Camera Lucida: Reflections on Photography*. New York: Hill and Wang.

Benjamin, W. (1968). Theses on the philosophy of history. In *Illuminations*, pp. 253–264. New York: Schocken.

Benjamin, W. (1976). Critique of violence. In *Reflections*, pp. 277–300. New York: Schocken.

Browne, S. (2015). *Dark Matters: On the Surveillance of Blackness*. Durham: Duke University Press.

Butler, J. (1993). Endangered/endangering: Schematic racism and white paranoia. In R. Gooding-Williams (ed.), *Reading Rodney King/Reading Urban Uprising*, pp. 15–22. London: Routledge.

Doane, M.A. (1990). Information, crisis, catastrophe. In P. Mellencamp (ed.), *Logics of Television. Essays in Cultural Criticism*, pp. 222–239. Bloomington: Indiana University Press.

Doane, M.A. (2002). *The Emergence of Cinematic Time: Modernity, Contingency, the Archive*. Cambridge, MA: Harvard University Press.

Feldman, A. (2000). Violence and vision: The prosthetics and aesthetics of terror. In V. Das, A. Kleinman, M. Ramphel, & P. Reynolds (eds), *Violence and Subjectivity*, pp. 46–78. Berkeley: University of California Press.

Fischer, M. & Mohrman, K. (2016). Black deaths matter? Sousveillance and the invisibility of black life. *Ada: A Journal of Gender, New Media, and Technology*, 10. Available from: http://adanewmedia.org/2016/10/issue10-fischer-mohrman/ [19 April 2018].

Frosh, P. (2015). The gestural image: The selfie, photography theory, and kinesthetic sociability. *International Journal of Communication*, 9, pp. 1607–1628.

Gilbert, B. (2016). Facebook refuses to accept it's a media company: Here's why that's terrible for you. *Business Insider*, 30 August. Available from: www.businessinsider.de/why-facebook-is-a-media-company-even-though-it-says-its-not-2016-8?r=US&IR=T [19 April 2018].

Isaac, M. & Ember, S. (2016). Live footage of shooting forces Facebook to confront new role. *New York Times*, 8 July. Available from: www.nytimes.com/2016/07/09/technology/facebook-dallas-live-video-breaking-news.html [19 April 2018].

Juhasz, A. (2016). How do I (not) look? Live feed video and viral black death. *JSTOR Daily*, 20 July. Available from: https://daily.jstor.org/how-do-i-not-look/ [19 April 2018].

Koliska, M. & Roberts, J. (2015). Selfies: Witnessing and participatory journalism with a point of view. *International Journal of Communication*, 9, pp. 1672–1685.

Kulwin, N. (2017). Streaming trouble: Facebook Live has a big problem with live-streamed violence. *Vice News*, 6 January. Available from: https://news.vice.com/en_us/article/mb985y/facebook-live-has-a-big-problem-livestreamed-violence [19 April 2018].

Kuntsman, A. (2017). Introduction: Whose selfie citizenship? In A. Kuntsman (ed.), *Selfie Citizenship*, pp. 13–18. Cham: Palgrave Macmillan.

Matsuda, M. (1996). *Memory of the Modern*, New York: Oxford University Press.

Mazzarella W. (2006). Internet X-ray: E-governance, transparency, and the politics of immediation in India. *Public Culture*, 18(3), pp. 473–505.

Mott, N. (2016). Lavish Reynolds wanted Facebook shooting video to "Go viral." *Inverse Culture*, 7 July. Available from: www.inverse.com/article/17978-falcon-heights-police-shooting-details-facebook [19 April 2018].

Nicholson, J. (2016). Don't shoot! Black mobilities in American gunscapes. *Mobilities*, 11(4), pp. 553–563.

Nicholson, J.A. & Sheller, M. (2016). Race and the politics of mobility: Introduction. *Transfers*, 6(1), pp. 4–11.

Noble, S. (2014). Teaching Trayvon: Race, media and the politics of spectacle. *The Black Scholar*, 44(1), pp. 12–29.

Papailias, P. (2016). Witnessing in the age of the database: Viral memorials, affective publics, and the assemblage of mourning. *Memory Studies*, 9(4), pp. 437–454.

Papailias, P. (2018). (Un)seeing dead refugee bodies: Mourning memes, spectropolitics, and the haunting of Europe. *Media, Culture & Society*. Available from: http://journals.sagepub.com/doi/pdf/10.1177/0163443718756178 [19 April 2018].

Peralta, E. & Corley, C. (2016). The driving life and death of Philando Castile. *NPR*, 15 July. Available from: www.npr.org/sections/thetwo-way/2016/07/15/485835272/the-driving-life-and-death-of-philando-castile [19 April 2018].

Perez, S. (2015). The live stream goes mainstream. *TechCrunch*, 27 March. Available from: https://techcrunch.com/2015/03/27/the-livestream-goes-mainstream/ [19 April 2018].

PoliceActivity (2017). Police dashcam footage of Philando Castile fatal shooting. YouTube video, 20 June. Available from: www.youtube.com/watch?v=PMKc Wz5nNoM [19 April 2018].

Reading, A. (2009). Mobile witnessing: Ethics and the camera phone in the "war on terror." *Globalizations*, 6(1), pp. 61–76.

Right Now News (2016). RAW FOOTAGE: Philando Castile SHOT **FULL VIDEO**. YouTube video, 7 July. Available from: www.youtube.com/watch?v=K_J3sYIgvUE [19 April 2018].

Vezner, T. & Horner, S. (2016). St. Anthony Police Data Shows Disproportionate Arrests of Blacks. *Twin Cities Pioneer Press*, 13 July. Available from: www.twincities. com/2016/07/13/st-anthony-police-data-shows-disproportionate-arrests-of-blacks/ [19 April 2018].

Chapter 9

Eye, flesh, world

Three modes of digital witnessing

Paul Frosh

Ours is an era of "witnessing fever", to use Kurasawa's telling phrase, "whereby public spaces have been transformed into veritable machines for the production of testimonial discourses and evidence" (Kurasawa 2009, p. 93). "Witnessing fever" is no less apparent in putatively private spaces (or more properly, in the multi-scale interpenetration of public and private), thanks to the increasing ubiquity of mobile digital devices and the density, scope and variety of media networks that make ordinary individuals always already witnesses-in-potential in their everyday lives (Frosh & Pinchevski 2014). One conspicuous feature of this transformation is the increasing circulation of image testimonies, videos and other texts on digital and social media platforms. Encompassing a variety of topics and sub-genres—such as the self-witnessing of "celebration selfies" sent to loved-ones by refugees who have survived the perilous Mediterranean crossing to Europe (Chouliaraki 2017; Literat 2017), and video "citizen camera-witnessing" (Andén-Papadopoulos 2014) of suffering in zones of violence and war—these testimonies evoke a range of emotional, social, ethical and political relations with distant viewers.

For all their diversity of approach and example, however, most analyses of these image testimonies share a significant emphasis: that while digital networks and social media act as the agents of circulation for witnessing, they rarely provide its "content". What we witness via Facebook, Twitter, Instagram, etc., tends not to be Facebook, Twitter, Instagram, etc. In an implicit privileging of the "transmission view of communication", famously identified by James Carey (1992, p. 15), the witnessing potential of digital networks is largely derived from their role as conduits through which image testimonies are conveyed between witnesses and their addressees. Notwithstanding the importance of this role, and the new temporal, spatial and social scales at which it operates, this transmissive focus tacitly promotes an a priori distinction between circulation and representation, media form and image content, that fails to capture the complexities of contemporary media witnessing.

In contrast to this emphasis, I will ask what we can learn from instances where image testimonies are not just distributed through digital platforms, but also foreground key processes and aspects of the medium itself and of our implication and indeed interpellation within it, where our interactions with digital networks and social media are also part of the representational and performative work of an image testimony. Proceeding through the close-reading of three examples, I will invoke a well-known distinction in the conceptualization of witnessing: between an observation-based witnessing aimed at imparting detailed and accurate perceptions of an event to others "objectively", and a sensibility-based witnessing which emphasizes the emotional and sensory intensity of subjective experience. Harari (2009), in a discussion of the emergence of these forms of witnessing in the context of modern warfare, names the first by the conventional expression "eye-witnessing" ("I was there, this is what I saw, now you know"), and calls the second "flesh-witnessing" ("I was there, this is what I experienced, you can never truly understand"). I will then supplement these two categories—in the analysis of the third example—with the concept of "world-witnessing", arguing that digital networks themselves constitute witnessable worlds operating in adjacency to the life worlds of physical existence. My claim is that the emotional and moral power of these image testimonies derives not only from the stories and topics they convey (injustice, suffering, death), but also from their poetic ability to reveal the underlying techno-cultural conditions, potentialities and vulnerabilities of our networked lives.[1]

Eye-witnessing and the ethics of kinaesthetics

On 20 January 2017, Shahak Shapira, an Israeli artist based in Berlin, launched a website in English and German called Yolocaust. An exercise in online shaming, the site was replaced a week later with a (similarly bilingual) letter that began thus:

Dear internet,
last week I launched a project called YOLOCAUST that explored our commemorative culture by combining selfies from the Holocaust Memorial in Berlin with footage from Nazi extermination camps. The selfies were found on Facebook, Instagram, Tinder and Grindr. Comments, hashtags and "Likes" that were posted with the selfies are also included.

https://yolocaust.de.

The shaming exercise was apparently successful. Not only was it visited, according to Shapira, by more than 2.5 million people, and covered fairly extensively by mainstream news outlets, it also reached the 12 individuals whose "selfies" had been exposed, leading to the extraction of confessions, expressions of contrition and regret, and apologies, along with promises to remove the offending images from their social media accounts.[2] The message of penitence from the most egregious of the 12 offenders, who had captioned an image of himself joyfully leaping among the memorial stones with the words "Jumping on dead Jews @ Holocaust Memorial" is reproduced on the website in full. The work of shaming completed ("The Yolocaust is Over" declared an article in Israel's *Ha'aretz* newspaper, see Sommer 2017), the images were removed from Yolocaust as a gesture of generous absolution to the offenders. The internet, however, is not as forgiving as Shapira. A postscript to the message sent by the main "offender" adds: "Oh, and if you could explain to BBC, Haaretz and aaaaallll the other blogs, news stations etc. etc. that I fucked up, that'd be great". Yet the images are still available if you search for them.[3]

Yolocaust is a shockingly poetic project. It exemplifies Jakobson's (1960) "poetic function" of communicative interaction in that it accentuates the material palpability of signs, but it is also poetic in Agamben's (1999) sense: poesis as revelation and making present, as bringing forth into being, unexpectedly—and violently—producing a heightened encounter with a disclosed world. In fact, Yolocaust deliberately discloses worlds in order to shock. On the original website the shock was created by a clever interactive feature. When visitors moved their cursors over the image taken from social media, it was immediately combined with an image from the Holocaust: the original "selfie" of someone jumping, leaning, posing, smiling or otherwise appearing to have fun at the Berlin Holocaust Memorial was instantly merged with a documentary photograph from the Holocaust—piles of corpses, mass graves, barracks full of emaciated survivors—which would appear as a background to the main figure, replacing the rows of giant stone slabs of the memorial, while leaving the main figures of the "selfie" in the foreground (for examples of these transitions see Sommer 2017). Hence "Jumping on dead Jews" is almost literally visualized, as the monumental yet abstract stone edifices of the site among which the jumper jumps in the "selfie" are replaced by piles of dead Jews. Such substitutions give body to those commemorated by the memorial site, exchanging the material weight and heft of the stones as structures of memory and mourning with the flesh and bones, bodies and faces, of photographed victims realized in a weightless, virtual medium: the digital screen. Even the name "Yolocaust" is a poetic performance, drawing attention to the palpability of the sign and the worlds it discloses through shocking conjunction. This works by combining the internet acronym "Yolo" (which stands for "you only live once"), whose usage is associated with acts of wacky enthusiasm and even physical recklessness, with the moral and historical gravity of the Holocaust. Through this juxtaposition, "Yolocaust" reveals the true poetic gravity of "you only live once", not as a justification for flighty social behaviour or extreme sports, but as a profound statement of existential limits and their appalling realization in genocide. Yes, the dead Jews only lived once.

Shahak's use of documentary Holocaust images constitutes a conventional technological delegation of witnessing, collapsing the two dimensions of witnessing defined by John Durham Peters (2001): the perception or experience of an event and its transformation into discourse for others who were not present when it occurred. The photograph, an indexical trace anchored by presence at the scene, is also an image of that scene in replicable form, making it visible to others who are removed in time and space.[4] More particularly, the photographic images in Yolocaust act as technological prostheses for "eye-witnessing". Taken largely by third-party observers (the Allied liberators), they remind viewers what the Holocaust "really" looked like. Shahak, of course, is not himself a primary eye-witness of the Holocaust, as he was not there to see it, but he is—along with the technologies he employs and the cultural framework that imbues his actions with authority and significance—an agent of technologized eye-witnessing, since he has made a moral judgement that photographs of the Holocaust need to be re-articulated, for the edification and judgement of others, by their insertion into contemporary public discourse. Yolocaust thus manifests the last two dimensions of "media witnessing" defined as "the witnessing performed *in*, *by* and *through* the media" (Frosh & Pinchevski, 2009, p. 1, original italics). It witnesses the Holocaust by media (photographs taken during and immediately after the Holocaust), and through media (the website established in 2017 via which the images are displayed).

Yet it obviously does far more: it also demonstrates ways for witnessing *in* the media, ways that foreground new witnessing potentialities characterizing the medium itself. First, it stitches together pairs of images into composites—the foregrounded figures from the "selfies" and the contextual surroundings from the Holocaust photographs. Creating such composites, while certainly possible in the pre-digital era, is greatly facilitated by the modular or "fractal structure" (Manovich 2001, p. 30) of digital and digitized images: their elements can be easily recombined into new assemblages without compromising their independent formal identity. This modularity, down to the level of the pixel, eases the task of making these composites compositionally continuous, in that the new ground of each image—provided by the old Holocaust footage—is made compatible with the dimensions, placement within the frame and physical poses of the individual foregrounded figures from the social media "selfie". Paradoxically, it is this compositional compatibility which underpins these composites' profound ethical discordance: the naturalistic postures of the individuals in the "selfies", signalling obliviousness to the catastrophic mnemonic purpose of their surroundings as they pose and smile for the camera, become obscene upon transferal to the photographic real of the Holocaust. In photography and film theory "obscene" also means "off-scene", that which the image alludes to through exclusion: Yolocaust makes the "off-scene" of the "selfies" (and indeed of the Berlin memorial itself)—Holocaust victims—into the primary *mise en scène* of the composite images.

No less significantly, the composites reverse the conventional temporal relations of witnessing. Traditionally, witnessing presumes a linear temporality in which perception or experience of the event precedes discourse about the event (one sees and then one speaks): witnessing transports the past into the framework of the present through representation. In Yolocaust, however, visual figures from the present are transported back into the past, made present in visible relation to it, a feature also enabled by the "database logic" of digital media objects, whereby sequential relations are detached from their anchorage in the technical procedures of media and become subject to multiple potential reconfigurations (Manovich 2001, p. 218). We could call this temporal transportation of figures "transposition", because diverse persons are trans-posed, visibly posed across the chasm of otherwise unrecoverable space and time, across the abyss of mortality itself. Part of the outrageousness of this transposition results from the animation and sociability of the "selfie" figures posed anew among the assemblies of the dead. Furthermore, those individuals who are transposed into the Holocaust photographs are thereby cast as flawed witnesses, or flawed recipients of testimony, since through their own imaging-practices they are judged to have either ignored or denigrated those whose absence is commemorated at the Berlin memorial—a neglect and denigration which their poses continue to convey even as they are placed among corpses. By reversing and collapsing the temporal relations between the "selfies" and the Holocaust photographs, the composites themselves display non-witnessing in conditions that demand witnessing. The composites are image testimonies, technologized eye-witness observations, of the very failure of witnessing.

To whom was this testimony of failed witnessing offered? To visitors to the Yolocaust website (including those whose images appeared on the site), and the audiences for subsequent reports about it. Crucially, visitors to the original website were required not merely to see the "selfies" and their transformation into composites with Holocaust photographs, but to execute this transposition by moving the cursor over the "selfies" to make the images change: without this movement the composites did not appear. Yolocaust's poetic disclosure and conjunction of disparate worlds was performed through an embodied physical gesture. Continuous with the sensorimotor operative procedures of mainstream digital interfaces—pointing, clicking, swiping, tapping—this gesture is semi-habitual, one of the "ways of the hand" (Moores 2014) through which we routinely orient our bodies towards and within digital media.

The reception of witnessing is thus entangled within an entire ecology of corporeal relations with contemporary media technologies: the habitual and nimble gestural movements of hands, fingers and eyes by which we navigate the interfaces of our digital devices. Networked digital platforms such as the Yolocaust website constitute an increasingly palpable world in which we, as witnesses-in-potential, are somatically enmeshed. While Yolocaust's use of these gestures can be interpreted as a mere gimmick, it also foregrounds another distinctive feature of witnessing in digital media: that it is now bound up with the multisensuous apprehension of image testimonies through an ensemble of routine kinaesthetic bodily and technological interactions. Thanks to digital interfaces, we find ourselves in a historically novel situation: the burden of our exposure to image testimonies, our response to them and potential responsibility for them, depends on the smallest habitual and volitional gestures of our eyes and hands. This burden is the "ethics of kinaesthetics" (Frosh 2018). Given what can now be done to an image testimony via a digital interface, by my own hands and through a simple and almost cost-free movement, not attending to, engaging with or acting on it becomes a moral decision performed in minutely embodied contact with a disclosed world. It is this burden that Yolocaust both operated and manifested as a fundamental transformation of eye-witnessing in digital times.

Flesh-witnessing and the gesture of discomposure

While Yolocaust made the "off-scene" obscenely visible, demanding of viewers' own bodily gestures that they reveal and thereby potentially repair the failed witnessing of social media images, another example shows how there are some experiences that can best be made visible to others through their conspicuous invisibility in a digital image testimony. Between 20 August and 30 September 2017, Noa Jansma, a student in Amsterdam, set up an Instagram account called #dearcatcallers. Its mission statement read as follows:

> #dearcatcallers, it's not a compliment.
> This Instagram has the aim to create awareness about the objectification of women in daily life.
> Since many people still don't know how often and in whatever context "catcalling" happens, I'll be showing my catcallers within the period of one month.
> By making the selfie, both the objectifier and the object are assembled in one composition. Myself, as the object, standing in front of the catcallers represents the reversed power ratio which is caused by this project.
> Please join me in the fight and post your own #dearcatcallers or send me a DM.

Twenty-two selfies were posted in total during the month that the account was operational, each one showing an unsmiling Jansma looking into the camera, with a man or group of men, her catcallers, pictured beside or behind her, mostly smiling into the camera. The image would often be accompanied by a brief description or quotation of the catcall.

These images (see Figure 9.1) demonstrate the poetic force of the selfie as an intervention in the world, whereby a genre of communicative sociability (the selfie) aimed at distant, anonymous others, is used to witness the gendered power structures of embodied sociability in the street. Following Kompridis, we could argue that Jansma's selfies perform "reflective world-disclosure": through them, "background structures of intelligibility are reopened and transformed through novel interpretations and cultural practices" (Kompridis 2006, p. 34). In particular, they open up and transform the everyday performance of sociability as a self-evident phenomenon.

Yet in one sense it is odd to say that these images really disclose anything. They are certainly not technological proxies for eye-witnessing, as the Holocaust photographs are. Jansma is not an observer of an event; her photographs do not

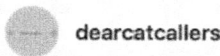

❤ 4,375 likes 🗨 282 comments

Mmmmmm beautiful sweet girl #dearcatcallers

AUGUST 30

Figure 9.1 Noa Jansma, Mmmmmm beautiful sweet girl, #dearcatcallers, 30 August 2017.

Source: © Noa Jansma.

record or depict catcalling, and are not evidence of it. Instead, the selfies are themselves new communicative events that Jansma has created across physical and digital spaces. They are examples of "flesh-witnessing": they say "I was there and this is what I experienced", though they do so in a very arresting and troubling fashion, one which both instantiates and manifests catcalling's character as invisible or inaccessible to subjective understanding for large sections of the population. They constitute a particular mode of reflective world-disclosure, which Kompridis calls "decentring", since they "stand in strikingly dissonant relations to already available meanings and familiar possibilities, to already existing ways of speaking, hearing, seeing, interpreting, and acting" (Kompridis 2006, p. 35).

Jansma's selfies are decentring in several obvious ways. First, composition-ally and spatially: Jansma's face is frequently cropped by the frame, and even when it is not she is still positioned to the side of her own image. Her catcallers are usually, in contrast, depicted in full. At the same time, however, she is always in the foreground, and they are usually in the background: she commands our attention and is clearly the creator and source of the selfie as a "gestural image", a deictic performance designed not only for the presentation of self but as an invitation to sociable companionship with viewers (Frosh 2018). Additionally, and against the long-standing convention of expressive consistency among participants in both group selfies and traditional group snapshots (we all try to smile together, or we all look serious and respectable at the same time), Jansma never smiles at the camera: her expression is hard to fathom precisely from the photograph alone, but it seems to combine determination, earnestness and defiance. The catcallers, in contrast, always smile, and often wave or gesticulate extravagantly.

These multiple decentrings suggest that the main topic of the image is located somewhere in between the human figures, in the non-figural and literally invisible relations between them, in the fact that far from the photographer of the selfie being pictorially and socially "composed" along with the male participants in the photographic scene, she, like the image itself, is thoroughly discomposed—"having lost one's self-possession; disturbed, agitated, unsettled" (OED, 2018)—as a result of the experience of catcalling. A further decentring put to work here is temporal: the event of the image, its reason for being, precedes the selfie (in this respect Jansma's images do follow the conventional temporality of witnessing). The selfie is a response to the catcalls, and not, as noted earlier, a record of them or, for that matter, a re-enactment of them (thus it is also the performance of a sensory decentring, from sound to vision). Again, the selfie presents its own centre of meaning and purpose as testimony to an event and an experience that is out of view, hidden, incapable of disclosure except elliptically, by the exposure of its very invisibility.

The final decentring is the mode of address. On the one hand the selfies are Noa Jansma's riposte to the catcallers, her censure of their behaviour, of their inability to distinguish between sociability in the street and harassment: this is the overt significance of the project name "dear catcallers"—the images are supposedly addressed to them. Yet the image does not show her admonishing them, but rather her and them addressing us, their unknown future viewers, by looking at the camera. It is not even as though they communicate with each other "through" us. Rather, the fact that the men smile and wave at us, and Jansma does not, generates a contrast that makes visible to their unseen viewers the men's inability to distinguish photographic sociability from reproach, selfie from critique, because their understanding of sociability is not put into crisis in the way that women's presence and visibility in the streets is constantly assailed by catcalls. This is made apparent in the number of (frequently insulting) comments on the #dearcatcallers Instagram page—alongside much support for her project—that maintained, continually, that the men were "just being friendly" (in the catcalls and in the selfies), and which blamed Jansma for misunderstanding their intentions.

#dearcatcallers is a powerful example of digitized flesh-witnessing. It enables the reflective disclosure of habitual, repetitive discomposure—of women by men—as a pervasive subjective experience of the lifeworld, one that remains, to very many of those who share its public spaces (catcallers), utterly concealed behind a lived ideology of "friendliness" and "flattery" (the perception that a catcall is a compliment). At the same time, it discloses how the selfie itself, and the mesh of bodily techno-social routines to which is has become bound (primarily the performative and behavioural norms of self-presentation within social media platforms), promote an ideology of networked sociability-at-a-distance that limits what can be witnessed. And the project performs this double disclosure in the form of a crisis in image testimony, a discomfiting crack in the self-evident signals of compositional equality and harmony—and putative levity—that have quickly become endemic to the selfie as a genre of digital communication with established conventions of appearance and performance. As image testimonies, Noa Jansma's photographs continually make viewers oscillate between recognition of the selfie as an embodied mode of sociability at a distance (the men are smiling), and critical judgement of a gendered "friendliness" that disguises harassment (the men are smiling). As with oscillations in the perception of optical gestalt illusions, it is difficult to engage with these modes of sociability simultaneously, yet each is haunted by the operations of the other. The catcalls of the men in the street are seemingly "rewarded" by a responsive act of apparent friendliness initiated by Jansma, their inclusion in her selfies; the compositional contrast between Jansma's stoical-defiant facial expression and the men's gregarious poses exposes the latter to critique both for their unembarrassed sociability in the selfie and for the harassment they have performed off-scene. The selfies repeatedly decentre conventions of acceptable and self-evidently "natural" interaction both on the street and in the digital network, keeping their conditions of intelligibility and legitimacy on the cusp of in/visibility through the very form that witnesses them, testing our ability to judge and respond.

World-witnessing and vital signs

If Yolocaust foregrounds how witnessing "in" digital media now enables and demands involvement at the minutest scales of habitual bodily interaction with our devices, and #dearcatcallers makes conspicuous the potentialities and limitations of new digital genres to witness the experience of victims of asymmetrical power structures, my final example takes witnessing to another level. It suggests that digital media networks and social media, by their very ubiquity and liveness, have become fully-fledged worlds of existence intimately and routinely intertwined with physical existence, and that image testimonies can bear witness to them. Digital media platforms are witnessable worlds. As such they are amenable to a third mode of witnessing which supplements the work of eye-witnessing and flesh-witnessing: world-witnessing. This third mode emerged with the rise of modern visual and audio-visual media, and its conceptualization draws on Ellis's (2000) analysis of the radically inclusive character of twentieth-century mass media "witness". By "world-witnessing" I mean that contemporary media do not just witness through conveying "objective" information or "subjective" experiences, but by routinely presenting for judgement actual worlds— or at least worlds generically interpreted by viewers as being actual. The profound ethical and ontological stakes attending digital media as witnessable worlds of existence, and of the world-witnessing that discloses them as such, is most acutely foregrounded at moments of extreme crisis: those potentially life-defining occasions where the fragility of life is made unbearably tangible.

On Monday 9 January 2017, the front page of *Yediot Ahronot*, one of Israel's most popular daily Hebrew newspapers, was devoted to the victims and survivors of an event that happened on the previous day (see Figure 9.2): a Palestinian driver had deliberately driven his truck into a group of soldiers disembarking from a bus on a popular promenade in Jerusalem, killing four of them. Unusually, the front page had no traditional headline. Instead, below the masthead, the entire upper half of the page was dominated by a screenshot from the smartphone of the mother of one of the dead soldiers, Shir Hajaj. The screenshot shows her WhatsApp instant messaging application and—as described by a caption—"the last message sent by Shir's mother to her daughter". The lines of text in the screenshot begin with the name of the person with whom contact is being attempted, including the name "Shiri", her WhatsApp profile image, and the formula—familiar to anyone who uses the app—"Last seen today at 12.39". Then there are these two messages which make up the main headline:

Shiri speak to me urgently 13:47
My darling [literally, "My life"] speak to me 16:46

Both of these lines are followed by two beige ticks.

This screenshot is nothing less than an "about to die" image (Zelizer 2010), a genre traditionally associated with photography, and which operates through the

Figure 9.2 Front page of print edition of *Yediot Aharonot*, 9 January 2017.

Source: © *Yediot Ahronot*.

intense oscillation between the photograph as evidence—the "as is"—and the photograph as a subjunctive cut in time—the "as if" of what could have transpired, but which we know did not.[5] It evokes a poetic sensibility of world-disclosure that is extraordinarily powerful. Part of the power of this screenshot has to do with the tragic irony of a conventional figure of speech no longer being figural. "My life", a common term of endearment in Hebrew among certain social groups, especially between parents and children, is made shockingly literal, becoming the question: you are my life, but are you alive? However, much of the poetic power has to do with inclusion of the commonplace indicators of "live" social media connectivity reproduced by the screenshot, and their sudden transformation: the word "last" in "last seen", now given terrible finality.[6]

Above all, the presence of the two ✓s and their telltale beige colour, showing that the message has been sent but—since they aren't blue—that it has not been read on the app by the intended recipient, because the intended is no longer either live, or alive. Abducted by the screenshot from the flux of the WhatsApp interface, these ordinary phatic signs of routine system functioning suddenly become poetically palpable as something far more serious. Extraneous details accompanying the main text of the mother's message, the wrongly-coloured ✓ are an existential glitch in the otherwise noiseless functioning of the communication channel (Menkman 2011, p. 12), as well as the site of a wound in the witnessed world. They are the accidental element "which rises from the scene, shoots out of it like an arrow, and pierces me" (Barthes 2000, p. 26): they are the punctum of the screenshot. They reveal the termination of connection not only within the mediated world the screenshot displays, but beyond it, disclosing the "grand interruption" of death (Lagerkvist & Andersson 2017).

No doubt there are biographical and contextual factors explaining the particular emotional resonance of these ticks and this screenshot for this author: cultural proximity to those killed, a pervasive (though far from unique) Israeli discourse which frames soldiers as "our children", a resemblance in parental position to Shir's mother (one child, so far, conscripted into the Israeli army), and other connections to this incident. Others less personally invested, or on the other side of the Israeli–Palestinian conflict, may feel differently. However, while the affective intensity of this particular screenshot is not universalizable, the screenshot's ubiquity and functioning as an image testimony which both attests to and makes present the worldliness of digital platforms, grant it this world-disclosing—and world-destroying—power. The pervasiveness of digital networks and devices and the "channel persistence" (Carr & Hayes 2015) of social media, our habituation to their live permeation and registration of everyday interactions and bodily movements, mean that symbols such as ✓ are no longer simply tokens of message delivery or task accomplishment: they have been delegated with existential powers as indicators of life, or to borrow an appropriate medical expression—vital signs.

W.J.T. Mitchell uses this term to argue for a consideration of the "varieties of animation or vitality that are attributed to images" (Mitchell 2005, p. 6).

However, the ticks in this screenshot are signs of life itself as a (fragile, finite) state of being, signifying life through technical infrastructures of connection and cultural conventions of imputed presence. And they are vital as some of our organs are vital: critical to the being of an organism. Moreover, the ticks stand in for a more general category of vital signs, which includes all multisensory indicators of connectivity conveyed through our devices. We carry these devices around, they are close to our bodies, frequently in direct, sensuously experienced contact with clothing or skin. Imagine Shir's mother not only seeing the ticks but also waiting for her smartphone to vibrate or emit a sound signalling an incoming message from her daughter. Vital signs routinely testify to the intense embodied presencing of others through our digital devices as near-perpetual companions in life, perhaps as never before. Tragically, the vitality of these signs is principally foregrounded, as it is here, when disclosed in a state of critical disconnection. An image testimony of that state, this screenshot shows us that social media and digital networks have become so intimately intertwined with our existence that they are far more than new infrastructures for circulating messages or managing social relationships. They are domains in which life and death are performed, experienced, and laid bare.

Conclusion

My three examples all emphasize the significance of social media witnessing as modes of explicit disclosure. At base, witnessing involves the representation of aspects of our world, which we have beheld or experienced, to others who have not. It is a deliberate communicative practice, rooted in notions of representational adequacy to the real, and designed to produce a part of the world before others, to bring it into their presence through disclosure. It is, of course, by no means a new phenomenon. Witnessing occupies a central position in legal, religious, scientific and philosophical traditions of thought that long predate both mass and digital media. Yet the advent and expansion of these media have transformed it, forcing us to encounter with ever greater frequency reports of far flung and often horrifying events, related by people whom we do not know personally. This unremitting exposure to the discourse of strangers about their lives has become a defining characteristic of what it means to be modern.

Yet something more has emerged in the case of networked digital technologies: a radical intensification of the possibilities for witnessing that reflect the existential conditions of contemporary "always on" mediation (Lagerkvist 2017). It is not simply that digital technologies expand the field of witnessing by conveying user-generated testimonies over social media networks. It is that digital media devices operate at new, often minute, scales of bodily action, registered by live networks of perpetual presence, which implicate us as witnesses-in-potential more than ever in the demand for responsiveness to others. The old dichotomies no longer hold (if they ever did): the technologized eye-witnessing of Holocaust photographs used in the Yolocaust website requires the fleshly responsiveness of viewer's hands on their digital devices; the flesh-witnessing of personal experience via selfies in #dearcatcallers demands viewers' optical scrutiny of a barely visible core of offence. And, above all, image testimonies reveal digital media themselves as witnessable worlds—vital domains of being—that are constantly immanent to our bodies and our lives with others.

Notes

1 This chapter extends ideas and examples that are discussed in my book, *The Poetics of Digital Media* (2018).
2 I have put "selfies" in quotation marks because many of the social media images designated inappropriate by Yolocaust were not actually selfies, but were clearly taken by others. Hence "selfies" is used on the Yolocaust site (and in much of the subsequent media coverage) as a term of moral opprobrium for all of the offending photographs. See Burns (2015) on the denigration of the selfie in public discourse.
3 The faces in them are often pixelated, however. Designed by Peter Eisenman and Buro Happold, The Berlin Holocaust Memorial, also known as the Memorial to the Murdered Jews of Europe, follows an abstract design characterized by long rows of huge concrete slabs arranged in a grid formation on a large field, and can easily be perceived by visitors as a space of play. See Dekel (2013) for an extensive discussion of mediation and memory at the memorial.
4 I use the term "scene" to indicate the ontological non-priority of the event over its mediation: photography produces a scene—a visual mediation—which is then established as a version of the event (and which retrospectively contributes to the eventfulness of the event). I also use it to indicate—in line with much photography theory—that the socio-cultural significance of photographic indexicality is highly variable, discursively shaped and not naturally given.
5 For a detailed exploration of the aesthetics and poetics of the screenshot as a digital document, a remediated photograph and a mode of witnessing, see Frosh (2018).
6 On WhatsApp, as of writing, while the default "last seen" feature can be turned off in the system settings, the "online" indicator cannot. There are additional forms of graphical remediation performed by this screenshot, such as the slight angle at which the screenshot seems to have been "pasted" onto the news page, which reinforce its connection to pre-digital documents as physical objects and to their evidential "know-show" function (Gitelman 2014).

References

Agamben, G. (1999). *The Man without Content*. Stanford, CA: Stanford University Press.
Andén-Papadopoulos, K. (2014). Citizen camera-witnessing: Embodied political dissent in the age of "mediated mass self-communication". *New Media & Society*, 16(5), pp. 753–769.
Barthes, R. (2000). *Camera Lucida: Reflections on Photography*. London: Fontana.
Burns, A.L. (2015). Self(ie)-discipline: Social regulation as enacted through the discussion of photographic practice. *International Journal of Communication*, 9, pp. 1716–1733.
Carey, J.W. (1992). *Communication as Culture: Essays on Media and Society*. London: Routledge.

Carr, C.T. & Hayes, R.A. (2015) Social media: Defining, developing, and divining. *Atlantic Journal of Communication*, 23(1), pp. 46–65.

Chouliaraki. L. (2017). Symbolic bordering: The self-representation of migrants and refugees in digital news. *Popular Communication*, 15(2), pp. 78–94.

Dekel, I. (2013). *Mediation at the Holocaust Memorial in Berlin*. London: Palgrave Macmillan.

Ellis, J. (2000). *Seeing Things: Television in the Age of Uncertainty*. London: I.B. Tauris.

Frosh, P. (2018). *The Poetics of Digital Media*. Cambridge, UK: Polity.

Frosh, P. & Pinchevski, A. (2009). Why media witnessing? Why now? In P. Frosh & A. Pinchevski (eds), *Media Witnessing: Testimony in the Age of Mass Communication*, pp. 1–19. London: Palgrave Macmillan.

Frosh, P. & Pinchevski, A. (2014). Media witnessing and the ripeness of time. *Cultural Studies*, 28(4), pp. 594–610.

Gitelman, L. (2014). *Paper Knowledge: Toward a Media History of Documents*. Durham: Duke University Press.

Harari, Y.N. (2009). Scholars, eyewitnesses, and flesh-witnesses of war: A tense relationship. *Partial Answers: Journal of Literature and the History of Ideas*, 7(2), pp. 213–228.

Jakobson, R. (1960). Linguistics and poetics. In T. Sebeok (ed.), *Style in Language*, pp. 350–377. Cambridge, MA: MIT Press.

Kompridis, N. (2006). *Critique and Disclosure: Critical Theory between Past and Future*. Cambridge, MA: MIT Press.

Kurasawa, F. (2009). A message in a bottle: Bearing witness as a mode of transnational practice. *Theory, Culture & Society*, 26(1), pp. 92–111.

Lagerkvist, A. (2017). Existential media: Toward a theorization of digital thrownness. *New Media & Society*, 19(1), pp. 96–110.

Lagerkvist, A. & Andersson, Y. (2017). The grand interruption: death online and mediated lifelines of shared vulnerability. *Feminist Media Studies*, 17(4), pp. 550–564. Available from: www.tandfonline.com/doi/pdf/10.1080/14680777.2017.1326554?need Access=true [6 July 2018].

Literat, I. (2017). Refugee selfies and the (self-)representation of disenfranchised social groups. *Media Fields Journal*, 12, pp. 1–9.

Manovich, L. (2001). *The Language of New Media*. Cambridge, MA: MIT Press.

Menkman, R. (2011). *The Glitch Moment(um), Network Notebooks*. Amsterdam: Institute of Network Cultures.

Mitchell, W.J.T. (2005). *What Do Pictures Want? The Lives and Loves of Images*. Chicago: University of Chicago Press.

Moores, S. (2014). Digital orientations: "Ways of the hand" and practical knowing in media uses and other manual activities. *Mobile Media & Communication*, 2(2), pp. 196–208.

OED (2018). Oxford English Dictionary Online. Oxford: Oxford University Press.

Peters, J.D. (2001). Witnessing. *Media, Culture & Society*, 23(6), pp. 707–724.

Sommer, A.K. (2017). No more Shoah selfies: Why the controversial "Yolocaust" project was taken down. *Ha'aretz*, 27 January. Available from: www.haaretz.com/jewish/.premium-why-the-yolocaust-project-was-taken-down-1.5491110 [6 July 2018].

Zelizer, B. (2010). *About to Die: How News Images Move the Public*. Oxford: Oxford University Press.

Part IV

Witnessing destruction

Chapter 10

"Living martyrs"

Testifying what is to come

Verena Straub

Research addressing new forms of witnessing on social media tends to focus on the phenomenon of citizen witnesses. Online platforms such as YouTube, Facebook or Twitter, however, have also provided new spaces for perpetrators to articulate their views and make them easily accessible to global audiences. Terror organizations such as the so-called Islamic State produce and distribute a variety of audio-visual material online.[1] These videos document brutal executions, the destruction of cultural heritage sites (see the contribution of Christoph Günther and Tom Bioly in this volume) and serve as testimonies to their belief. Any discussion concerning online practices of image testimony thus cannot limit itself merely to the accounts of victims, innocent bystanders or human rights activists, but must also consider testimonies disseminated by militant groups or terror organizations. As philosopher Sybille Schmidt has recently pointed out, perpetrator testimony remains a blind spot in theories of witnessing (Schmidt 2017, p. 87). While much has been written about the witness as a moral and ethical figure, perpetrator testimonies remind us that witnessing is not per se "good" or ethically valuable, as Schmidt has noted, but "normatively ambivalent, depending on what purpose it serves" (Schmidt 2017, p. 90). Following Schmidt, in this text I aim at shifting perspectives to ask how perpetrator testimonies require us to re-examine concepts of witnessing and our approaches to understanding them. In what follows, I will discuss videos of suicide bombers as one special genre of perpetrator testimonies. These audio-visual recordings are commonly referred to as "video testimonies" (Hasso 2005). The labelling of these videos as testimony, of course, raises a number of questions: what exactly is being testified in these videos, who acts as the witness, and what modes of witnessing are at play? Before I take a closer look at the different modalities of witnessing, I will first consider more broadly how these videos emerged as a "genre".

The genre of suicide bombers' videos: a historical perspective

A quick look at the history of suicide bombers' videos demonstrates the sheer diversity of the political, ideological and religious contexts in which these videos appeared. The practice of recording suicide bombers' videos first appeared amongst secular and left-wing militant organizations in the mid-1980s in Lebanon. After the Israeli army invaded Lebanon at the height of the civil war in 1982, various competing militant groups staged suicide attacks against Israeli military bases in southern Lebanon. In the first video testimonies released by the Syrian Social Nationalist Party and the Lebanese Communist Party, the future suicide bombers are seen rigidly seated facing the camera while announcing their intentions and motivations for committing their attacks. Even though these early suicide bombers and their attacks were not framed in religious terms, the individuals nonetheless established the convention of identifying themselves as martyrs in front of the camera (in Arabic: ash-shaheed/a). Martyrdom, in these contexts, primarily referred to self-sacrifice for the nation and for the party's political conviction. In one of the earliest examples, a 17-year-old girl who would commit a suicide attack on 9 April 1985, commences her video address with the words: "I am the martyr Sanā' Yūsif Muhaydlī. [...] I am not dead, but alive among you" (Khalili 2007, p. 13). The locution "I am the martyr" has since become the central characteristic of suicide bombers' videos. Another prominently recurring motif in these early videos was the verbal and visual reference to previous self-declared martyrs. In most of these videos, the future suicide bombers are seen in front of walls covered with images of preceding martyrs, often taken from previous video testimonies (Figure 10.1). By establishing a visual net of reference and re-enacting the video testimony of previous suicide bombers, these early videos helped consolidate a recognizable audio-visual genre. According to Stanley Cavell, the affiliation of films to a certain genre is defined precisely by the relations they form: "They are what they are in view of one another" (Cavell 2003, p. 29).

Figure 10.1 Screenshot retrieved from the video testimony of Lebanese Communist Party member Jamāl Sāti who committed a suicide attack on 6 August 1985.

Source: www.youtube.com/watch?v=pRICEAYXmqw, uploaded by "ellaoz kamed" on 23 October 2013 [17 July 2018].

Since the 1990s, both Shiite parties such as the Lebanese Hezbollah, as well as Sunnite Islamic militant groups, have adopted this video practice from secular parties. Each adaptation developed the genre further by implementing additional scenes, incorporating the party's own "corporate design" or adding a more developed choreography to the visual narrative of this genre. A peak of suicide bombers' videos occurred during the second Palestinian Intifada (2000–2005), when suicide attacks against Israel were employed in huge numbers by various militant groups such as the Al-Aqsa Martyr Brigades, Hamas or Islamic Jihad. In addition to reading their testimony to the camera, the self-declared living martyrs were seen kneeling down to pray and striking various poses with a Qur'an and a Kalashnikov. In recent years, video testimonies of suicide bombers have mainly been produced by radical Islamic Jihadi groups such as the Taliban in Afghanistan, Al-Shabab in Somalia, Boko Haram in Nigeria as well as globally acting terror networks such as Al-Qaida or the so-called Islamic State. I want to emphasize again that the political and ideological contexts in which organizations make use of suicide bombings differ significantly. The aims connected with suicide bombings in the above-mentioned examples vary from regional struggles against foreign occupations and the liberation of the homeland (as in the Lebanese and Palestinian contexts), to the religious rhetoric of a global jihad. When I talk about these videos as a "genre," it is therefore not to level out these political differences and regional specificities, but to present distinct instances of how this specific type of image came to be appropriated, modified and further developed.

What started as simple one-shot messages increasingly turned into dramatically complex productions. The so-called Islamic State in particular has expanded the genre of suicide bombers' video testimonies in recent years by creating feature-length videos, assembled by a variety of different video footage and computer-animated graphics. Compared with the home-video aesthetic of early video testimonies, IS-productions are distinguished by a high level of technical know-how and careful aesthetic deliberation informed by popular culture. Further, the distribution of these videos changed significantly: while the video recordings of suicide bombers during the Lebanese civil war were sent to public TV-stations, were sold as VHS-cassette copies at kiosks in Beirut (Maasri 2009, p. 123) or—in the case of Hezbollah—disseminated via their own TV channel,[2] the digital audio-visual recordings today almost exclusively circulate online. In the digital age, video testimonies of suicide bombers are shared, downloaded, appropriated and re-posted in manifold ways and migrate between different devices and locations. The Islamic State in particular has maximized its reach by exploiting a variety of social media platforms, but also by decentralizing its media productions. Their video content is produced by a number of autonomously operating media companies from West Africa to the Caucasus (Koerner 2016). Yet, despite various technical, media and dramaturgical developments, the centerpiece of suicide bombers' videos today still remains the reading of their testimonies (Figure 10.2). The 45 minute long video produced by the IS in 2008, which I will discuss in more

Figure 10.2 Still image showing the suicide bomber Abū Usāma al-Maddanī reading his testimony (al-waṣīya). Islamic State Iraq/al-Furqān media production: "Fursān aš-šahāda" ("Knights of the testimony of faith"), 45:17 min., 2008.

Source: https://archive.org/details/Forsan-Ashahada5 [17 July 2018].

detail below, also contains the characteristic testimony scenes introduced by the subheading, al-waṣīya, meaning "the testimony." The rigid aesthetic setting still draws from earlier models and makes reference to a number of visual conventions advanced since the 1980s. For instance, the individuals are typically filmed frontally, facing the camera while reading their testimony; they are seen surrounded by Kalashnikovs and copies of the Qur'an, while the background is delimited by ornamented cloths or flags with party emblems. In addition to their statements of intention and words of farewell, the future suicide bombers recite Qur'anic verses that mention the rewards of martyrdom in Paradise. Regardless of their political or religious affiliation, the most common characteristic that defines these videos as a genre is the future suicide bombers' self-reference as shaheed, as martyr.

Suicide bombers' videos as anticipatory testimonies

The figure of the shaheed can serve as a starting point for thinking about the issues of testimony or witnessing. Like the Greek word martyr, the Arabic term shaheed means "witness." It is derived from the Arabic verbal root shahada, which literally means to "see," to "witness," to "testify," to "become a model and paradigm" (Ezzati 1986). In the current discourse on testimony, the martyr is often described as one of three modes of witnessing. Both Michal Givoni (2011) and Didier Fassin (2008) differentiate between three different witness-figures or modalities of giving testimony. The first kind, derived from the Latin word testis, is the modality of the eye-witness whose testimony is based on the observation of facts. "The truth of the testis," Fassin notes, "is deemed objective" and often conveyed as a third-person account of the events that happened (Fassin 2008, p. 535). In contrast, the testimony of the survivor-witness, derived from the Latin term *superstes*, is a decidedly subjective account of the events. This second modality of witnessing is based on personal experience and is conveyed in the first person. Fassin concludes that "the latter [superstes] has merit by virtue of the affects it involves, the former [testis] by virtue of those it eliminates" (Fassin 2008, p. 535). Finally, a third modality of witnessing is indicated with the figure of the martyr whose testimony is based on action, meaning the act of self-sacrifice. At first sight, this form of witnessing seems to be the predominant mode with suicide bombings. Both secular and religious militant groups glorify their suicide bombers as shuhada, as martyrs, following the attack. According to the supporters' view, the bombers sacrifice their life in order to testify to a higher political and/or religious truth. Thus, the act of suicide bombing itself is interpreted by them as an act of witnessing. According to Didier Fassin, the testimony of the martyr is a testimony not with words, but with the body. He writes: "Unlike the survivor or the observer, who speak in the first or third person, the martyr bears witness without speaking: he testifies through the sacrifice of his life" (Fassin 2008, p. 541). In the case of video testimonies of suicide bombers, however, the self-acclaimed martyrs do speak. The bodily testimony of the martyr is anticipated by an image testimony in which additional modes of witnessing become operative. By giving a first-person account about their new status as shaheed, the depicted individuals seem to take on the impossible position of a survivor-witness. This becomes especially obvious in an utterance such as "I am not dead, but alive among you" (Sanaa Muhaydli, see Khalili 2007, p. 13) or "I am still alive."[3] The would-be suicide bombers do not announce "I will become a martyr once I have died," or "I promise to die as a martyr and gain eternal life"—statements that would have been plausible in the situation of video recording. Instead they proclaim: "I am the martyr." Far more than an announcement of intention, a promise or an oath, this spoken statement acts as a kind of testimony to an already-sustained martyrdom. Unlike typical survivor testimonies, however, the self-acclaimed martyrs do not bear witness to something that has happened to them in the past, but to an event that has not yet taken place. The witness speaks to us viewers from an imagined future, which—in the moment of videotaping—is yet to come. Thus, neither the testimony of the martyr, nor the testimony of the survivor-witness suffices to describe the unique character of these image testimonies. Since the temporalities of testimony play out in reverse, it is necessary to expand the typology of testimony. Bearing this in mind, I suggest that we consider these videos as forms of anticipatory image testimonies.

Introducing the possibility of an anticipatory testimony, however, also means challenging some common and fundamental assumptions about the nature of testimony/witnessing (see Schmidt 2015). Following the "Evidential View" on witnessing, one could easily dismiss the testimony-status of the suicide bombers' video statements. After all, the notion that testimonies provide evidence or proof to an event that already happened in the past, is here turned upside down. Many scholars have turned away from a singular focus on the evidentiary nature of testimony, emphasizing instead the social and relational character of giving testimony.[4] Yet, what has become known as the "Assurance View" within testimony research turns out to be not very fruitful, either, when talking about the videos of suicide bombers. Testimony, according to this view, is dependent on both the witnesses' assurance to tell the truth as well as the trust of the audience members, who need to accept the witnesses' accounts as testimonies. The act of testimony, then, would only be fulfilled and realized by the time supporters accept the death of the depicted as "martyrdom." By the time of the video performance, however, one could hardly speak of the individuals' testimonies as "believable," since the "truth" of the spoken words was still to come. Thus, if we decide to refer to these videos as testimonies, it becomes clear that neither their evidentiary character ("Evidential View") nor their "credibility" ("Assurance View") capture the unique position and the special force of these testimonies. One could argue, of course, that the videos merely employ the rhetoric of survivor witnesses and constitute purely imaginary or fictional testimonies. Yet, what gives these audio-visual recordings their eerie character is that reality eventually catches up with them. By the time the video gets published, one can be quite certain that the depicted has in fact died, even though one might not accept this death as "martyrdom." There are, of course, video testimonies of individuals who did not go through with their attack, who were detained and imprisoned. In these cases, however, the audio-visual recordings remain hidden or get destroyed by the responsible party. Since the prerequisite for their visibility is the actual death of the individual, suicide bombers' video testimonies are connected to the reality of the so-called martyrdom operation in quite disturbing ways, and can hardly be dismissed as purely imaginary or fictional.

Despite the dissonance with common lines of testimony theory, I suggest that thinking about the suicide bombers' videos as anticipatory testimonies can offer fruitful insights into the unique status of mediatized testimonies and their intricate relation to time. Because, what is most crucial here is that we are dealing with testimonies for the camera. As the words of the self-acclaimed martyrs gain validity and significance only after their so-called martyrdom attack, the mediatization of their words is the very condition for their status as testimonies. Unlike other mediatized testimonies, which could be received by a live audience without losing their status as testimonies, the meaning of the suicide bombers' video testimonies depends on their deferred mediatization to a future audience. As soon as we accept that image testimonies can also testify to an event in the future, we are faced with an entirely new set of questions about the agency of these images. What is the image testimonies' relation to the referred event, if they do not represent, document, or recount the event, but precede its happening?

As a proof of commitment and determination before the deed, the video testimony of the suicide bomber serves as a fatal record. Joshua Simon has pointed out:

> when filmed, the Shaheeds do sentence themselves to death, simply because the existence of tapes in which they are seen swearing to die as martyrs [...] makes them what military intelligence calls "ticking bombs," meaning they will be tracked down and targeted.
>
> (Simon 2009, p. 43)

Given the fatal risk in producing these videos, the question arises as to why individuals and organizations create such incriminating material before carrying out their attacks. According to several organizers of suicide attacks during the Second Palestinian Intifada, who were interviewed in Israeli prisons by psychologist Ariel Merari, these video recordings fulfill important purposes. A member of Hamas stated: "The videotaping is actually a contract between the candidate and the organizer" (Merari et al. 2009, p. 113). In a similar vein, a Fatah organizer said: "The videotaped reading of the testament creates a situation of commitment to complete [the mission]. There is no way back!" (Merari et al. 2009, p. 113). These self-declarations resonate with Mark Harrison's interpretation of the martyr video as a "contract" between the organization and the individual. Harrison argues for a reading of suicide bombing as "a voluntary agreement between the faction and the young person to trade life for identity" (Harrison 2006, p. 1). He claims that, in addition to other political, religious or individual motivations, the promise of gaining an identity as a martyr is one driving factor for mobilization. The practice of videotaping forces these individuals to actually go through with the attack, while also assuring that they will leave a lasting image of themselves as martyrs and heroes. As I have argued, these image testimonies indeed result from a contract between individual and organization when they are recorded as videos, and therefore not only anticipate the future suicide attack, but also in fact set the stage for it to occur (Straub 2016). Viewed in this light, the video-recordings are constituent agents in the construction of the event that is set into motion by the image testimonies. To put it another way, video testimonies of suicide bombers do not give evidence but create evidence. This is not to say that without the image testimony, the suicide bombing would not take place. Or, that every suicide bombing is necessarily preceded by the recording of a testimony. But once the video recording exists as physical evidence, it functions as a motor and driving force towards the fulfillment of the promise and the anticipated martyr identity.

In order to fully grasp the agency of these anticipatory testimonies, it is necessary to put a special emphasis on their bodily and affective dimensions. Another way of describing the video performances of would-be suicide bombers is to draw on the concept of (p)reenactment (Czirak et al. 2019). As I argued above, the recording of the video testimony is closely entangled between past, present and future. On the one hand, the individuals re-enact preceding martyr testimonies from the past by relating to the aesthetic, rhetorical and performative qualities of the genre and by explicitly referring to their predecessors. On the other hand, the performances are just as much directed towards the future, and can be viewed as pre-enactments of their imagined persona as martyrs. The unique temporal disposition of (p)reenactments is fundamentally characterized by a multilayered assemblage of affective dynamics (Czirak et al. 2019; Schneider 2011). In the case of suicide bombers' camera performances, the affective potentiality of the recording situation oscillates between the emotional value ascribed to preceding martyrs (e.g., admiration, pride, veneration) and an affectively charged vision of their own status as martyrs in the future. The corporeal experience of the individual who states "I am the martyr" in front of the camera thus constitutes and shapes a certain affective orientation towards the upcoming suicide attack, making it feel like a desirable and noble endeavor. Similar to what Richard Grusin has described as the "affective prophylactic" of "premediations," the video anticipations of suicide bombers impact and modulate future affective states, while at the same time drawing on examples from the past (Grusin 2010, p. 46). This affective (p)reenactment can thus be described as one key element of how these videos set the stage for what is about to happen.

Postproduction as a form of co-witnessing

Thus far, I have discussed the different roles of the suicide bombers as witnesses, and the transformative agency of the act of recording the testimony. As I indicated earlier, martyr videos of suicide bombers are today highly edited artefacts that employ techniques of montage and slow-motion, and expand the video testimonies with additional footage. The second argument that I want to put forth is that the producers and editors of these videos act as co-witnesses to the martyrdom of the depicted. I substantiate this claim by discussing the example of a video testimony, produced by one of the Islamic State's media agencies, al-Furqān. The video, which is 45 minutes long, was released in 2008, and combines the testimonies of three Saudi suicide bombers who detonated bombs in different locations in Iraq. In the course of the feature-length production, each of the three suicide bombers is introduced by a voice-over and text, giving the viewer some biographical details about the individual and praising his willingness for jihad. The first intro of "the martyr Abū Usāma al-Maddanī" is followed by the recording of his testimony (see Figure 10.2) and several scenes of farewell in which the individual is seen reciting verses, praying with his comrades and hugging them goodbye. The scenes are compiled with Qur'anic verses, divided by computer animated subheadings, and complemented by speeches of Islamic State's authorities. Eventually, a sequence at around 14 minutes into the video starts with the subheading tanfīḏ al-ʿamalīya, meaning "Execution of the Operation" (Figure 10.3).[5]

First, we see footage shot from a camera mounted on the outside of the explosive-laden truck showing the would-be suicide bomber Abū Usāma al-Maddanī driving to the target. The following scene is filmed at a distance and shows the vehicle driving on a street behind a concrete wall. As the truck is blocked from sight by the wall most of the time, a superimposed red arrow traces its barely visible movements. In addition, a didactic caption explains the context and route of the vehicle. It says: "Brother al-Maddanī drives towards the station," meaning the police station in Tigris, where the attack took place. Right before the explosion, the video image is slowed down and the footage of the blast is repeated three times in succession, with the third time played back in slow-motion. I would like to suggest that this scene introduces yet another mode of witnessing to the video as a whole. The—what I call—anticipatory testimony of the "martyr" is juxtaposed with camera eye-witness accounts of the actual explosion: a visual strategy that corresponds with the testimony of the testis. The video documentation of the attack as well as the didactic charting and explanation of what happened claims to provide evidence to the operation and to verify the martyr's promises. The distant camera-observer acts as co-witness to the act of martyrdom. This is by no means a new visual strategy in suicide bombers' video testimonies, as examples by Hezbollah demonstrate. As early as 1995, Hezbollah started to incorporate footage of the attack itself, which functions as the dramaturgic climax of the video testimony. In contrast, however, the explosion in the Islamic State's video does not mark the video's conclusion. Footage by the blast is superimposed by a revisited sequence of al-Maddanī's testimony, in which he is seen saying "I will surrender myself to God, I will support this Religion and achieve Paradise where I will face God" (Figure 10.4). First, his image is seen surrounded by representations of rubble, a clear reference to the destructive effects of his suicide attack. Shortly after, the rubble transforms into red tulip blossoms, which in Shiite Islamic iconography symbolize martyrdom in the name of God.[6] Today, this symbol is increasingly borrowed by Sunni Islamic groups, such as the Islamic State, in reference to their "martyrs." The final syllables of the recorded testimony ("facing God") are repeated three times until the image of the martyr vanishes behind a shower of

(a)

(b)

(c)

Figure 10.3 (a)–(c) Three still images of a sequence starting with the subheading tanfīḏ al-ʿamalīya, "Execution of the Operation"
(13:57–15:10). Islamic State Iraq/al-Furqān media production:
"Fursān aš-šahāda" ("Knights of the testimony of faith"),
45:17 min., 2008.

Source: https://archive.org/details/Forsan-Ashahada5 [17 July 2018].

(a)

(b)

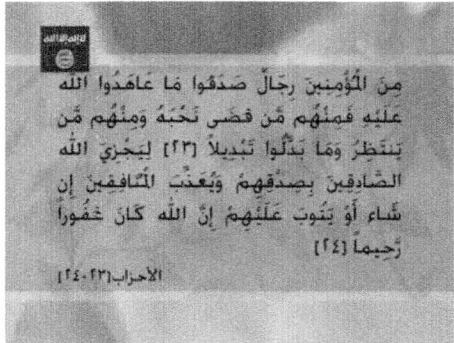

(c)

Figure 10.4 (a)–(c) Three still images of a sequence following the filming of the explosion (15:10–16:03). Islamic State Iraq/al-Furqān media production: "Fursān aš-šahāda" ("Knights of the testimony of faith"), 45:17 min., 2008.

Source: https://archive.org/details/Forsan-Ashahada5 [17 July 2018].

red blossoms. The montage finally culminates with the display and recitation of the Qur'an sura 33:23–24 that commences with the words:

> There are some remarkable men among the believers who have been true to the covenant they made with Allâh. There are some among them who fulfilled their vow (and fell martyrs). [...] Allâh may reward the truthful for their having been true (to their covenant).
>
> (The Qur'an: 33:23–24)

The transformation from the earthly to the heavenly (the reward of becoming a martyr) as indicated by this sura, is manifested here by means of audio-visual postproduction. What al-Maddanī anticipates in the reading of his testimony— namely him entering Paradise as a martyr—is visually testified by ways of montage. A similar aesthetic strategy is employed at the end of the video, when the video images of all three suicide bombers appear amidst a computer-generated blue sky (Figure 10.5). We could describe these postproduction

Figure 10.5 Still image of suicide bomber Abū al-ʿAbbās al-Makkī's testimony mounted in front of a computer-animated sky (39:51–40:48). Islamic State Iraq/al-Furqān media production: "Fursān aš-šahāda" ("Knights of the testimony of faith"), 45:17 min., 2008.

Source: https://archive.org/details/Forsan-Ashahada5 [17 July 2018].

sequences as fabricated eye-witnessing accounts that symbolically testify that the depicted individuals are not dead but gained God's esteem as martyrs in heaven.

At no point in the video, however, do these eye-witness-accounts claim to speak from the position of an objective or non-involved witness. On the contrary, the postproduction of the video material and its dramaturgic development appeals to the viewers' affective reactions. This holds especially true for the soundtrack of nasheed-songs, which permeates the entire video. So-called nasheeds are Islamic acapella chants, which in militant and jihadi contexts often invoke topics of holy war and martyrdom and call for participation in combat (Said 2012). Jihadi nasheeds are very popular on the internet and, for instance, are circulated in huge numbers on YouTube. As Behnam Said emphasizes, nasheeds can be considered especially powerful recruitment tools as they appeal to sympathizers on both a rational and emotional level (Said 2012, p. 875). The strongly affective and appellative character of the video reminds us that the visual strategies of co-witnessing in the videos must also be understood as propaganda tools that aim at the mobilization of potential recruits, and ultimately at the creation of future martyrs.

Deconstructing truth-claims

What video testimonies of suicide bombers demonstrate is that every witness depends on a co-witness to accept and to testify to their truth. As I have suggested with the Islamic States' video, the act of co-witnessing can take place on the level of the image itself. However, as media theorists such as John Ellis, Paul Frosh and Amit Pinchevski have argued, the act of co-witnessing also extends to viewers in front of the screen, who share responsibility for the testimony process simply by taking part in it (Ellis 2000; Frosh & Pinchevski 2009). If we accept the assumption that an act of testimony is a relational process that also involves mediated forms of witnessing, we have to ask: what is our own position as viewers when watching and discussing these videos that have become so easily accessible online? While this question is relevant for all kinds of testimony, it is especially pressing when confronted with perpetrators' testimonies such as the videos produced by the Islamic State. Sibylle Schmidt has pointed to the moral dilemma that results from a study of perpetrator testimony. She argues that if we want to learn from testimonies as a source of truth, it "presupposes the authorization of the witness and that this act of accreditation is a form of recognition and empowerment" (Schmidt 2017, p. 102). Schmidt continues: "In the case of perpetrator testimony, this brings up a moral problem, since it runs the risk of re-enacting the authoritarian violence, and victimizing the victims once again" (Schmidt 2017, p. 102). However, as I argued earlier, in the special case of anticipatory testimonies, this problem has to be posed differently. In highlighting the agency of these testimonies, I have put forth the argument that suicide bombers' testimonies should not be regarded as epistemic documents that could tell us anything about what "really" happened. Equally misleading is the question of whether the speakers' accounts seem "believable" or not, and whether we can trust or mistrust their words. Instead, the chronological inversion that characterizes these anticipatory testimonies necessarily shifts our focus to the transformative power of the testimony performance itself. The act of recording serves as a critical force in the (affective) construction of "martyrdom," which is then co-witnessed and further fabricated by the producers of the video. Therefore, rather than asking what we can learn about a "truth" by viewing these videos, the relevant question is how the perpetrators' truth is constructed by audio-visual strategies of testimony. Describing and analyzing suicide bombers' videos as anticipatory testimonies does not mean to accept these testimonies as sources of evidence. On the contrary, an anticipatory perspective deconstructs the truth-claims that these videos attempt to make.

Notes

1 According to the 2015 report *Documenting the Virtual Caliphate* by the Quilliam Foundation, the Islamic State releases, on average, 38 new items per day, many of them images, ranging from photographs and short clips to feature-length videos (see Koerner 2016).
2 Hezbollah's own TV station Al-Manar started broadcasting in June 1991. For a comprehensive discussion see Jorisch (2004).
3 Ali Ghazi Taleb, another suicide bomber of the SSNP, says in his video testimony preceding his attack on 31 July 1985: "My last request to you is not to wear black on my death—because I am still alive" (cited in Graitl 2012, p. 234).
4 As Sibylle Schmidt discusses in more detail, this view on testimony was particularly shaped by Angus Ross and Richard Moran (Schmidt 2015, p. 117). Angus Ross, for example, defined the process of testimony as follows: "The speaker, in taking responsibility for the truth of what he is saying, is offering his hearer not evidence, but a guarantee that it is true, and in believing what he is told the hearer accepts this guarantee" (Ross 1986, p. 79).
5 I am grateful to Christoph Günther for the translation of the Arabic language video.
6 In the Shiite–Persian tradition the red tulip is one of the most common symbols for martyrs. It refers to the belief that from martyrs' blood red tulips will blossom. Iranian poet Arif Qazvini evoked this symbol (whose genealogy is not fully investigated yet) at the time of the Iranian Constitutional Revolution (1905–1911) in a poem talking about fallen revolutionaries: "From the blood of the youth of this homeland/Tulips have grown/ Mourning their tall fallen figures [...]" (cited in Dabashi 2012, pp. 268–269). Many murals and posters commemorating martyrs during the Iranian war with Iraq, as well as martyr posters by the Shiite Lebanese Hezbollah are typically adorned with red tulips.

References

Cavell, S. (2003). *Pursuits of Happiness: The Hollywood Comedy of Remarriage*. Cambridge, MA: Harvard University Press.
Czirak, A., Nikoleit, S., Oberkrome, F., Straub, V., Walter-Jochum, R., & Wetzels, M. (2019). (P)reenactment. In J. Slaby & C. von Scheve (eds), *Affective Societies: Key Concepts*. New York and London: Routledge.

Dabashi, H. (2012). *The World of Persian Literary Humanism*. Cambridge, MA: Harvard University Press.

Ellis, J. (2000). *Seeing Things: Television in the Age of Uncertainty*. London: I.B. Tauris.

Ezzati, A. (1986). The concept of martyrdom in Islam. Al-Islam.org, 12. Available from: www.al-islam.org/al-serat/vol-12-1986/concept-martyrdom-islam [2 May 2018].

Fassin, D. (2008). The humanitarian politics of testimony: Subjectification through trauma in the Israeli: Palestinian conflict. *Cultural Anthropology*, 3, p. 531.

Frosh, P. & Pinchevski, A. (eds) (2009). *Media Witnessing: Testimony in the Age of Mass Communication*. Basingstoke: Palgrave Macmillan.

Givoni, M. (2011). Witnessing/testimony. *Mafte'akh: Lexical Review of Political Thought*, 2, pp. 147–169. Available from: http://mafteakh.tau.ac.il/en/wp-content/uploads/2011/01/Witnessing_Testimony-.pdf [2 May 2018].

Graitl, L. (2012). *Sterben als Spektakel: Zur kommunikativen Dimension des politisch motivierten Suizids*. Wiesbaden: Springer.

Grusin, R.A. (2010). *Premediation: Affect and Mediality after 9/11*. New York: Palgrave Macmillan.

Harrison, M. (2006). An economist looks at suicide terrorism. *World Economics*, 7(3), pp. 1–15.

Hasso, F.S. (2005) Discursive and political deployments by/of the 2002 Palestinian women suicide bombers/martyrs. *Feminist Review*, 81, pp. 23–51.

Jorisch, A. (2004). Al-Manar: Hizbullah TV, 24/7. *Middle East Quarterly*, XI(1), pp. 17–31.

Khalili, L. (2007). *Heroes and Martyrs of Palestine: The Politics of National Commemoration*. Cambridge, UK: Cambridge University Press.

Koerner, B.I. (2016). Why ISIS is winning the social media war. *WIRED*, April issue. Available from: www.wired.com/2016/03/isis-winning-social-media-war-heres-beat/ [2 May 2018].

Maasri, Z. (2009). *Off the Wall: Political Posters of the Lebanese Civil War*. London: I.B. Tauris.

Merari, A., Fighel, J., Ganor, B., Lavie, E., Tzoreff, Y., & Livne, A. (2009). Making Palestinian "martyrdom operations"/"suicide attacks": Interviews with would-be perpetrators and organizers. *Terrorism and Political Violence*, 22(1), pp. 102–119.

Ross, A. (1986). Why do we believe what we are told? *Ratio*, 28(1) (June issue), pp. 69–88.

Said, B. (2012). Hymns (nasheeds): A contribution to the study of the Jihadist culture. *Studies in Conflict & Terrorism*, 35(12), pp. 863–879.

Schmidt, S. (2015). *Ethik und Episteme der Zeugenschaft*. Konstanz: Konstanz University Press.

Schmidt, S. (2017). Perpetrators' knowledge: What and how can we learn from perpetrator testimony? *Journal of Perpetrator Research*, 1(1), pp. 85–104.

Schneider, R. (2011). *Performing Remains: Art and War in Theatrical Reenactment*. New York and London: Routledge.

Simon, J. (2009). Thoughts on the aesthetics of terror in general and suicide bombers' videos in particular. In J. Simon & M. Slome (eds), *The Aesthetics of Terror*, pp. 28–47. Milan: Charta.

Straub, V. (2016). The making and gendering of a martyr: Images of female suicide bombers in the Middle East. In J. Eder & C. Klonk (eds), *Image Operations: Visual Media and Political Conflict*, pp. 137–150. Manchester, UK: Manchester University Press.

The Qur'an, English translation by Abdul Mannan Omar. Available from: http://englishquran.com/ [2 May 2018].

Chapter 11

Testimonies for a new social order

The Islamic State's iconic iconoclasm

Christoph Günther and Tom Bioly

Introduction

Ever since the Islamic State successfully contested the power of state authorities in Iraq and Syria and declared the establishment of the "Caliphate" in June 2014, still and moving images of its fighters and other representatives have been disseminated across the globe, drawing worldwide attention to this *Jihadist* movement. For the most part, these images were elaborately produced, skillfully crafted, and widely circulated by the Islamic State and its supporters. They helped the movement to structure, create, and produce a Manichean world order that the Islamic State presents as an alternative to a secular and pluralist organization of governance and society. The Islamic State also uses these images to display its social-revolutionary project and the various ways it competes with its opponents. Within this display, brute force prominently structures this state of symbolic and concrete competition. The movement frames the use of violence as being embedded in a timeless fight between monotheism (*tawḥīd*) and its antipodes, put into effect on both an ideational and a material level. Violence constitutes one means to engage in this fight, with the Islamic State setting its sights on establishing divine ordinances, and accordingly exerting legitimate social, political, and theological authority. A vital part of this endeavor is the "purification" of the earth from any representatives or material and immaterial manifestations of monotheism's antipodes. Consequently, the Islamic State's ideologues barely distinguish between human opponents and inanimate representations of *shirk* (polytheism, idolatry), *kufr* (disbelief), and *ṭāghūt* (tyranny, lit. juggernaut), but rather equate many of these instances. This equivalence becomes apparent not only textually and ideologically, but also affectively in the construction and representation of the world by means of visual media.

In this chapter, we will shed light on how the Islamic State visually presents its fight against the material representations of what it identifies as idolatry. We argue that the spectacular destruction of these objects, their visualizations, and the visual testimonies of these acts of iconoclasm are key parts of the Islamic State's strategy to bring about fundamental social change. The destruction of visual representations is a historically established and well-known means of displaying the transition from one dominion to another. Nevertheless, we argue that the Islamic State's particular commitment to visually staging its iconoclasm is unprecedented. We will furthermore show that the Islamic State does not content itself to merely remove idolatrous representations, but rather seeks to capture these moments in pictures in order to produce and perpetuate visual memories of the destruction and of the resulting empty spaces.

The Islamic State

The Islamic State's rigid take on cultural properties is primarily informed by the movement's history as one of the warring parties in conflicts of power in Iraq and Syria. The Islamic State's ideational and organizational nucleus was formed as early as 2003 by al-Tawḥīd wa 'l-Jihād (Monotheism and Jihad), one of the many groups within the broad spectrum of Sunni resistance against the socio-political reformation of Iraq. The group later merged with al-Qaida and declared the emergence of Dawlat al-ʿIrāq al-islāmīya (Islamic State of Iraq) in Fall 2006. Since its early days, the Islamic State's ideologues developed the vision of an alternative mode of operating governance and society. Their approach is based on a firm belief in the rigorous implementation of their specific interpretation of divine ordinances derived from the Qur'an, Sunna, and the exegetical literature. The Islamic State's genesis from a small Jihadist group to one of the most powerful movements contesting state power in Iraq, Syria and beyond can only be understood in light of the social and political framework in both countries and the broader region, which cannot be discussed within the scope of this paper (Gerges 2016; Günther 2014; Lister 2015). What interests us more is the Islamic State's social-revolutionary approach: that is, the movement's ideological and practical engagement with the intellectual concepts, social practices, and cultural properties that it regards as material and immaterial manifestations of idolatry (*shirk*).

In general terms, the Islamic State frames the concept of *shirk* as the major antipode to monotheist faith and practice, and hence, to "genuine" Muslimness. According to the Islamic State, Muslims cannot achieve salvation in the here-after solely through faith, obeying their creator in all spheres of life, and con-forming to the provisions of religious practice. Muslims must also "keep far from the gateways to shirk and its various shades" (Al-Hayat Media 2014). Shirk, therefore, has become the overarching category used by the Islamic State to judge individual and collective conformity to "true" Islam. In this view, the domains of the secular and the religious have become so inseparable that the word shirk has become "a catch-all phrase used to describe how the Islamic State defines itself: fighting the shirk of Bashar, the shirk of passports, the shirk of national poets and museums, the shirk of Shia mosques" (Hall 2014).

Systematic and historical remarks on iconoclasm

Although rooted particularly in the history of Christianity[1] and deeply linked to the history of Judaism and Islam as well, one can also identify certain historical patterns and features of iconoclasm that point beyond the religious nature of iconoclastic deeds, specific socio-political actors, and the cultural properties they target (Apostolos-Cappadona 2005).

In what follows, we shall highlight three of those features that capture the communicative context of iconoclasm and that are crucial for a systematic understanding of the Islamic State's actions. First, iconoclasm is a highly complex phenomenon, as public images are always entangled with cultural, social, and political narratives. Images in the public sphere are therefore more often than not intertwined with truth claims and discourses of power. We thus have to potentially regard art as a medium of social conflict (Bredekamp 1975) where both idolatry and iconoclasm are in the first place accusations—from a religious as well as a power-political perspective (Freedberg 2009). Second, iconoclasm connects deeds, words, and images very closely. More than just a material act of destruction, iconoclasm must be understood as an act of communication. Targets, and often dates, are chosen carefully (Elias 2013). In some cases, certain features of targets are removed instead of the whole object being annihilated. A typical example of this would be the smashing of faces or eyes of images of living beings, attempting to bereave them of their "vitality." As a consequence, the destruction of the "old" images creates "new" ones. These acts therefore do not aim at an annihilation of memory, but at creating the memory of the annihilation (Brubaker 2013). Third, the dispute over the relation between reality and representation—and, thus, the power—of images (Freedberg 1991) constitutes the crystallization point of any discourse of iconoclasm. Ironically, (self-)proclaimed "enemies of images" become the actual "friends of images" in this context, since it is they who acknowledge the irresistible power of images that arises from the fusion of the signifier and the signified (Brock 1988). It is only in light of this assumption that it becomes necessary to destroy images at all.

In addition to these general features, two specific historical events can be regarded as role models for the Islamic State's ideological and practical engagement with material manifestations of idolatry: the Saudi-Wahhabi expansions and the destruction of the Buddha statues at Bamiyan in Afghanistan. As for the former, the alliance between the House of Saud and the reformist preacher Muhammad ibn Abdalwahhab (1703–1792) and his followers ultimately led to the establishment of the Kingdom of Saudi Arabia in 1932. During their conquests in the Arabian peninsula and southern Iraq, they destroyed Shi'i sites, but also several Sufi shrines, and even targeted some graves of companions of the Prophet Muhammad. The Wahhabis considered all these monuments to be sites of veneration of other entities than the one true God (Elias 2013; Noyes 2013; Peskes 2002). Thus, the Wahhabis are seen not only as ideological defenders of a strict divide between the realms of monotheism (*tawḥīd*) and idolatry (*shirk*), but also as material defenders against what they identified as manifestations of idolatry. For this reason, those Wahhabis have become a shining example—if not idols—for modern Jihadism itself.

Following in the lines of this modern Sunni reform movement, the destruction of the two great Buddha statues in the Bamiyan Valley in March 2001 by the Afghan Taliban[2] was framed within this recurrent polarizing ideological pattern with similar functions, aims and effects. But the event also foreshadowed other aspects of the Islamic State's iconoclastic actions. It was, first of all, a media coup, staged on an international scale.[3] Having achieved worldwide attention, the Taliban were able to communicate several important matters. First, they demonstrated power over and independence from the United Nations, a powerful opponent that had attempted in vain to prevent the destruction (Elias 2013). Second, they exposed an alleged hypocrisy of the West, which would be shown to present more of an outcry over "stones" than about the humanitarian crisis in the country that was itself caused by intentional sanctions (Crossette 2001; Freedberg 2001). And third, they highlighted that the objects in question were actually still "venerated"—namely in the form of the appreciation of cultural heritage (Falser 2010; Flood 2002).

An overview of the Islamic State's destructions

While the Islamic State's iconoclasm is not unprecedented, it is nevertheless remarkable. One could argue that the Islamic State has combined—or even cautiously suggest that it has perfected—both the excessiveness of the destructive acts during the Saudi-Wahhabi expansions and the communication strategy that was adopted by the Taliban with regard to the Buddha statues at Bamiyan.

Although it is difficult to give exact numbers, we can safely assume that the Islamic State carried out several hundreds of deliberate assaults on cultural property since the Summer of 2014. This marks a massive increase compared with the years before (Danti 2015), even though the status of cultural property has not fared well in the region since the outbreak of the Iraq War in 2003 (Baker, Ismael, & Ismael 2010). Among the properties attacked by the Islamic State are mosques, shrines, graves, churches and other minority religious sites, museums, archaeological sites, libraries and archives, as well as objects connected with national history, especially with the history of the Hussein and al-Asad families. About two-thirds of the religious properties are Islamic, over half of which are Shi'i. The remaining properties are mostly Yezidi and Christian, with around 10 percent each. Ancient sites and objects have, in contrast to Western public perception, only a share of 3 percent (Danti 2015). Without being able to go into detail here, this apportionment is telling in several ways. The predominance of Islamic properties reflects their disproportionate share of cultural properties in Iraq and Syria. More importantly, it demonstrates the Islamic State's perception of these sites—and of the religious and socio-cultural institutions related to them—as bona fide rivals to its social-revolutionary project. In removing them, the Jihadists are on the one hand able to inhibit practices they deem nonconformist or heretical. On the other hand, by annihilating these sites, the Islamic State aims to create spatial and intellectual voids to fill with its own institutions and ideas of "genuine" social and religious practice. The destruction of these sites and related social infrastructures are designed to alter the structure, appearance, and function of particular urban or rural spaces, and impede the identity-creating function of distinct social practices such as pilgrimages, saint venerations, spiritual exercises, and other rituals. Such destruction may also hinder further identity-creating social practices, such as intellectual debates and scholarly education in local seminaries, bookshops, or clerical circles. As argued elsewhere (Günther, forthcoming), this all-encompassing spatial, material, ideational, and intellectual purification of the socio-religious landscape makes the Islamic State's iconoclasm rather a form of socioclasm in the first place.

In contrast, the destruction of ancient sites and objects follows the example of Bamiyan. It targets, in addition to a local or national sense of belonging (Harmanşah 2015), the very concept of cultural heritage itself, which is identified with an alleged global order dominated by Western universalism. The Jihadists sought to further a polarized conflict between the latter and "genuine" Islam propagated by the Islamic State, as well as to set a warning example for the future. They therefore chose to target some particularly famous sites, including the Mosul Museum and the ancient cities of Niniveh, Nimrud, and Palmyra. Meanwhile, the affective power of destroying ancient properties and sites used by contemporary communities lies in the same presuppositions as the attacks on sites of Muslim religious practice: namely that an attack on a material representation of a certain community is equivalent to an attack on the community itself. In other words, the objects in question can perform such a constitutive role for the identity of a community that, rather than just representing it, they are treated as if they were this community themselves (Bredekamp 2016; Freedberg 1991). The Islamic State, however, only seldom specifies the various cultural properties in question. Rather, the movement's media label many of its targets indiscriminately as "manifestations of idolatry" (maẓāhir al-shirk) or refer to them in other generic terms. Such a generalizing approach mirrors the Islamic State's Manichean ideological framework, which allows the movement to present itself as the only legitimate manifestation of an "authentic" Islam through an omnipresent and exclusively religious framing of its deeds, and by using traditional Islamic vocabulary, references to Islamic sources, and certain Islamic visual elements (Bioly 2016). Further, this generalizing approach also reflects the Islamic State's understanding of these sites as manifestations of forces of evil lying outside time and history, and against which the trustees of divine ordinances must stand their ground.

Destruction and communication—three examples

The Islamic State did not limit itself to bringing about social change by destroying cultural properties regarded as material manifestations of shirk. The movement rather took many of these destructions as an opportunity to produce images, which bear witness to the implementation of the Islamic State's ideology in certain territories. As such, they are part of the "image wars" (Rossipal 2016) in which the Islamic State is engaged, using images to address and relate to their audiences and potential followers, to articulate its ideological framework, and to accord appraisals of social and political facts and developments. As images are an indispensable element of human communication, the Islamic State, just as other socio-political actors, uses visual means to propose future visions, aims to link up with their (potential) followers' aspirations, and provides an alternative to their opponents' offers. In doing so, the Islamic State seeks to shape their targeted audiences' perception of the world, elicit their emotions, and orchestrate their behavior.

The Islamic State does not document every single iconoclastic act it commits. But when its media outlets do so, they usually produce very professional material in the form of photographs or videos. A typical example of this is a ten minute clip entitled "The Axe of the Khalil (Ibrahim)" (Figure 11.1), which was released in Ramadan 2016 (Nīnawā Media Office 2016). The video displays the destruction of different ancient sites, including several of the famous gates of the ancient city of Niniveh dedicated to the Mesopotamian gods Nergal, Mashki, and Adad as well as the Nabu Temple of Nimrud (Jones 2016a; 2016b). The video begins with a few short impressions of "heretical" Islamic, Jewish and Christian practices that appear to be chosen at random. The practices are annotated with a general narrative about men, especially Muslims, going astray from the purportedly "straight path" of monotheism. What follows is an indiscriminate display of certain ancient and modern "idols" such as the Giza Pyramids and the Burj Khalifa in Dubai, portrayed as the paramount representations of disobedience to God and of tyranny and injustice. Only afterwards does a spokesman of the Islamic State appear. The spokesman is shown standing before one of the Niniveh gates, preaching about the obligation to mercilessly destroy any manifestation of idolatry. Behind him, bulldozers are seen tearing down the structure as the spokesman continues to explain and guide the audience through the depicted destructions. Sanctioned by divine ordinances, his speech-act adds to the image-act. Together they testify to the deceitfulness of these monuments and of any attempt to ascribe a positive capacity to them as parts of local or national identities, as remnants of an estimable past, or as symbols of universal cultural heritage. Further "evidence" for the righteousness of this approach is presented in the form of a hadith promoting the destruction of images and exalted graves. Both the acoustic and visual dimension of this account are thus powerful reminders that these moving images depict a reality that the Islamic State created through the act of destroying these artefacts. Additionally, the

Figure 11.1 Word, deed and image intermingled: a representative of the Islamic
State explains the obligation to destroy any manifestation of idolatry, 02:26 min., 2016.

Source: Nīnawā Province Media Office, 2016, Fāʾs al-khalīl (The Axe of the Khalil).

movement created reality by declaring these monuments what they "really" are:
"Today we destroy and obliterate another landmark of polytheism, which had
been held in high esteem by the people, whereas they did not know that these
relics are idols and statues, which had been worshiped besides God" (Nīnawā
Media Office 2016). After a short scene with a caravan marching through the
desert, the video proceeds with the blowing-up of the Nabu Temple remains at
the site of Nimrud. This time, two representatives give similar reasons for this
act, the second one additionally promising that the Pyramids of Giza will eventually share the same fate. In contrast, the end of the video depicts scenes of
"everyday life" in the Islamic State. These scenes portray a religious life above
all, prominently consisting of prayer, public sermons, and the distribution of
propaganda material. Some parts of the clip are accompanied by *anāshīd*, religious a cappella hymns, which further the viewer's multisensory experience.

What interests us here though is a specific portion of what can be seen in the
film, namely what the Islamic State wants its audiences to witness and the way
in which it guides them through this audiovisual testament to the Islamic State's
righteousness and power. The video presents the fundamental victory of a social
order sanctioned by divine ordinances, inspired by a past remembered as glori-
ous, and by a future imagined as resurrection of "true" Islam. In the Islamic
State's vision, the (re)creation of this order is paralleled by the obliteration of
any immaterial and material representations of *shirk, kufr, ṭāghūt* or other opposing concepts and forces. The movement uses videos and images of this kind to

make its audiences witness the simultaneity of its own ascension and of the deterioration of its enemies. In so doing, it seeks to affect concepts of cultural heritage as well as of local and national identities. In addition, its audiences are about to witness acts that mark fundamental ethical, normative, religious, political, and social transformations. Although the iconoclastic acts in some way speak for themselves, the Islamic State uses verbal and textual explanations to put this message across, enforce its classificatory power, and reduce the polysemy inherent in images, leaving no room for doubts about the meaning of what is displayed. Altogether, the framing of the events is extremely dense and multi-layered. We can therefore call this kind of communication "guided" or even "enforced witnessing," the latter stressing the role of the depicted physical violence, making it utterly impossible to keep the stance of a neutral beholder.

It furthermore becomes clear that the destruction of "idols" is of greatest importance for the general strategy of the Islamic State. First of all, explicitly defining the material representations of its enemy[4] serves as a means to illustrate and sharpen the perceived bipolarity of the situation of conflict, which the Islamic State seeks to fuel. In further suggesting an analogy between themselves and the first generations of Muslims, the followers of the Islamic State claim both legitimacy and authenticity for their actions. This elevates iconoclasm to a virtuous expression of "genuine" Islam as well as to the struggle for a new system of social order, a "new world" so to say.

No such "official" images exist for another memorable destruction carried out by the Islamic State. On 24 July 2014, the Jihadists blew up the Mosque of the Prophet Jonah in Mosul, including its minaret (Figure 11.2). According to Muslim beliefs, the mosque harbors the grave of the biblical Prophet Jonah

Figure 11.2 Collage of the destruction and the remains of the Mosque of the Prophet Jonah by a local citizen, 2014.

Source: https://twitter.com/RorateCaeli/status/492350393775816705/photo/1, 24 July 2014 [5 October 2017].

(Yūnus in Arabic). During the long history of the city that is now Mosul, an Assyrian Palace originally stood on the site followed by a Christian church, which was rebuilt into a mosque surrounding the Prophet's grave (Wilmshurst 2000). By the time the city was seized by the Islamic State in early June 2014, rumors of the mosque's destruction had already been spreading (Jones 2014). These rumors may have given the Islamic State another incentive to actually put the planned destruction into action. Official announcements and explanations as we have seen them in "The Axe of the Khalil" took place here as well, but locally and immediately: "ISIL terrorists ordered everyone out of the Mosque of the Prophet Yūnus before detonating and demolishing it, declaring that 'the mosque had become a place for apostasy, not prayer'" (Mamoun 2014).

It therefore seems like this event stands out in the first place due to its inevitability. When it finally happened, the news spread like wildfire with dozens of locals posting photos and pieces of information on various social media platforms. As they were dispersed through the internet, these snippets proved the power of the Jihadists. In the Islamic State's view, its regulative authority had been established by the sheer fact that this alleged site of shirk was destroyed, regardless of debates about the necessity to further this act and make local populations accept its legitimacy as divinely sanctioned. Rather, accounts of local people, international journalists, and activists were used as mere testimonies of the Islamic State's superiority and power. It is, nevertheless, surprising that the Islamic State did not seek to capitalize on this event beyond a local level by means of its own media output. One possible explanation would be that they indeed relied on the independent spreading of the news alone. On the other hand, it is not unlikely that the Islamic State faced some difficulties in justifying the destruction of an entire Sunni mosque when, for example, the removal of the shrine around the grave alone could have generated an impressive effect as well. In the end, a combination of both explanations seems probable (Bioly 2016).

In cases like the aforementioned ones, representatives of the Islamic State blew up entire architectural structures or razed them to the ground. However, they acted differently in the course of a raid on the Catholic St. George's Monastery on the northwestern edge of Mosul in early March 2015. The perpetrators "purged" the area by smashing statues, images and tombstones, and by removing crosses and replacing them with the black flag of the Islamic State (Jones 2015). Doing so was supposed to represent the triumph not only over Christians in this particular territory, but also over Christianity in general. This becomes even more evident in an image testimony of this act, published by the Islamic State itself. It shows a bell tower with a fallen cross and the raised flag right next to it (Figure 11.3). Taken from a low-angle shot, there is no space for context. All you can see is the objects, the "soldier" carrying out the deed, the bell tower and the sky. The caption— "removal and smashing of the crosses"—confirms the ahistoricity of the event and renders it completely interchangeable. The same is true for another picture from the raid. Framed by the caption "removal of manifestations of idolatry," it depicts a boy who wields a hammer against an image of Mary, Jesus and an angel (Figure 11.4).

Figure 11.3 An "old" image replaced by a "new" one: removing a cross from the St. George's Monastery, 2015.

Source: https://gatesofnineveh.files.wordpress.com/2015/03/171.jpg, 17 March 2015 [5 October 2017].

Figure 11.4 Breaking and making images: smashed out faces of an iconic depiction at the St. George's Monastery, 2015.

Source: https://gatesofnineveh.files.wordpress.com/2015/03/151.jpg, 17 March 2015 [5 October 2017].

However, the picture is still arranged, as can be seen from the diagonal position in which the boy holds the hammer (Bioly 2016). Thus, one is tempted to say that, beyond the immediate local impact of these acts, those "old" images of the St. George's Monastery were destroyed solely for creating these "new" ones.

Conclusion

We have shown that the Islamic State's destruction of cultural properties are more than mere acts of "blind vandalism." Exclusively framed in religious terminology, the movement presents its iconoclasm as part of a continual, timeless struggle of "genuine" believers in monotheism fighting for the establishment of divine ordinances. In this understanding, the destruction of cultural properties regarded as material manifestations of idolatry is conducive to the purification of this world and mankind from anything that potentially leads people astray from the "right" path. Moreover, it is a means to underline the Islamic State's classificatory power to define "genuine" Islam and its borders and to enforce these definitions. Iconoclasm therefore makes the distinction between "right" and "wrong" religious and social practices tangible for local populations. It leaves little doubt about which practices and sites are allowed since any other practice is impracticable in public, or the site is simply destroyed. In this way, the strategic use of iconoclasm helps the Islamic State to suppress deviant religious, social, or political practices and enforce the movement's own interpretation of "genuine" Islamic beliefs and practices among local communities.

At the same time, the visualization of iconoclasm becomes iconic itself and thus lends potential stability to the Islamic State's establishment of an alternative system of social order in the minds of both its followers and its adversaries. As can be seen from the three examples we chose to highlight in this paper, the movement has destroyed certain sites not only as a means to display its regulative authority, but also to produce annotated images and videos that establish the meaning of these acts once and for all. Because they were integral to the conceptual framing of these acts of destruction, these images could shape how the Islamic State's audience witnessed and appraised the destruction of cultural artefacts. They thus acted as testimonies to the rise of a powerful entity sanctioned by divine ordinances to obliterate these alleged sites of idolatry and, thereby, to (re)create a "true" Islam. Finally, it should be noted that local people did not always accept the movement's attempts at classifying both acts and targets in this way. They too used visual means to testify to the Islamic State's cruelties, thereby undermining its classificatory power and keeping local identities alive.

Notes

1 In this narrower context, the term refers to two concrete periods of "active hostility towards images" (Cancik 1993, p. 217), namely the Byzantine Iconoclasm in the eighth and ninth century and the various outbreaks during the Protestant Reformation.

2 At the same time, but almost unnoticed by the broader public perception, the Taliban also demolished tens of thousands of historical objects, mainly at the National Museum in Kabul (Stein 2015).

3 The act was publicly announced and, when the day had come, several journalists were transferred to the location to ensure international attention (Elias 2013).

4 We prefer to use the singular at this point since it reflects the Jihadists' ultimate indiscrimination, although this specific iconoclastic act aims at in fact at least three distinct levels: the sovereignty of the Iraqi government, the cultural and national memory of the Iraqi people, and the international community's strive for the protection of cultural heritage.

References

Apostolos-Cappadona, D. (2005). Iconoclasm: An overview. In L. Jones (ed.), *Encyclopedia of Religion*, 2nd edn, pp. 4279–4289. Detroit: Macmillan Reference USA.

Al-Hayat Media (2014). Hādha wa'd Allāh (This is the Promise of Allah).

Baker, R.W., Ismael, S.T., & Ismael, T.Y. (2010). *Cultural Cleansing in Iraq: Why Museums were Looted, Libraries Burned and Academics Murdered*. London: Pluto Press.

Bioly, T. (2016). *Die Zerstörung von Kulturgütern durch den "Islamischen Staat."* MA Thesis, University of Leipzig.

Bredekamp, H. (1975). *Kunst als Medium sozialer Konflikte: Bilderkämpfe von der Spätantike bis zur Hussitenrevolution*. Frankfurt am Main: Suhrkamp.

Bredekamp, H. (2016). *Das Beispiel Palmyra*. Köln: Verlag der Buchhandlung Walther König.

Brock, B. (1988). Der byzantinische Bilderstreit. In M. Warnke (ed.), *Bildersturm: Die Zerstörung des Kunstwerks*, pp. 34–40. Frankfurt am Main: Fischer Taschenbuch Verlag.

Brubaker, L. (2013). Making and breaking images and meaning in Byzantium and early Islam. In S. Boldrick, L. Brubaker, & R. Clay (eds), *Striking Images, Iconoclasms Past and Present*, pp. 13–24. Farnham and Burlington: Ashgate.

Cancik, H. (1993). Ikonoklasmus. In H. Cancik, B. Gladigow, & K.-H. Kohl (eds), *Handbuch religionswissenschaftlicher Grundbegriffe III*, pp. 217–221. Stuttgart: Kohlhammer.

Crossette, B. (2001). Taliban explains Buddha demolition. *New York Times*, 19 March. Available from: www.nytimes.com/2001/03/19/world/taliban-explains-buddha-demolition. html [19 April 2018].

Danti, M.D. (2015). Ground-based observations of cultural heritage incidents in Syria and Iraq. *Near Eastern Archaeology*, 78(3), pp. 132–141.

Elias, J.J. (2013). The Taliban, Bamiyan, and revisionist iconoclasm. In S. Boldrick, L. Brubaker, & R. Clay (eds), *Striking Images, Iconoclasms Past and Present*, pp. 145–163. Farnham and Burlington: Ashgate.

Falser, M.S. (2010). Die Buddhas von Bamiyan, performativer Ikonoklasmus und das "Image" von Kulturerbe. In M.C. Frank & K. Mahlke (eds), *Kultur und Terror*, pp. 82–93. Bielefeld: Transcript.

Flood, F.B. (2002). Between cult and culture: Bamiyan, Islamic iconoclasm, and the museum. *The Art Bulletin*, 84(4), pp. 641–659.

Freedberg, D. (1991). *The Power of Images: Studies in the History and Theory of Response*. Chicago: University of Chicago Press.

Freedberg, D. (2001). The power of wood and stone, the Taliban is not the first to fear the mysterious lure of art. *The Washington Post*, 25 March, p. B.02.

Freedberg, D. (2009). Iconoclasm and idolatry. In S. Davies, K.M. Higgins, R. Hopkins, R. Stecker, & D.E. Cooper (eds), *A Companion to Aesthetics*. 2nd edn, pp. 341–343. Oxford: Blackwell Publishing.

Gerges, F.A. (2016). *ISIS: A History*. Oxford: Princeton University Press.

Günther, C. (2014). Ein zweiter Staat im Zweistromland? Genese und Ideologie des "Islamischen Staates Irak." PhD thesis, University of Leipzig. Würzburg: Ergon Verlag.

Günther, C. (forthcoming). *The Islamic State: Entrepreneurs of Identity*. Oxford and New York: Berghahn Books.

Hall, M. (2014). Iconoclasm and the Islamic State: Razing shrines to draw new borders, a Q&A with Dr. James Noyes, Part I of III. *Atlantic Council*, 26 September. Available from: www.atlanticcouncil.org/blogs/menasource/iconoclasm-and-the-islamic-state-razing-shrines-to-draw-new-borders [19 April 2018].

Harmanşah, Ö. (2015). ISIS, heritage, and the spectacles of destruction in the global media. *Near Eastern Archaeology*, 78(3), pp. 170–177.

Jones, C. (2014). And now it's gone: Shrine of Jonah destroyed by ISIS. Blog post, 24 July. Available from: https://gatesofnineveh.wordpress.com/2014/07/24/and-now-its-gone-shrine-of-jonah-destroyed-by-isis/ [19 April 2018].

Jones, C. (2015). Damage around Tikrit, destruction in Mosul. Blog post, 17 March. Available   from: https://gatesofnineveh.wordpress.com/2015/03/17/damage-around-tikrit-destruction-in-mosul/ [19 April 2018].

Jones, C. (2016a). The cleansing of Mosul. Blog post, 6 June. Available from: https://gatesofnineveh.wordpress.com/2016/06/06/the-cleansing-of-mosul/ [19 April 2018].

Jones, C. (2016b). ISIS destroys Temple of Nabu at Nimrud, Nergal Gate at Nineveh. Blog post, 8 June. Available from: https://gatesofnineveh.wordpress.com/2016/06/08/isis-destroys-temple-of-nabu-at-nimrud-nergal-gate-at-nineveh/ [19 April 2018].

Lister, C.R. (2015). *The Syrian Jihad: Al-Qaeda, the Islamic State and the Evolution of an Insurgency*. Oxford and New York: Oxford University Press.

Mamoun, A. (2014). URGENT: ISIL destroys Mosque of Biblical Jonah, Prophet Yunus. Iraqi News, 25 July. Available from: www.iraqinews.com/features/urgent-isil-destroys-mosque-biblical-jonah-prophet-yunus/ [19 April 2018].

Nīnawā Media Office (2016). Fāʾs al-khalīl: (The Axe of the Khalil), Video.

Noyes, J. (2013). *The Politics of Iconoclasm: Religion, Violence and the Culture of Image-breaking in Christianity and Islam*. London: I.B. Tauris.

Peskes, E. (2002). Wahhābiyya (1). In P. Bearman et al. (eds), *Encyclopedia of Islam*, 2nd edn, pp. 39–45. Leiden: Brill.

Rossipal, C. (2016). ISIS and the global image war: An archival perspective on iconoclastic performance and bio-political authority. *Inquiries Journal*, 8(11). Available from: www.inquiriesjournal.com/a?id=1489 [19 April 2018].

Stein, G.J. (2015). The war-ravaged cultural heritage of Afghanistan: An overview of projects of assessment, mitigation, and preservation. *Near Eastern Archaeology*, 78(3), pp. 187–195.

Wilmshurst, D. (2000). *The Ecclesiastical Organisation of the Church of the East*, pp. 1318–1913. Louvain: Peeters Publishers.

Chapter 12

From Cape Town to Timbuktu

Iconoclastic testimonies in the age of social media

Tobias Wendl

Vandalism and iconoclasm—targeting political as well as religious imagery—are well-documented phenomena throughout history, from antiquity to modern times. The erasure of monuments, the destruction of architecture, the smashing, burning or drowning of images and works of art have occurred in multiple and various ways. Yet as Bruno Latour (2002) has reminded us, the negative connotation, inherent to the term "icono-clasm" (as "image-breaking"), is somewhat misleading and incomplete, since every image broken is at the same time a new image made. Their traces and remains, the voids and replacements create afterimages, echoing the memory and message of destruction, and thus give testimony to antecedent conflicts, loss and pain. As David Freedberg (2016, p. 68) explains "to censor or destroy a work is to testify to its hold over its public." And in a similar vein, Michael Taussig (1999) has argued that defacement in general tends to simultaneously unmask and enhance the power of images.

This chapter focuses on three recent cases of iconoclasm, which occurred between 2012 and 2016 in South Africa and Mali. First, the "Rhodes Must Fall" campaign at the University of Cape Town, which led to the removal of a statue of Cecil Rhodes from the university campus in 2015 and quickly grew into a broad student movement addressing the legacies of white supremacy in post-apartheid South Africa. Then the vandalizing of a painting entitled "The Spear" by Brett Murray in a gallery exhibit in Johannesburg in 2012, executed by two men who felt that the painting had insulted President Jacob Zuma. And finally, the mass demolition of sacred Sufi sites, mosques, shrines, mausoleums and books by Salafist jihadist militias in Timbuktu, Mali, in 2012 and 2013. Although the cases under study have particular agendas and contexts, which I will elaborate in some detail, they have in common that they were all heavily re-mediated and triggered myriad response images and secondary image testimonies on social media, such as Twitter, Facebook and WhatsApp.

I argue that in order to really understand the dynamics of vandalism, iconoclasm and censorship in the era of social media, it is necessary to not limit oneself to the destructions as the primary iconoclastic testimony, but to also include the multiple and multifaceted re-mediations as secondary testimonies.

They can be conceived of as afterimages adding new layers and contours to the controversies and conflicts fought by the protagonists and parties involved.

#RhodesMustFall in Cape Town

Since the end of apartheid in 1994, South African politicians, architects and artists have faced the task of overcoming the inherited structures of racial segregation and creating new spaces, symbols and monuments of reconciliation and shared history. This was done by the vision of a new "Rainbow Nation," heralded by Desmond Tutu and Nelson Mandela as well as by prestigious buildings such as the Constitutional Court in Johannesburg, which is very impressive in its architectural transparency as well as by its new function as a link between the neighborhoods of Braamfontein and Hillbrow (Coombes 2003; Gevisser 2004). Until 2015, this gradual reconfiguration of the public space went on rather smoothly. Places where the resistance to apartheid had been initiated, were often turned into national heritage sites, monuments and statues of apartheid politicians were successively disposed and replaced by ANC politicians or other heroes and heroines of the anti-apartheid struggle and the long road to freedom.[1]

In March 2015, however, the issue of monuments and memory became heated again. Students in Cape Town requested the removal of a statue of the British colonialist and diamond magnate Cecil John Rhodes on the UCT campus. In their "Rhodes Must Fall" campaign they declared Rhodes a symbol of oppression and imperialism. Student activists poured a bucket of human excrements over the monument, defaced it with paint and covered it with black garbage bags. Within a few days the iconoclastic testimony became widely circulated through Twitter, Facebook and WhatsApp and sparked a remarkable protest movement among students and staff throughout the country. Rallied by the hashtag #RhodesMustFall, further actions followed, including the occupation of the central administrative building. Students saw the statue as a disturbing reminder of the university's colonial complicity, and the failure of the university to take action made Rhodes a focal point (Nyamnjoh 2016).

After three weeks of ongoing protests, the administration decided to remove the statue, acknowledging the importance of the debate around symbols on campus and the depth of student feeling about this particular instance. The removal of the colonial Rhodes was celebrated in a euphoric manner and the victory was well documented and shared by hundreds on their smartphones.

During the removal—while the statue was still hanging on the crane—a remarkable afterimage was produced by the performance artist Sethembile Msezane, ascending like a phoenix from the ashes (Figure 12.1). She had dressed in a costume with wide wings and was mounted on a white plinth she had installed for the occasion. Her back was turned to the event being witnessed by the crowd. The costume, a beaded headdress and feathered arm adornments, referenced a historical stone bird sculpture that Rhodes had acquired in Great Zimbabwe for his Groote Schuur castle in Cape Town; an antiquity that the Rhodes

Figure 12.1 Sethembile Msezane, Chapungu: "The Day Rhodes Fell", performance in Cape Town, 9 April 2015.
Source: © Carlie Shoemaker/Getty Images.

estate has refused to return to Zimbabwe, despite official requests (Simbao 2017,
p. 2).[2] In addition, the artist's pose evoked an infamous cartoon from 1892 of
Rhodes as a lonely colossus bestriding the African continent from the Cape to
Cairo.

In April 2015 the "Rhodes Must Fall" movement spread across the country
like wildfire, fueled by the energy of young Black student activists, who directed
their hurt, pain and disappointment against statues and monuments celebrating
colonial and apartheid protagonists—as if there had never been a break in the
country's history. Statues of Johannes Strijdom and Paul Kruger were vandalized with paint; the statues of King George in Durban, of Queen Victoria in Port
Elizabeth and even Mahatma Gandhi in Johannesburg suffered a similar fate.[3] In
Uitenhage, enraged members of a radical youth movement burned and charred a
monument—dedicated to British soldiers who had died in the Anglo-Boer War
(1899–1902)—qualifying it as a "colonial legacy." The protesters "necklaced"
the soldier by putting a burning tire over the statue—a lynching method, quite
common during the apartheid era and the riots of the early 1990s (Marschall
2017, p. 212).

The affective dynamics, unleashed by these iconoclastic acts, were reinforced
by social media, which—for the first time in South African history—provided a
major platform for the participating actors to circulate and share their image

testimonies. As a response, white right-wing South Africans started to organize local defense committees to protect and secure their heritage from further defacement or removal. In Pretoria, Afrikaans singer Sunette Bridges chained herself to a vandalized soldier statue at the bottom of the Ohm Kruger monument celebrating the "father of the Afrikaner Nation." The statue had been covered with green paint shortly before. The controversial singer expressed her fear of the Boers becoming "victims of a genocide by the Black majority" (Thamm 2015).

While the debate about the heritage war in South Africa slowly calmed down in the second half of 2015, the "Rhodes Must Fall" campaign spread across national boundaries. In June 2015—two months after the victory of Cape Town—"Rhodes Must Fall" reached the University of Oxford in Britain. Its main target was the Rhodes sculpture attached to the façade at Oriel College. Students expressed their determination to decolonize the physical space in Oxford, particularly the plague of colonial iconography (in the form of statues, plaques and paintings) which they considered as an uncritical whitewashing of British history and its colonial legacy. In comparison to their South African peers, however, students at Oxford were less successful, since the university officially declined their request to removing the Rhodes statue. As the university spokesperson announced, the college had decided that the statue should remain in place and that the college would seek to provide a clear historical context to explain why it is there. Later it became known that the college had been warned of the possibility that it would lose roughly £100 million in gifts if the statue were to be taken down (Rawlinson 2016).

In Cape Town, students soon articulated additional concerns and arguments to underscore the issue of white supremacy. They protested against the precarious housing situation for black students, the lack of black teachers and the eurocentrism of their curricula. "Rhodes Must Fall" was quickly followed by "Fees Must Fall" and by "Homeless at UCT," and in February 2016 a new wave of iconoclasm swept across the campus. Student activists stormed through the campus buildings, grabbed paintings from the walls and started to burn them. Most of the 24 paintings they heaped on a bonfire were portraits of historical white settler figures. Protesters proudly posted their picture trophies on social media. And one of their tweets testified: "Whiteness is burning!" A couple of students were arrested, three of them were put on trial for malicious damage to university property. But the charges were later withdrawn and the accused were given community service.[4]

A month after these events, the Institute of African Studies at UCT opened a student-curated photo exhibition on the "Rhodes Must Fall" (RMF) campaign. A somewhat self-congratulatory act, reminiscent of Sarah Ahmed's concept of "conditional hospitality": "People of color are welcomed on condition that they return that hospitality by integrating into a common organizational culture or by 'being' diverse, and allowing institutions to celebrate their diversity" (Ahmed 2012, p. 43). The exhibit, entitled "Echoing Voices from Within," assembled 75 photographs of the toppling Rhodes monument and the ongoing struggle for decolonizing the campus. However, much to the surprise of the organizers, the opening was disturbed by members of a student "Trans Gender Collective" who smeared the photographs and texts with red paint and blocked the entrance to the gallery with their naked bodies (Figure 12.2). With this intervention the collective protested against the RMF narrative of the exhibition and their own exclusion. Only three out of more than a 1000 images of and by trans people, which the collective had provided, ended up making it into the show. This erasure of the transpeople's contribution to the RMF movement by cis-male and cis-female curators was considered as scandalous and as disgraceful. The exhibition was closed down and did not reopen again, despite the fact that the trans-collective declared on their Facebook page two days later, that they did not "destroy" the pictures of the exhibition, but only "defaced" them by using washable paint so that the archive remained intact (Weinberg 2018, pp. 1–4).

The events exposed the internal frictions and fault-lines within the student movement and their decolonizing project. Yet, as an iconoclastic testimony, the case is extremely revealing, since it represents an iconoclasm of a kind of second degree—the defacement and annihilation of the photographs as earlier image testimonies, which laid the ground for turning an iconoclasm into an icon.

Figure 12.2 Rhodes must fall exhibit vandalized in UCT protest on 9 March 2016.

Source: © and courtesy of Ashraf Hendricks/GroundUp.

Brett Murray's "The Spear" in a Johannesburg art gallery

Let us now turn to my second example, which occurred in an art gallery context and also showed clear references to race issues, however with a somewhat different agenda. Brett Murray's painting "The Spear" from 2010 shows Jacob Zuma, the former South African ANC President with naked genitals. Zuma, a proud polygamist, officially married to four women, had already faced different trials for corruption and rape. During his rape trial Zuma admitted to having unprotected intercourse with his accuser who he knew to be HIV positive, but he claimed that he took a shower afterwards to minimize the risk of contracting HIV. This statement had made Zuma an easy target for cartoonists. Jonathan Shapiro started to integrate a shower-head affixed to Zuma's skull which soon became a distinctive mark of Zuma's presidency (Freedberg 2012, p. 37).

Brett Murray shows Zuma stretching out his arm and gazing prophetically to the future. At first glance, the pose—modelled after Viktor Ivanov's iconic Lenin poster—seems fitting to a leader, but then one notices his unzipped trousers with the open fly from which hangs a penis. The painting was controversially discussed in both, social media and the South African press, and the ANC issued a condemning statement, requesting an immediate removal of the painting from the exhibition in the gallery. Renowned senior artists such as William Kentridge and David Goldblatt expressed their solidarity with Murray and referred to the freedom of artistic expression. Critics and opponents judged the painting as obscene, insulting and as a racist denigration of all Black South Africans. Enoch Mthembu, the spokesman of the Nazareth Baptist church, called for Murray to be stoned to death. Matters threatened to escalate, when the *City Press*, a weekly newspaper, which presented the painting on its website did not bow to the ANC's pressure to remove the painting from the internet. While the painting went viral on the web, enraged protesters marched through the streets of Johannesburg—burning copies of the *City Press* weekly and shouting: "We say NO to the abuse of artistic freedom!" (Freedberg 2012, p. 37).

Social activist and writer Gillian Schutte expressed her empathy with the protesters and wrote in her blog:

> The point, people, is this is not the president's penis. It is the grotesquely huge Black male "dick-ness" that resides somewhere in the deep collective consciousness of the White psyche—a primal and savage "dick-ness" that was entrenched about 500 years ago as a White supremacist plot to control the world of women and racism. The image suggests that [...] this is the essential "nature" of the Black man, because although in a suit, the unzipped dick confirms his failure to gain access to "culture."
>
> (Schutte 2012)

On 22 May 2012 two men entered the Johannesburg gallery and started to paint over the offensive art work (Figure 12.3), obviously a spontaneous and

Figure 12.3 Brett Murray, "The Spear," 2010, acrylic on canvas, 185 × 140 cm, before and after the attack on 22 May 2012.

Source: © and courtesy: the artist, Everard Read CIRCA Gallery and Goodman Gallery, Johannesburg.

uncoordinated action. While the first, the 58-year-old white South African Barend Lagrange started to paint over Zuma's nakedness and face two red crosses; the second, Lowie Mabokela, a 26-year-old black South African covered additional parts of the body with black paint. The action was filmed by a television crew, randomly present at the gallery, and both men were immediately arrested. In a TV interview on the next day, Lagrange justified his action by explaining that the conflict had shifted from a political to a racist issue and that he "could not allow the racial conflicts in South Africa start again." In April 2013, both stood trial before the Hillbrow magistrate for malicious damages to property. Mabokela pleaded not guilty, saying he had done nothing wrong, but was merely protecting the image of the president. He was condemned to a suspended sentence of six months in prison. Lagrange accepted a fine of 1000 Rand (the equivalent of €80) after admitting his guilt.[5]

When we compare the iconoclastic testimonies articulated in the "Spear" and in "Rhodes Must Fall" we can discern similarities as well as differences. Both cases are testimonies against the unsettled issue of white supremacy in South Africa. In both cases, images were judged as offensive, and both images triggered reciprocal offensive acts by defacement or banning them from view. In both cases social media practices contributed first in heating up the arena and then in circulating the iconoclasms and further afterimages. However, in the

"Rhodes Must Fall" campaign, the image was much closer linked to what it represented. It stood in as a substitute and the defacement was motivated by the belief that whatever is done to the material "signifier" is also done to the "signified". In the case of the "Spear" however, the question of "signifier" and "signified" is more complexly layered. Here, it was not president Zuma (neither in person nor as substitute for an incompetent ANC government) that triggered the offensiveness of the image. The offensiveness of the image resulted from a presumed antecedent iconoclasm, committed by the artist, who had desecrated the image of the president in his painting. The outrage and subsequent defacement did not target the president as the "signified," but the painting as the "signifier." The two vandalizers intended to defend and protect Zuma against an artist who had offended him. As a protective gesture they "corrected" the painting by veiling the parts they judged offensive. In this respect the case of the "Spear" is very similar to the defacement of Chris Ofili's "Holy Virgin Mary" at the Brooklyn Art Museum in 1999 by Dennis Heimer who smeared white paint all over the artwork in order to undo an antecedent blasphemy and offense, committed by the artist Ofili who had applied excrements of elephants on his canvas (Mitchell 2005, pp. 135–136).

Timbuktu 2012

My third example, on Timbuktu, sheds further light on the intermingling spheres of religion and politics and on how material signifiers can accumulate additional layers over time. In March 2012, after a military coup in the Malian capital Bamako, members of the Tuareg Movement for the liberation of Azawad were able to seize control of the northern part of the country. They quickly formed a coalition with ANSAR DINE and AQMI,[6] two Salafist militias, who had gained support through the exodus of Tuareg soldiers from Libya after the liquidation of Muammar al-Gaddafi. On 6 April 2012 they proclaimed Azawad as an independent state. Later they went on to introduce Sharia and started to commit atrocities against the population and the built environment. The ferocity and violence were such that the Azawad Liberation movement quickly pulled out of the coalition. But the occupation of Northern Mali by ANSAR DINE and AQMI—all in all about 3000 jihadists—continued for nine months before the joint SERVAL military intervention of French and Malian troops succeeded in dispersing the occupiers.

A particular feature of the urban fabric and architecture in the cities of the inner Niger delta is its emphasis on anthropomorphism—on the human body as the basis of architectural design. As Labelle Prussin (1986) has shown in her study of architecture in West Africa, houses in the region often incorporate a highly symbolic façade which is imagined as a human figure, topped with a parapet. This anthropomorphism extends into the interior of houses and mosques in which the layout of the different spaces reflects the human anatomy. In addition, the incorporation of protective medicines and amulets into the buildings is a common practice (Marchand 2009); and many of the local Sufi saints are honored with mausoleums and tombs which people consult for prayers. These structures—often somewhat simplistically categorized as "Islamic"—are in fact spiritually much more complexly layered and express the culture-historical syncretism prevailing in Northern Mali.

In 1988, UNESCO declared the old towns of Djenné and Timbuktu as World Heritage Sites, which attracted a growing number of international tourists. The new heritage status not only meant that the architectural structures had to be sustained, but that they also acquired new meaning as articulations of translocal histories to a global public—as "vessels of ancestral presence" and "repositories of memory" (Apotsos 2017, p. 104). Although the world heritage status bestowed the inhabitants with a certain pride, the policy measures put into action started to transform the architectural landscape into an "idol of Western imagination" (Apotsos 2017, p. 106)—a transformation that was locally often perceived as cultural colonization—imposed by Western policymakers and backed by the disdained Malian state. The continuous funding of heritage and preservation operations in Timbuktu at the expense of social programs reinforced the long established geopolitical division between North and South and became a key catalyst in ANSAR DINE's subsequent iconoclastic campaign. As a site of frustration and despair, "Timbuktu had a lot to offer in terms of ideological ammunition [...]" (Apotsos 2017, p. 106).

In June 2012, after the first wave of demolitions was over, UNESCO declared the monuments of Timbuktu as an "endangered world heritage site" and requested that the destruction of graves and mosques end immediately. ANSAR DINE spokesman, Sanda Ould Boumana, responded that the worship of Sufi saints and their tombs were contrary to the Sharia and pure Islam (Figure 12.4).

Figure 12.4 ANSAR DINE spokesman Sanda Ould Boumama, still from the documentary Salafistes, France 2016.

Source: © and courtesy of Francois Margolin and Lemine Ould Salem.

He announced that all shrines would be destroyed and ridiculed the UNESCO request by stating: "This is haram. We are all Muslims. UNESCO is what?"[7]

The second wave of destruction followed immediately, and within a few days the Jihadist group had morphed from a local grassroots movement to an internationally known terrorist organization. The outcry against their savagery fueled the group's campaign by producing and circulating ever more violent images, first online in social media and later diffused by global TV channels. The jihadists levelled monuments and sacred buildings all over the city in an untamed furor of destruction. Their iconoclasm became propaganda for disseminating intimidation and for celebrating their military power. They demolished 16 mausoleums and inflicted significant damage to numerous tombs embedded in the exterior surface of some of the mosques (Figure 12.5). Michele Apotsos (2017, pp. 108–109) refers to

> a well-oiled choreography of violence, that characterized these acts, typically beginning with the dramatic entrance of a militant-laden truck flying the black flags of their organization [...]. Chanting "Allahu Akbar" or "God is Great," these militants would then disembark and surround the targeted site with their trucks, blocking onlookers from interfering [...], but always maintaining clear avenues of visibility so that onlookers became involuntary participants in the action as well. Then using shovels and pick-axes the militants would proceed to systematically dismantle the targeted structure [...].

Figure 12.5 ANSAR DINE jihadists destroy a Sufi mausoleum in Timbuktu, 1 July 2012.
Source: anonymous video still, © Getty Images.

One witness said: "There are many of us watching them destroy the mausoleum. It hurts but we can't do anything. These madmen are armed, we can't do anything but they will be cursed that is for sure."[8]

According to the 2012 report of the UN High commissioner for Human Rights, crimes by ANSAR DINE and AQMI Jihadists included "summary executions, rape, torture and the recruitment of child soldiers, violations of freedom of expression and of right to information and violations of the right to education and health"; the number of refugees and displaced persons quickly mounted up to 300,000 (UN Report 2012, pp. 1 and 8). Abderrahmane Sissako's award-winning film Timbuktu (2014), which I consider as an artistic afterimage, is based on the events during the occupation as the author and his fellow filmmakers Margolin and Salem (2016) reconstructed them. It opens with an iconoclastic vignette, featuring a group of jihadists shooting at wooden pagan sculptures placed on a desert dune. The film was a box office hit and triggered a massive international wave of solidarity with the victimized people of Northern Mali. It ridiculed and at the same time humanized the jihadists, but reinforced the dichotomy of "good Sufi Islam" versus "bad Salafist Islam." Critics, familiar with the political realities on the ground, also pointed to some historical inconsistencies, particularly concerning the role of the Tuareg, whose initial welcoming of the jihadists and whose active participation in the violent secession of Azawad is completely obscured and whose culture is heavily romanticized (Cazenave, Taoua, Sow, & Harrow 2016). A basic paradox of the jihadists' world—as depicted in the movie—is the combination of antiquated and despotic social values with ultramodern technology, and in this respect the iconoclastic acts, re-staged in Sissako's film, become disengaged and almost comedy-like.

After the invasion of French and allied ECOWAS troops in January 2013 the jihadists were quickly dispersed into the desert. The situation stabilized, although kidnappings and guerilla attacks—particularly by suicide bombers—have continued. In 2014, UNESCO, in partnership with the European Union and other donors, launched an ambitious plan to rehabilitate the heritage landscape in Timbuktu. UNESCO officials, in cooperation with local masons and craftsmen, started to rebuild and renovate the historical structures—relying on photographs and the heritage documentation. By February 2016, all 16 mausoleums had been reconstructed. Renovations of some of the city's libraries followed in order to accommodate the historic book manuscripts that were saved by a group of heroic smugglers before the jihadists torched the Ahmed Baba Centre in January 2013 (English 2017). As Apotsos (2017, p. 115) summarizes, all these activities of reconstruction and rehabilitation emphasized the fact that the

attacks have been solidly assimilated into Timbuktu's cultural and architectural history—an event which acknowledges, yet fundamentally disempowers ANSAR DINE's and AQMI's legacy as a defining characteristic of the city's identity.

The destructions have thus increased Timbuktu's symbolic capital, strengthened its iconic status as a transnational crossroad and fostered people's emotional engagement with their location. Ben Assayouti, the Iman of the Djinguere-Ber mosque declared: "To us it is a new birth to Timbuktu"; and Andrzej Bielecki, the EU political counsellor added that "By rebuilding these monuments we will destroy the work of the jihadists."[9] This renewed interest and admiration for the built environment is indeed striking since it required the destruction and loss in order to emerge. In September 2016 the responsible person for the destructions, Ahmad al-Mahdi, was sentenced by the international criminal court at The Haag to nine years in prison. It was the first trial in history to judge cultural destructions as a war crime. However, the political situation in Northern Mali is still unsettled and the hope that tourism could be revived in Timbuktu has largely faded.

Conclusion

What are the lessons we can take from these three case studies? The Timbuktu case is by far the most complex one. Its iconoclastic testimonies were part and parcel of a larger geopolitical conflict and followed a particular dramatic trajectory. The vacuum in which the Timbuktu events took place, was a direct result of the destabilization in Libya which spread into West Africa. The first destructions in May 2012 were rather side effects (or collateral damage) following the gradual transformation of the self-proclaimed "État indépendant de l'Azawad" into a Sharia state. An "Islamic police" was established. Its members imposed drastic changes to the everyday life of inhabitants (full-face veils for women, no music, no football, no alcohol, no smoking, etc.). In addition, the jihadist occupiers staged brutal executions and punishments—such as the stoning of unmarried couples and adulterers or the amputations of hands and feet for thieves. At this early stage, the Sufi sites remained in the background. Initial attacks were rather isolated and targeted the monument of the city's guardian djinn Al-Farouk or the practice of venerating the Sufi saints. The offensiveness of the mausoleums and tombs was associated with heresy and the iconoclasms were much more "expressive" than "instrumental"—to take up the useful distinction introduced by Finbarr Barry Flood (2002, p. 646). The jihadists wanted to "express" their power and disgust rather than to perform an "instrumental" act for achieving a higher goal. However, the perceived offensiveness of the Sufi sites abruptly increased on 28 June, when UNESCO director general Irina Bokova proclaimed that Timbuktu was now officially listed as a "World Heritage in Danger" site. Her widely mediated "speech act," aimed at raising international solidarity and support for a region under terrible siege, suddenly added new political layers to the hitherto predominantly religious signifiers. The immediate response by ANSAR DINE spokesman Sanda Ould Boumama was: "We are all Muslims. What is UNESCO? Now we will destroy every mausoleum in the city!"[10] Only two days later, on 30 June, the iconoclasm turned into a frenzied spectacle, which was first circulated by local witnesses on social media and then re-mediated and condemned by international TV channels and press. The new icon-oclastic furor now combined both "expressive" and "instrumental" testimonies and was directly destined for the UNESCO—as the extended arm of the imperial powers of France and the US, backing the detested Malian state. In this respect, Timbuktu is very different from the South African examples, but has some simil-arities to the Taliban blowing-up of the Bamiyan Buddhas in Afghanistan in 2001. In both cases, the notion of "world heritage" became a crucial parameter. As Dario Gamboni (2001, p. XX) has explained,

> the notion of world heritage, intended as a shield, may instead act as a target. [...] Tying certain objects to certain values—sometimes has contrary effects. It recommends certain objects to the care of those who share these values but attracts the aggression of those who reject them or who feel rejected by them.

All the cases discussed in this essay reveal such oscillations between the different layers of the "signified" which were continuously shaped and re-shaped by the actors who eventually engaged in vandalism and iconoclastic acts. Yet, as Sabine Marschall (2017, p. 204) has reminded us, the term vandalism describes these phenomena exclusively from the perspective of the prevailing order and those in power:

> Acts such as breaking pieces off a monument, scrawling graffiti or protest messages, or setting a monument on fire could also be described in terms such as "intervention," "modification," "alteration," "appropriation," "rein-scription," "addition," or "rearrangement": in other words, terms that carry more positive connotations of innovation, creativity, and hope for change.

W.J.T. Mitchell (2005, p. 18) argues quite similarly when he writes,

> Iconoclasm is more than just the destruction of images. It is a "creative destruction" in which a secondary image of defacement or annihilation is created at the same moment that the "target" image is attacked.

The production and dissemination of such secondary images and image testimo-nies was—in all three examples—heavily triggered and fueled by the immediacy promise of social media and their potential to communicate a multiplicity of voices and viewpoints. Social media's bubbling echo chambers boosted the affective currency of image testimonies and paved the way for consuming icono-clasm in the form of a global spectacle, in which images of destruction super-seded the destruction of images.

Acknowledgments

This chapter was written within the Collaborative Research Centre 1171 Affective Societies at Freie Universität Berlin. I am grateful to the German Research Foundation for financial support and to Kerstin Schankweiler, Verena Straub, Landon Little and Kerstin Pinther for discussions and suggestions. I also thank Paul Weinberg for sharing his impressive photo archive and text on the vandalized student exhibition "Echoing Voices from Within" at the University of Cape Town (2016).

Notes

1 A telling example for this ongoing process was the inauguration of the National Heritage Monument in Groenkloof near Pretoria in 2015, which displays ca. 80 life-sized bronze statues of historical South African heroes from the sixteenth century up to the end of apartheid. Upon completion, the "Long Walk to Freedom" site will include 400 figures. See the project website: http://nhmsa.co.za/#!Project [1 August 2018]. Such projects signal a clear rupture with the politics of the former National Monument Council (NMC) which was responsible for the fact that in 1989, at the dawn of the new democratic era, 97 percent of all declared South African monuments reflected the values of the immigrant White community while only 3 percent represented the art, architecture and artifacts of the country's Black population. See Franco Fresura, National or Nationalist: The Work of the Monument's Council, 1936–1989. www.sahistory.org.za/franco/historical-conservation-nationalist.html [1 August 2018]. For a discussion of earlier artistic engagements with colonial and apartheid monuments see Peffer (2005).

2 See the interview by Erica Buist with the artist "Sethembile Msezane performs at the fall of the Cecil Rhodes statue," 9 April 2015 in the *Guardian*, May 15, 2015 – available at: www.theguardian.com/artanddesign/2015/may/15/sethembile-msezane-cecil-rhodes-statue-cape-town-south-africa [1 August 2018]. Further information about the artist's intentions are available from her lecture performance, Sethembile Msezane at TEDGlobal 2017 "Living sculptures that stand for history's truths" at: www.ted.com/talks/sethembile_msezane_living_sculptures_that_stand_for_history_s_truths/up-next [1 August 2018].

3 The South African online Heritage Portal lists 20 cases of statues vandalized from March 2015 up to February 2016, www.theheritageportal.co.za/thread/vandalisation-statues-south-africa [1 August 2018].

4 www.economist.com/middle-east-and-africa/2016/02/18/whiteness-burning. A list of the 24 artworks destroyed during the Shackville protest can be found at: www.groundup.org.za/article/here-list-art-destroyed-uct/ [1 August 2018]. See also: Tammy Petersen, Charges withdrawn against UCT students who burnt paintings, at news24, 6 December 2016, www.news24.com/SouthAfrica/News/charges-withdrawn-against-uct-students-who-burnt-paintings-20161206 [1 August 2018].

5 See the eNews channel interview with Barend Lagrande at: www.youtube.com/watch?v=064pkF5lr8U and an article on the trial against the iconoclasts in *The Citizen*, available at https://citizen.co.za/news/south-africa/293651/the-spear-finally-rests/ [1 August 2018].

6 ANSAR DINE (Defenders of Faith) is a militant Islamist group, founded by Iyad Ag Ghaly in 2012, who has participated in the Tuareg rebellions against the Malian state

since the 1980s. AQMI (Al-Qaida au Maghreb islamique), was founded in Algeria in 2007 and joined ANSAR DINE in the Jihad in Northern Mali in 2012.

7 Quoted from the article "Timbuktu shrine destruction 'a war crime'" in the *Telegraph*, available at: www.telegraph.co.uk/news/worldnews/africaandindianocean/mali/9369271/Timbuktu-shrine-destruction-a-war-crime.html [1 August 2018].

8 Quoted from the article "Timbuktu shrine destruction 'a war crime'" in the *Telegraph*, available at: www.telegraph.co.uk/news/worldnews/africaandindianocean/mali/9369271/Timbuktu-shrine-destruction-a-war-crime.html [1 August 2018].

9 Quotes from the article "Timbuktu Seeks Rebirth after Militants' Destruction", 5 April 2014, www.denverpost.com/2014/04/05/timbuktu-seeks-rebirth-after-militants-destruction/ [1 August 2018].

10 See the article "Timbuktu shrine destruction 'a war crime'" in the *Telegraph*, available at: www.telegraph.co.uk/news/worldnews/africaandindianocean/mali/9369271/Timbuktu-shrine-destruction-a-war-crime.html [1 August 2018].

References

Ahmed, S. (2012). *On Being Included: Racism and Diversity in Institutional Life*, Durham: Duke University Press.

Apotsos, M.M. (2017). Timbuktu in terror: Architecture and iconoclasm in contemporary Africa. *International Journal of Islamic Architecture*, 6(1), pp. 97–120.

Cazenave, O., Taoua, P., Sow, A., & Harrow, K. (2016). Timbuktu—The Controversy—Abderrahmane Sissako, Director. Timbuktu. Original title: Timbuktu, le chagrin des oiseaux. 2014. 97 minutes. *African Studies Review*, 59(3), pp. 267–293.

Coombes, A. (2003). *History after Apartheid: Visual Culture and Public Memory in a Democratic South Africa*. Durham: Duke University Press.

English, C. (2017). *The Book Smugglers of Timbuktu*. New York: HarperCollins.

Flood, F.B. (2002). Between cult and culture: Bamiyan Islamic iconoclasm, and the museum. *The Art Bulletin*, 84(4) (December), pp. 641–659.

Freedberg, D. (2012). The case of the Spear. *Art South Africa*, 11(1) (September), pp. 36–41.

Freedberg, D. (2016). The fear of art: How censorship becomes iconoclasm. *Social Research: An International Quarterly*, 83(1) (Spring), pp. 67–99.

Gamboni, D. (2001). World heritage: Shield or target? *The Getty Conservation Institute Newsletter*, 16(2) (Summer). Available from: www.getty.edu/conservation/publications_resources/newsletters/16_2/feature.html [1 August 2018].

Gevisser, M. (2004). From the ruins: The Constitution Hill Project. *Public Culture*, 16(3) (Fall), pp. 507–519.

Latour, B. (2002). What is iconoclash? Or is there a world beyond the image wars? In B. Latour & P. Weibel (eds), *Iconoclash: Beyond the Image Wars in Science, Religion, and Art*, pp. 14–37. Cambridge, MA: MIT Press.

Marchand, T. (2009). *The Masons of Djenné*. Indianapolis: Indiana University Press.

Margolin, F. & Salem, L.O. (2016). *Salafistes*, Documentary film (France – 72 min.).

Marschall, S. (2017). Targeting statues: Monument "vandalism" as an expression of sociopolitical protest in South Africa. *African Studies Review*, 60(3) (December), pp. 203–219.

Mitchell, W.J.T. (2005). *What Do Pictures Want? The Lives and Loves of Images*. Chicago: University of Chicago Press.

Nyamnjoh, F.B. (2016). *#RhodesMustFall: Nibbling at Resilient Colonialism in South Africa*. Oxford: African Books Collective.

Peffer, J. (2005). Censorship and iconoclasm: Unsettling monuments. *RES: Anthropology and Aesthetics*, 48 (Fall), pp. 45–60.

Prussin, L. (1986). *Hatumere: Islamic Design in West Africa*. Berkeley: University of California Press.

Rawlinson, K. (2016). Cecil Rhodes statue to remain at Oxford after "overwhelming support". *Guardian* (international edition). Available from: www.theguardian. com/education/2016/jan/28/cecil-rhodes-statue-will-not-be-removed-oxford-university [1 August 2018].

Schutte, G. (2012). The president's penis. *The South African Civil Society Information Service*. Available from: http://sacsis.org.za/site/article/1302 [1 August 2018].

Simbao, R. (2017). Situating Africa: An alter-geopolitics of knowledge, or Chapungu rises. *African Arts*, 50(2), pp. 1–4.

Sissako, A. (2014) *Timbuktu*, Film (Mauretania/France – 97 min.).

Taussig, M. (1999) *Defacement: Public Secrecy and the Labor of the Negative*. Stanford, CA: Stanford University Press.

Thamm, M. (2015). Afrikaner singer chains herself to vandalised South African statue. *Guardian* (international edition). Available from: www.theguardian.com/world/2015/ apr/10/afrikaner-singer-chains-herself-to-vandalised-south-african-statue [1 August 2018].

UN Report of the United Nations High Commissioner for Human Rights on the Situation of Human Rights in Mali (2012). Available from: https://reliefweb.int/sites/relief web.int/files/resources/Report%20of%20the%20United%20Nations%20High%20 Commissioner%20for%20Human%20Rights%20on%20the%20situation%20of%20 human%20rights%20in%20Mali%20A-HRC-22-33.pdf [1 August 2018].

Weinberg, P. (2018). *Curation in times of Fallism*. Unpublished manuscript, SAVAH Conference, Stellenbosch (July 2018).